Of Poetry and Poets

OF POETRY AND POETS

Richard Eberhart

University of Illinois Press   *Urbana Chicago London*

Library of Congress Cataloging in Publication Data

Eberhart, Richard, 1904–
Of poetry and poets.

1.   Poetry—Addresses, essays, lectures.
2.   Eberhart, Richard, 1904–   —Interviews.
I.   Title.
PS3509.B456035   809.1   78–11597
ISBN 0–252–00630–5

To Ivor and Dorothea, Jack and Moira,
Betty, Dikkon, Channa, Lena, Malya,
Alex, Gretchen, and Benjamin

Contents

Foreword *by James Dickey*

The sovereign characteristic of Richard Eberhart's literary assessments is that he praises well. Criticism like his is seldom encountered and not easily come by. In an age when the word criticism means to *be* critical—that is, averse to whatever the work in question might be—Eberhart's writings in the field of poetry are heartening and life enhancing. He deals with various works he *likes*. His naïveté is what we all have wished for, without knowing it. This appellation is by no means pejorative. One thinks of a critic as a small, perhaps mangy man in a houseful of books and huge files of three-by-five cards, sitting at an old typewriter in a formal suit with a tightly buttoned vest, determined at all costs not to be wrong. Richard Eberhart is entirely different from anything of that sort. He is a man standing in the full sun. His criticism of other poets is also a criticism of the human condition. Matthew Arnold would have approved. Eberhart's critical work is essentially an affirmation. He is possessed of a natural animal exuberance that has been famously lacking in our critics. His generosity toward poets and poetry proceeds from what one might call, in his case, an overwhelming acceptance of and delight in life. He is closed off to nothing.

How much the literary, the human imagination needs this kind of approach, we all instinctively know. Poetry is commonly supposed to be an act of faith and a vindication of the human imaginative and creative capacity. These qualities are found in abundance in Richard Eberhart's work: in his poetry, in his plays, and now in these essays and reviews. His poetic values are evidenced in his critical assessments of thorny poets like William Empson, but most especially in his dealings with young poets, to whom he extends cordial and incisive advice.

When one reads through Eberhart's critical pieces, one is caught by two characteristics: an imaginative sympathy and a personal concern. Eberhart loves poetry, but he is not gullible about it. He can be tart, but he is not given to literary tartness as a way of life and reputation. The quality which we most associate with Eberhart as a critic—and also as a man—is that of fellow feeling: an intelligent rapport.

This isn't to say that he is not as good as the best in the area of close reading. He was, for example, with William Empson at Cambridge in the literary Twenties when Empson was coming to prominence, and he fixed unerringly on the strange, baffling but haunting scholastic element in Empson's verse and defined its nature before anyone else did. He quotes a poem which was never collected, but which pins down Empson's queer over-learnèd and intriguing quality.

UFA Nightmare

Gramophony. Telephony. Photophony.
The mighty handles and persensate dials
That rule my liner multi-implicate
Ring round, Stonehenge, a wide cold concrete room.
(I run the row from A to O, and so
—To and fro; periscope, radio—
We know which way we go)
  "If we can reach the point
Before the tide, there is another style.
I shall checkmate, given the whole board;
Juggling the very tittles in the air
Shall counterblast the dreadnought machiner."
  (Scamper, scamper, scamper.
Huge elbows tumble towards chaos.
Lurch, sag, and hesitation of the dials.)
  A tiny figure, seated in the engine,
  Weevil clicking in a hollow oak,
  Pedals, parched with the fear of solitude.

In Eberhart's words:

Here was a remarkable poem, timely then as it still is. Its title, wickedly foreign, excused its oddity, let one wander in the dream, yet there was something scientifically precise about it. It had wit; originality in every line; very subtle music; drama; lines that strode across the years, summing up the age; and, as in most of Empson's poetry, a strange quality of hiding the meanings, hoarding its strength, elusively secreting delicacies of perception.

The first line was novel. One had not heard a poem start that way. The license, however, was not excessive: something balanced about the three terms, which you never knew whether you were pronouncing properly, a fact giving the more pleasure—you wondered whether the author calculated even on that, or whether it was merely your stupidity—and there was the other level of meaning in the sound of "phony." Line two went off with a great swish, quite released from the first, or even a Miltonic dignity. One had the tendency in Empson to enjoy single successful lines, savoring them as they were, out of context with their grammatical relation to previous or succeeding lines; and this was one. What his "liner" was one did not yet know; "multi-implicate" was new; "Stonehenge" was thrown up in your face. You finally derived pleasure from using this last as a verb, certainly a novel notion, but you could take it as a noun singly, giving a different and yet quite similar suggestion to "wide cold concrete room." Contrast of the static with the dynamic, ancient simplicity with modern complexity. Then the musical lilt of the next three parenthetical lines, how accurately the music controlled! I recall a vague feeling of similarity with Hart Crane here, the only place in Empson, quite evanescent, probably wrong. "We know which way we go" struck me as masterful, for I never knew in those years which way I was going—would have loved to know—but that is going out of context again.

Now supposedly the technician is speaking. Something dramatic and opu-lent in the first two lines. Switch to a chess image; odd, but provocative, keeping it from being too nautical. "Juggling the very tittles in the air" was a ravishing line. It was what the greatest critical insight always did: it lifted you up high into the rarefied air of exquisite contemplation. I always thought of it as what Empson as poet and critic was doing. Again that nice contrast between two lines, in the heavier consonantal values of the "counterblast." "Juggling the very tittles in the air" was delicious! Juggling them, all most delicate thought or perception would finally overcome the heavy opposing weight of world or matter, put all in order.

All is not order in either the prose or poetry of Richard Eberhart. He is beyond that, and he, in his work, passes beyond any neatness. He has the gift of life, as well as the gift of the library. In his critical pieces he becomes, as he is in his poems, the adventurous lover of words. He belongs to no school but his own, which I personally hope and believe will enlist many followers. One reads his poems and his assessment of other poems with an exciting sense of one's own potentialities as to imagination and response to existence.

In our time we are in danger, not of being of the stature of the great sinners cast into Dante's Hell, nor of that of the saints in Paradise. We find ourselves in limbo: in Purgatorio. Richard Eberhart has the means and the skill to lift us out of this dim anti-kingdom by his enthusiasm, his intelligence, and his art. I believe everything he says as a critic, and as one of the finest poets, perhaps the very finest, of his time. In criticism and in verse he deals with ultimates, and the blood cannot but quicken on reading him, whatever his form. All of it is good. A poet's eye, ear, and sensibility control and are set free. We, also, are set free with these.

What shall I say to Walt Whitman tonight?
Reading him here in the springtime of bursting green,
Foreign from him, held by the same air he breathed of the world,
Looking at night to the same stars, white and radiant,
Obsessed with a kindred obsession, at a dark depth,
Inheritor of his America maybe at its great height,

I praise him not in a loose form, not in outpouring,
Not in a positive acclamation of frenetic belief,
Not in the simplicity of a brotherhood, such peace,
And not in the dawn of an original compulsion,
But speak to him in the universe of birth and death.

Preface

In 1968 I asked Dartmouth's library to get up my prose. Dorothy Beck spent the summer trying to find it. She turned up a manuscript of about five hundred pages, going back to the Thirties. This book is the result of that search. During at least three decades I had been so closely bent on poetry that I had not thought of myself as primarily a critic or prose commentator. I called that manuscript my *Selected Prose*. Over half of it consisted of the articles and essays found in this book; the rest was reviews and fugitive pieces which the editor thought not to publish, but which I regard as a careful index to my feeling about many current poets of the day. I regret the omission of all those scores of reviews through the years.

It is still a mystery how and why writers become what they are. Most poets are critics as well—and indeed, the act of criticism is implicit in every line of poetry written. But in some poets criticism overrides their creative gifts as poets, and they become known first as critics, or in some kind of balance between prose and verse. There is no ideal in this respect. Swift is generally praised for his prose, but I, with others, like him for his verse. The same for Johnson. With me, the main force was poetry—but I hope some of the pieces I have written on the making of poetry, and on contemporary poets, will be considered worthy of a place on the shelf alongside the poems.

I suppose prose, like poetry, is an endless effort to find and evoke meanings for your life as it goes by and you try to catch it, elusive, in the shortness of your stay on earth.

—Richard Eberhart

PART ONE

Notes on Poetry

I live in reality but have a sense of unreality. Like a fish out of water with a clairvoyant sense of waters.

I feel strong and sane, yet these called insane seem very much as I am.

I esteem a perfect poem as an impossibility yet would work a lifetime to make one, as many as I could.

I would not die for poetry, I would live for it.

Perfection is only possible in poetry, or in another art if you are not a poet. Yet it is unlikely. A so-called perfect poem is supposed to last five hundred or a thousand years. The mathematical possibilities of making one that will last that long are small.

Poetry is to overcome time. I want to overcome time because I cannot hold it in me. It is taking me away beyond my will, therefore I want to make something that is beyond time, that will be beyond my time. Art is in a sense timeless. A perfect poem is in a sense timeless, limited to the communication of its meaning through centuries. One reads Sophocles as if he wrote today.

I search my own identity through poetry. Each poem is a milepost along the way. How do I know who I was at twenty, thirty, forty, fifty, or sixty if I do not have poems to show for my life?

I penetrate my times through poetry. I cannot expect to know history as it is. An existential poetry could never catch up with existentialism. Too much immediacy in poetry defeats itself. Yet poems are in a sense necessarily limited to the moment, they express in a sense the day, the decade, the times. What you wrote in 1936 you cannot write in 1966.

First published in *Twenty-five/Dartmouth/Poems*, selected, with notes on poetry, and a postscript by Richard Eberhart (Hanover, N.H.: Dartmouth Publications, 1966), pp. 5–7.

3

I escape my times and prophesy the future in poetry. By seeing through one's times one transcends them. A poet feels ahead of his times because of his revolutionary dissatisfaction with everything about him. He heads into the future and may reach a beyondness which, if great enough, may become timeless in the sense of his perceptions lasting hundreds of years.

I am a vehicle of the spirit moving in me. All the intellect in the world cannot make a perfect poem. But the poet may be or become a sensitive vane or instrument through which a spirit blows beyond his will, a psychic draft of absolute reality may move his hand. This is a mystery of poetry.

A poet is a mystery to himself and to the world.

The world cherishes the poet because it recognizes that he has been touched by a divine stroke, drenched in holy fire, and speaks as an oracle.

To be wise is to know the world. To be unwise is to be a poet, who, becoming a child, gives wisdom back to mankind. Therefore he is wise.

The situation of the poet is unimportant to the poem. If the urge is strong enough, he will write no matter what he does. The light of poetry falls on farmers, teachers, businessmen, bums, scholars, the poor and the rich, the married, the hale.

Contradictions are everywhere. The poet may be said equally to depend on environment, to seek continuously the right environment, and the poem comes only when the environmental situation is such that it evokes poetry.

A poet secretes his audience within himself. He prefers to live by the audience he creates, but if he has no audience he creates anyway, as happened to Hopkins.

There is no one poet.

The reader must come up to the poet.

Ambiguous poetry stretches the mind. It is not plain as day because the day is not plain.

If a poet writes to save his soul, he may save the souls of others.

A young poet should throw his life away to win his poems. If he does not throw it away, he wins nothing. Denial precedes affirmation.

Struggles in the soul make poetry possible.

If a poet has sufficient self-criticism, he will not have to criticize others. The responsibility is on him. The pure do not blame the impure.

It is poetry that the light changes.

Poetry and society are hand in glove, but the poet can pull off the glove and salute the sun and the stars.

4

Poems of condemnation are not as profound as are poems of affirmation. Wrath is valuable but is soon spent and is not as valuable as love, which endures beyond it.

Poetry orders nature and tells it how it is.

Poetry evaluates science, science does not evaluate poetry.

Poetry is of the heart and head. If it is all heart, it may become soft. If it is all head, it becomes arid.

A poet's taste should be catholic. He should admit every poem to his pantheon, judge every poem according to excellence.

A poet must be true to himself, but he can only find himself by writing many poems. Part of himself will be in each poem. History may judge that his true self exists in few or many poems.

A poet lives dangerously, in constant danger of failure.

Poetic speech is a poised articulation of conscientiousness. It is not like prose speech, and is only like prose in that it is sensible. It is a magical fusion of thought and feeling. Throughout the centuries nobody has given a satisfactory definition of the difference between prose and poetry.

Poetry does not change the world, it changes the poet.

Postscript

Following this year's announcement of the Pulitzer Prizes I was asked to give a reading of my work in Hopkins Center. At this reading on May 19 I read the following paragraphs, entitled 'Note,' which were written for that occasion.

At the height of his career at the Inauguration of President Kennedy Robert Frost called for an age of poetry and power. As yet we have no Virgil to write the epic of Augustus Caesar. I call for an age of power in poetry, which is more modest and realistic. The power would be in the poetry but the question would be left open as to the relation of poetry and the state.

To have power in poetry would be to have poetry at its most viable, available to many, a true force of nature, limitless in its imagination, secret in its depths, the ambiguity of the voice of nature, the continuous excitement of a revelation of life, a deep message and meaning of art. It has been so in past centuries. May it come to be in our America. To have power in poetry is better than to have poetry in power. Plato long ago threw the poets out of the ideal commonwealth because they were too acquainted with the divine madness whereas sober men should hold the reins of state.

In ousting the poets Plato paid them a subtle compliment, as if to say that their dangerous ideas were admired because of a value beyond logic. In the *Ion* we read 'For the poet is a light and winged and holy thing, and there is no invention in him until he has been inspired and is out of his senses, and the mind is no longer in him: when he has not attained to this state, he is powerless and is unable to utter his oracles.

Let us then have all the power of poetry we can come by but let us not equate poetry and power in an age. Poetry may be from Plato's idea higher than the state. Our present state thinks it lower. Let us have power in poetry and if fate should give us a hundred years from now another Athens, another Elizabethan England, then it will be time enough to call it an age of poetry and power.

Poetry as a Creative Principle

When I was in Ireland on a walking trip during my Cambridge days, I dined with Yeats and AE in Dublin at the house of Oliver St. John Gogarty. I made a young and eager fourth to these venerable gentlemen. I was about to have my first book published and had no literary name. I was twenty-four years old. I sat beside Yeats all evening after dinner. He drew his long thin hands through his long straight gray hair. I distinctly recall the elders lapsing into Latin. They seemed to be telling jokes in Latin, on occasion. I heard Yeats quote a Latin author. Maybe it was Horace, maybe Catullus.

Last year when talking with a scholar from Harvard, Richard Ellmann, whose books on Yeats I liked, and having recounted the above event, he put up a strong argument that Yeats knew no Latin. He said that he could not possibly have spoken in Latin. He grew so forceful that I began to doubt my own memory. I kept protesting that I had sat only a foot from him and had distinctly heard him on several occasions speak in Latin, quoting a Latin author or authors. My friend had just published his book on Yeats after years of study. He became categorical. He said it was impossible. I felt that I was being authoritatively removed from that natural lucidity to which I was accustomed.

I had made a note at the time, after that memorable evening. The note plainly said that I had heard Yeats say some Latin.

Last month I told this story again to Frank O'Connor, now here on his first visit from Ireland. Frank O'Connor had known Yeats well for years. He corroborated the finding of Mr. Ellmann. He said that Yeats could not possibly have said a word of Latin.

This leaves me in a dilemma which I am going to pass on to you.

In youth we think everything is wonderful and indeed it may be.

Founder's Day Address, Wheaton College, Norton, Massachusetts, April, 1952.

You have been studying in this beautiful place. You have the world before you. And you are sure that you know reality, that you know what you are doing; that, as Hamlet said, you can tell a hawk from a handsaw.

But wait. What is a handsaw? A handsaw is not a handsaw. It has nothing to do with a saw. It is a heronshaw, another bird like a hawk. No, not like a hawk. It is a heron. Shakespeare's comparison is not so easy as that between a hawk and an instrument for sawing wood, but between one bird and another bird which have similarities, but whose individualities are quite distinct.

Reality is a hawk, and poetry is a heronshaw. They are at once very similar and very different. As the heronshaw is the more gaudy of the two, so, perhaps, is poetry. They both fly and partake of the universal air.

As for reality, may I suggest that years from now you may not be able to remember whether you received an *A* or a *B* in English? Of course, the advantage of receiving a very low mark is that you will be able to remember it more definitely!

Now how does this fit into the problems of poetry?

The longer we live, the more complex life becomes, the vaster seem its possibilities and its limitations, and the more we have to admit the deep nature of our ignorance. In the modern world, even if any of you should years hence master some facet of one subject, and write a definitive book, you will have been able to master what in fact will be only a small part of reality.

We cannot know everything, even if our desire for knowledge were insatiable. We cannot, apparently, even know what we think we know with finality. The truth is lost in the obscurity of memory. The scholar and the novelist, my critics, may well be right where I was wrong. Maybe one of the other guests said the Latin. Maybe I imputed Latin to Yeats because I thought he ought to know Latin. Maybe I had a pre-image in my mind of him as such a man, so that my will or my fancy distorted reality.

How does this bear on poetry? It bears because poetry is a new creation and it is a new creation because things as they are never stay as they are. The poet makes the world anew; something new grows out of the old, which he locks in words. A certain new order is imposed upon nature by art. Time keeps on flowing but the poet has re-created life as it flies. It is therefore a wonderful thing that you can read ancient poetry as if it were new, for it was thrown up out of life and left in print as vital imagination in which we can enter as really now as could a contemporary. Shakespeare is still new, so are Aeschylus and Sophocles. So is T. S. Eliot. It is the glory of great poetical utterances that they escape time and live beyond their time even as they epitomize their time.

I would like to make four points about poetry from the point of view of the creator, the poet, and then relate these to you, the reader, the receiver and ultimate enjoyer, and try to show how valuable can be the love of poetry, if you will persist in it from your present beginnings through the years, discovering in each new poem some wonderful richness, some startling or violent perception, some subtle rhythm to sing in your blood for days, some noble utterance creating an ideal by which to live. Poetry is ancient, it is older than the Magna Charta, than the Catholic Church, than the tombs of Egypt, or the first dynasties of China. It goes back to the rhythms of the human body, to wonder and to ecstacy, and also to that consciousness of death which must have been known to the first man and has been inseparable from man's consciousness since.

What is poetry?

First it is an adventure of the soul among mystifications. The truth is never fully known. Poetry lights us along the road to the discovery of truth. We may never find it, or we may find it in part, in individual illuminations. Coleridge said, "When no criticism is pretended to, and the Mind in its simplicity gives itself up to a Poem as to a work of Nature, Poetry gives most pleasure when only generally and not perfectly understood." The mind relaxes from the inhuman attempt at perfection and in poetry accepts the human condition of imperfection. It can thus revel in the delights of poetry, in its rhythm and music, and can expand and commit acts of intellectual enlargement among the infinite variety of the connotations of words. Each poem becomes a statement of some facet of truth.

Second, poetry is a spell against death. Poets are more conscious than others, perhaps, or are more articulate in the realization of our temporality. Poetry is thus produced as a monument against the passing of time, against death. I do not say that it is consciously so produced by the poet every time he writes a poem, but that is what it becomes.

It is mileposts of significance and realization along the way of life. I am old enough to remember World War I, but those times are like a dream; they have no reality in themselves. Yet the reality of those times is in the poems of Wilfred Owen, or of Rupert Brooke, or of Isaac Rosenberg. They wrote spells against their own deaths. Decades later we may capture their feelings and emotions locked in the spells of their words.

You are old enough to remember World War II. Yet even now, after a few years, it is getting out of focus. It is becoming history. And just as certainly as of World War I, when you are fifteen years older than you are now, you will best realize the attitudes toward World War II from the poems occasioned by its total impingement and awful involvement.

I, as I presume other poets do, write poems to discover the self, to say, to speak, to perform the self in acts of creation against the total loss of time were one silent. It is somehow good to read a poem one wrote twenty years ago; you recapture what you were: the poetry has made you become what you are. Poetry is a kind of pinching of oneself, as one used to do as a child, to see what you are like. When you read an old poem, you say, that is what I was then, that is what the world was to me then, in this instance. When you read a new poem you say, this is what the world means to me now, in this instance, in the framework and limitations of these words.

If the poet did not have the record of his poems, his past would be as shadowy and doubtful as the Latin of William Butler Yeats.

Third, poetry is a spiritual gyroscope. It keeps the mind on a true course, the true course of our common humanity.

Every time one reads a good or maybe a great poem, he instinctively recognizes its truth and its justice. His mind and feelings are trued up, so to speak. He is joined to the central feelings of mankind as a strut is joined to the main structure of a building by a carpenter. The reader casts off his idiosyncrasies, his peculiarities, his temporal concerns, and lives, while the poem works on him, in central, elemental, and profound human realizations. This brings a deep satisfaction, for it acts as a reintegration and restores the senses to a refreshed, vivid, and vital awareness.

Fourth, poetry is an aesthetic delight, without utilitarian value. It relates one thing to another in novel ways, creating new resemblances which, when perceived, seem true. You would not have perceived these resemblances, but the poet did. Once established, they seem as if they had always existed, and are true. Or, more truly, you had the perceptions but it was the poet who expressed them. As Pope said, the poet puts down "What oft was thought, but ne'er so well expressed."

Poetry is highly social as it is an act of communication; its purpose is to give delight, to please, to charm, to elevate. It is of no utility, it has not the taint of worldly use. It increases the soul and is thus allied to religion. No man can read the works of Shakespeare, Milton, Wordsworth, or the ancient Greeks without gain in moral stature. To this extent poetry is useful in that it improves the mind, and presumably the character. So there is a contradiction here which remains unresolved. But poetry can be indulged as an intellectual game or play, the play of wit. It can be enjoyed in the privacy of the study. Its meanings can be enjoyed in pure contemplation, without the necessity to act, which is what I intended by stating that, in one sense, it has no utility.

As poetry is a spell against death, so it is also a spell against birth, by which I mean that it establishes permanent relationships of mind and spirit. Sophocles did not know that I was going to be born in the twentieth century, but he set up profound dramatic truths, a spell for me or anyone to come to, whether in the fourteenth, this, or a later century. The spell of poetry is part of the adventure of the soul among mystifications. We can enhance our lives by aesthetic pleasures in reading poetry, and may keep our minds on the true course of our common humanity in the comprehension of great works.

You, as the readers of poetry, are also affected. How are you affected by poetry?

For you poetry can also be an adventure of the soul among mystifications, for the reader is just as mystified as the poet and can be as creative in his responses to the ultimate mysteries. By conscious study of the significant poems of each century, you as students and later as general readers can enjoy almost limitless pleasure, for the field is large and rewarding, and with the incorporation into your fibers of each masterpiece the mystification, for the time being, at least, will become less. The great poems are positive utterances of order and intelligence; they give a world view. I think of the *Divine Comedy* or of *Paradise Lost* and *Paradise Regained*. These are ultimately acts of confidence. We are being confided in. Each in its grand way limits life and puts it in a special order. Each work in its own way presents the significance of life and the world. And, of course, in your freedom you may take them or leave them, or take them and leave them.

As readers you may scotch the spell against death theory. You may read every poem as inevitably vibrant with life, and you may increase your life in the enjoyment of each poem without considering the poet's conscious or unconscious motive of outliving the present.

As a reader you may be creative in keeping your mind on the true course of our common humanity. This is hard to do. It involves the question of taste. You do not see the gyroscope. You will have to read hundreds of poems in what is probably a painful access of education, and learn to tell a good one from a bad one. You will have to distinguish the fads and fashions of this decade from those of past decades, learn to judge, to criticize, apportioning praise and blame.

It is not easy to achieve independence of mind. You ought not to follow the crowd, or repeat what others say, but certainly make up your own mind about the value of a poem. The admission of one type of poem, or indeed of a whole school of poetry, does not necessarily preclude the admission of other types or schools. In this country we enjoy freedom in thought and discussion. This right of ours ought to be kept vigorously alive. Each student should perfect his or her own taste.

As a reader, addressing point four, there is no limit to your aesthetic delight in the study and enjoyment of poetry.

Professor Douglas Bush has published the notion, in *The Kenyon Review*, Winter 1951, to put it simply, that literature makes us better. His words are, "What is the ultimate end, according to my creed, is that literature is ethical, that it makes us better."

Having a penchant for leaping to opposites, my first reaction was that maybe it makes us worse. The young headstrong poet may be so overwhelmed upon discovering Rimbaud that he may want to emulate his life, as well as imitate his verse. What a revolutionary possibility! If he should break all the rules of society for the glory of poetry, and come to a bad end, would not literature have made him worse? What if he tried to emulate the lives of Marlowe, or Chatterton, or Baudelaire, or Wilde, or Ezra Pound? You could hold that literature could make him worse.

Also, certain sensitive readers may become so enamoured of the world of Proust or Kafka as to imitate them, in any number of psychological and subtle ways, to drastic changes in their own course of action and maybe for the worse. Literature is a powerful resource, from either the poet's or the reader's approach. It can change the human character. So I do not know that I can agree with Professor Bush that literature makes us better, although I have not made up my mind that it makes us worse, and indeed these two propositions are too glaringly opposite. And in any case, as Dr. Johnson would say in any literary controversy, there is much to be said on both sides.

Considering the great weight of works of the past which have come down to us, it becomes obvious that they would not have persisted in men's minds for centuries if they were either immoral or amoral. Professor Bush is then correct in his assumption that man wishes to remember things that make him better and has preserved the works which do. Although this is a large generalization, it can probably be made with fair regard to the truth.

Yet I would remind you of Plato, who threw the poets out of his ideal republic. This scandal has been talked about ever since. Plato held two very clear notions: one, that the rulers of the world are to rule by reason; and, two, artists or poets, when they try to reason, become so emotional that they disturb society. The violence of the reasoning power in creative persons can become so extraordinary as to unsettle everybody. The idiosyncrasy of genius may be clairvoyant, but it may also be revolutionary. Plato thus threw out the poets from rule of the world because they made society worse.

But Shelley, in the nineteenth century, partially restored the poets to power by holding, as you recall, that they are "the unacknowledged legislators of the world."

We might turn now to the writing of poetry, to the creative act.

Since one has written many poems under many conditions throughout the years, it is difficult to make a definite statement as to how one writes poetry. Perhaps an anecdote will be in order.

Two years ago I woke up in the middle of the night with a swirl of words going about in my head. This condition seems to be a gift of the gods and in this instance I had done nothing consciously to bring it on. The condition is dramatic. The words and rhythms, seemingly endless numbers of them, are present in an expansive flow of ideation. You feel that you must get to a pencil quickly or they will be lost. You know this. If you stayed in bed they would be lost; in all probability they would never be caught, they would be lost and go back to the reservoir of memory unused. You would wake up as if nothing had happened, for it is not like having a dream all or parts of which are remembered upon waking. And there would be no poem.

Some poets have concrete imaginations. Frost told me once that he formed a poem in his head over long periods of time, say weeks, without any anxiety of losing a line or phrase. He would perfect it consciously and deliberately and when he was good and ready all he had to do was to write it down.

My mind is entirely different. It is as if the images and words were in a whirling chaos, a verbal spate wanting and waiting to be caught and fixed, but so tenuous and volatile that, unless an act of will should drive the body to the paper and make the hand capture the meanings from the flux, all would be lost. All would be lost very quickly, which gives a sense of anxiety and desperation to the time. If one waited five minutes, even a minute, the magic might stop as quickly as it had come.

I stumbled out in the darkness to my nearby study. I turned on a light. I found a pencil but could not find a paper. This was drastic. I had to find a paper. I could not find a paper, and in this maybe only one minute all these marvelous sounds and images, floating and prancing before the mind, were being lost, or not quite lost, liable to be lost.

Suddenly I found a three-by-five white pad of paper. This saved the situation. Immediately I began, in calmness and control and dominated by a certain mood which pervaded all the images, to draw off meanings and put down feelings. I could get just six short lines on a page. The size of the sheets of paper dictated the form of the poem. As I turned over page after page the poem became separate stanzas of six lines each. I wrote seventeen of these small pages, that is seventeen stanzas, before the mood was spent.

If there is anything I am certain of, it is that this poem, "The Herb Basket," has its form not from preconception but by the arbitrary caprice of the fortuitous appearance of the three-by-five pad of paper in the middle of the night.

I would like to quote one stanza:

> A cereal-fed fat oyster
> Kept for a winter dinner
> Is an example of sophistication
> And a case of debasement.
> I would rather have it thinner
> With some sea water in my dinner.

This rather odd experience leads us now to a consideration of the psychological aspects of the creative principle.

Thus far we have talked about poetry as a creative principle from some general approaches. We have not attempted to put our finger precisely on what causes a creative act of imagination. This is a difficult and a complex subject. We cannot expect to entertain numerous theories on the subject here, but we can choose one modern psychological theory and try to explain it.

Dr. Harry B. Lee of Chicago, in "On the Esthetic States of Mind," has an account of what causes the creative state, and in it you will find mordant realizations of what may, in fact, be true, or partially true, and perhaps interesting to entertain. He says:

The artist's depression is only the acute worsening of a chronic maladjustment to human relationships, evident in his traditional inner discord, vanity, isolation, aloofness, and "temperament." It results from his turning against himself, at the prompting of conscience, of the same destructive rage as he had directed at another. This manifests itself in an unconscious need to suffer and in the withdrawal from human ties and other objects of a large share of his interest, which he then diverts to the tasks of self-punishment and self-healing. He emerges from his illness upon achieving a cycle of mental tasks that include the unconscious psychic labors of inspiration and creation; and these labors, through restoring in him the functions of pity and love, restore inner harmony among the institutions of his mind, as well as gratify his excessive need for self-esteem and renew his previous interest in human ties.

The creative work of art, therefore, is not really undertaken as an end in itself. It is not simply the overflow of a generous nature, or the artist's special reaction to natural beauty, or his wish to communicate a message, or the consciously directed process that aestheticians have described. Neither is it the sublimation of nonrepressed pre-genital sexual wishes that Freud claimed it to be. Instead, the created work is something made to bridge the way back to mental health from the despondency into which the artist's destructive rage has plunged him. The creative artist is delivered to his genius *only at this time*; this is why he does not do creative work at all times, and why he cannot do creative work at will. He must await the bid of his Muse; and her bid comes only when he is out of favor with her, depressed.

The truly creative artist . . . is a man who is convalescing from a neurotic depression brought on by the effects of having hated too much.

This is a modern clue and we may as well accept it as an example of twentieth-century penetration. We do not have to accept it dogmatically, but can apply a tentative method to get what insight we can from it, and look into further psychological theories if we wish. The theory tends to make of the poet a kind of monster, which is poles apart from the notion of the poet as enlightened prophet, cultural disciplinarian, or unacknowledged legislator.

If Dr. Lee's theory is acceptable, the poet is no different or no more guilty than other mortals; he is simply more highly conscious of what he is doing. All share guilt and recognition; the creator brings consciousness to the general view.

When applied against the works of Shakespeare, this theory seems monstrous indeed! There must be something fundamentally wrong with it, which is, I take it, its limitation to the time-spirit. It would not have done in the eighteenth century and may not do in the twenty-first.

There is no doubt some truth in the theory of the monstrosity of the poet; he may be more or less monstrous at different times. He is society's nerve ends and cannot be asked to reflect and present more health than there is in the body politic.

The poet need not, of course, be monstrous at all. The gentle Milton was called "Angel Face" as a youth at Cambridge. It is that all men contain within themselves the potentiality of all action, of all modes of being. Various poets bring to the minds of men certain of these conditions; poets focus certain attitudes, and since they penetrate life, love, tragedy, and death they sometimes represent evil, just as they often represent the good, and as a few have permanently exhibited the sublime.

On reading the above excerpts from Dr. Lee's article to a friend of mine who is a psychiatrist, this doctor had an instantaneous reaction. Instead of immediately inquiring into the truth or justice of the theory, he at once began to probe into the reasons for Dr. Lee's holding such views! He began to psychoanalyze the psychoanalyst. He drew forth all sorts of reasons why Dr. Lee must have wished to set up such a theory. To this one must say that it is very hard to be scientific; psychiatrists seem creative to the extent that they rebel against the bounds of rules and invent new systems. I could not detect a mobile depression in my friend, nor a state of convalescence, but a freedom of mind to exercise a critical spirit against a theory reputed to be based on the examination of psychotics.

The trouble with Dr. Lee's theory is just that. He has concocted his notions from the study of psychotics. It is, however, a theory presuming to apply to true artists, to artistic creations. The jump is perhaps a wish-fulfillment inasmuch as artists are not usually true psychotics. If Dr. Lee could have studied numbers of artists of achievement, one wonders whether his theory would be sustained.

Another trouble with his theory, hinted at, is that it seems too modern, too limited to the time-spirit. I choose this term purposely as one not used predominantly in the past decade or so, but which was formerly much employed. Homer, Dante, Chaucer, Shakespeare, Spenser, Milton, and Wordsworth accomplished large and sustained works of the greatest artistic achievement—or Dryden, Pope, Marvell, Hardy, or Yeats—whom you will—by a steadier, more controlled, resolute and directive light of mind than is indicated in the neurotic theory of Dr. Lee. I may be wrong. But it seems unlikely that Chaucer or Dryden could compose poetry under any such compulsions. As the mind is a sorting machine, we must sort out the poets and limit Dr. Lee's theory to those to whom it might apply.

A further trouble with the theory is that its generalization is too great. It says that this is how the creative artist works or acts. It erects a dogma as if it were a universal truth, whereas it should only pretend to say that this is the way a certain type of mind, a certain type of creative artist, may operate.

Nevertheless, I find the theory fascinating, and to have some truth in it. It would not fit Virgil, Goethe, or Racine. It might fit poets like Hölderlin, Rimbaud, Hopkins, or Hart Crane.

It is bewildering to think about poetry, as I have been trying to get over to you, and I would like to recount an experience I had after I gave a reading a year or so ago in New York. At a party after the reading there were many people in a crowded room. After about two hours the crowd thinned and a young man, whose most noticeable feature was his fiery eyes, his coal-black, flashing, penetrating, startling gaze, came up and engaged me in conversation. Presently he was doing all the talking.

He said that he had been in a mental hospital for nine months and had just got out. I thought him little or no different from numbers of highly intelligent young men whose conversation one hears at Harvard. He said that after he had been incarcerated for some time he came across my poetry, which he had not known before, and read it voraciously, then meticulously. He came upon a poem which, he asserted, so impressed his mind and released his imagination that for days he lived in a kind of trance. I gathered that it was a state of great consciousness and ecstasy for him. He then peppered me with learned questions about Catholicism, Montaigne's ideas, the source of Saint Theresa's inabilities and strengths; he asked questions of scholarship which I could not answer, possessed of a rare intellectual zeal. As a matter of fact, he almost had me spellbound in the passionate recounting of his psychic experience. I did not feel that I was the author of the poem in question or that all this somehow had much to do with me.

Then with a deep kind of sigh he said, "But after it was all over, after the illumination, your poem made me feel worse than I had before and I had to go back to the psychotic ward for two weeks."

When I left the party and thought that a poem of mine had made a young fellow with the "divine madness" madder, I felt that there was no further use in criticism.

I have brought this story to your attention to show how wild and sporadic may be the unexpected uses of poetry; how unpredictable may be the response and the result of study; how beyond the control of the artist may become his art. A poem, in a sense, becomes all things to all men.

Pure Poetry

One of the reasons why modern poetry is said to be complex is that modern society is complex. This famous assertion of some forty years ago made a stir in its day and seemed to be much more profound than it was or is. It embodied a single truth, a direct ratio, but it said nothing about the value of complexity. It was as if complexity were a thing in itself, valuable because of itself. Yet nobody could reduce poetry to the quality of complexity as if this were uniquely fundamental, and critics went on talking about other phases of it.

The truth of the assertion must not be taken lightly, however, since we recognize Western civilization as a fact so complex, going so fast, that some theorize that it is about to fall apart. It is so complex that it is breaking down.

Perhaps because our society, our civilization, our culture are so complex, nobody has had the insight to question the old assertion that modern poetry is complex because modern society is complex. The world took this for granted once it was proposed and circulated, thinking little more about it.

I want to speak about pure poetry. I should like to isolate the purity of poetry and show this quality as prime, essential, fundamental, and rewarding.

My difficulty in writing about poetry, as opposed to freedom in writing it, is that I am not dogmatic, propose no dogmas, and since I am open minded, receptive to ideas, I hold wide, secular beliefs rather than hierarchical, closed ones. It is thus possible, due to ambivalence of mind, to hold the notion that I could as well write an essay on impure poetry as on pure poetry.

First published as "Poetry" in *Quality: Its Image in the Arts,* ed. Louis Kronenberger (New York: Atheneum, 1969), pp. 327–40.

19

The idea is intriguing. We see impurity everywhere, from the failures of the individual will to the failures of the death-collecting will of the war in Vietnam. Impurity is closely allied with the complexity of life as everyone senses, sees, and knows. We have grown so exorbitantly, as to numbers but not as to spiritual power or control, that there are now two hundred million Americans. The complexities of this situation are staggering to contemplate. It is as if quantity denied quality, as if the impurities of our complexities would deny purity of mind, purity of purpose, purity of action, purity of art. We live and have our being in the complex and the impure.

It would be possible to explore poetry in relation to its endless impurities as well as in its ancient stance within the complex. Compared with a stylized, totally structured poet like Dante, who may be termed pure as well as having a complexity well ordered and controlled, Shakespeare is impure and complex, like a vast landscape in parts of which grow purple flowers. He is sprawling, vigorous, and so sizable a creator that one can find anything in him as in the Bible.

There is a sense in which the greatest poets are the most impure and the most complex. There is more passionate acclaim, perhaps, in Milton's *Paradise Lost, Paradise Regained,* and *Samson Agonistes* than there is purity or simplicity of utterance. This is not to say that we think of Milton as a vast disorder, nor do we think this of Shakespeare, but it is to say that the greatest poets are not the most neat, the most tidy. Chaucer sprawls to some extent, as does Spenser. Much has been made of the sometime failing quality of Wordsworth's natural language. Blake's late works are so complex as to seem gigantic mouthings of an overly complicated mind, without the relief of clarity. We think of Whitman, too, as vast, sprawling, inchoate, a map of humane imperfections from which a great spirit shines.

This is not to say that we do not love these poets as much as any others, any of the less raw and colossal ones, but is to suggest, giving only short evidence of names, that impurity and complexity are central to poetry and that one could advance a thesis in their behalf. I have purposely avoided the word "ambiguity," with which I grew up, along with "ambivalence" and "irony," but these are in the field of impurity and complexity. Arguments have been put forward in my time that ambiguity is at the heart of poetry, is in fact its essence, and provides its most exquisite pleasures. Empson with his *Seven Types of Ambiguity* caused me to postpone for about forty years the notion of writing about purity in poetry, involving clarity, simplicity, and universality.

It is also felt in these times that poetry should be like life itself, as lived, not at a remove of art. Poetry should mate with the times. There is always the hankering to see whether it is true to life, where "to life" means life as lived here and now. Poetry should be inclusive rather than exclusive, should explain our life and lives to us "like now," like reality.

William Carlos Williams hammered for decades on the notion that American nervosity begets an American poetry unlike British poetry and that our mental, physical, vocal movements make outdated the iambic pentameter line. We breathe not in iambs, but in agitated forms which he was always trying to capture and assess.

Poetry should reveal us to ourselves, this is the cry. It should express and explain our motives, show our temper, reveal our secrets, name our aspirations, stand for our hopes as it shows our despairs. It should make plain our limitations and it should express our desires for perfection. It should digest every idea in the mind of man and measure his imagination in words. This is what poetry is felt to be in our times, a grasp on the actual, a significance of the real.

The wind has changed, let us say, and we have to set our sails another way. If it is true that poetry is a grasp of the actual, a significance of the real, may we not question the meaning of these terms and read them another way than that intended above?

William Empson wrote meticulously of ambiguity, as I said, and another contemporary, Kathleen Raine, announces ideas of poetry which I would like to detail. She holds (or could hold, as I do not quote her directly) that poetry should not be written about the quotidian but should express eternal things, the soul of man. The actual will be the actuality of spiritual reality, not the actuality of every day. The real will be a reality that transcends every day. The real will be, poetically, what is real for all time, not only for now. All time is a long time, yet every reader knows what is meant by immortal poems, immortal poetry. This is the best kind of poetry for Miss Raine. Recognizing the quickness of the passing hour, a certain senselessness in the scramble of events, imperfection everywhere in man's relation to man, the shifting of values in all societies, the changes of attitude from century to century, Kathleen Raine holds to the ancient idea that a poet lives in the reality of events, the events of his body and mind, and of his times, but that (she speaks only of poets she deems worthy of the name, a few) he pierces to the heart of the meaning of man, producing a poetry that is timeless. In time, he exceeds his time. He exceeds, at best, the times of centuries, as did Dante and Shakespeare, to produce a poetry valid at any time, now and in the future. The poet in her view is thus prophetic. While he grasps the immediacy of the real, the real is much

21

more than the actual, and he has the ability to communicate poems that are at once felt as true now but that will also be true forever or, better to mitigate this high possibility, as long as English is read.

For Miss Raine the poorest poets of a time are those who communicate only a sense of their time, limited to the feelings of the day, the style and tone of the period, while the best poets transcend their times, while necessarily embedded in their years and decades.

They have a take-off mechanism into the sublimity of the soul, total spiritual experience which makes them available to what can be called timelessness. They achieve universality. The best poets for her are the universal poets. The condition is so high that she naturally can name only a few, a few say of the past forty years, but these are considered the most important. The many who coped with their day, in any form of realism, will be lost to memory. The few who wrote to universal principles not only will exceed their time but may be generally accepted for centuries. This is a high claim for poetry but it is an ancient one, only reannounced by Miss Raine in our day.

Perhaps an example might be in order here. The poets of the Thirties who wrote Communist poems are for the most part forgotten. Perhaps several are remembered. They were limited to political poetry. Furthermore, the kind of Communism they wrote about no longer exists but has been radically altered, so they were doubly wrong by these changes. If you think poetry is a vehicle of the moment and has no further significance than the messages conveyed by Communist poets to readers of these messages, then it can be said that they summed up the then references of their poetry. From this point of view, it would be excessive to expect more from it. And it may be that the aesthetic pleasure enjoyed by the reader of one of these poems at that time would be equal to the aesthetic pleasure of reading a timeless poem. What are the measures for determining this argument?

However, it seems plain to me that poets who wrote only political poems in the Thirties and who are now living cannot speak to the Sixties unless they change with the times. As I said, there are only a few living, now writing, of the many who wrote political, sometimes Communistic poems in the Thirties, whose early works are read.

Involvement in political affairs involves the poet in writing political poems. There have been hundreds of anti-Vietnam war poems, but how many of these will have the purity to outlast this century? It is a difficult problem. Poets should speak out politically now and let time winnow their war poems as to long-term value.

I would remind the reader that Edna St. Vincent Millay, horrified and shocked at Nazi retribution in Lidice, wrote a poem by that title out of goodness of heart and the right reasons, but this political poem is regarded by every critic as inferior to her best poems, which, unpolitical, have already lived beyond their decade and have elements of the timeless.

To have a poetical voice in the Sixties if you began in the Thirties, it would have been necessary early to imagine leaping over decades and writing to a time beyond your time. Everything being relative, a time beyond your time may have only been three decades, but three was a long time beyond one. And the relatively few viable decades of even the longest writing life may leap only a few half-centuries ahead. But in all poets who try to penetrate to the heart of life there must be some deep hankering after timelessness, some feeling of the universal character of poetry, some belief that truth does not change.

Timelessness is still a relative term, based on time, so that we do not count up centuries the minute we say the word. Yet every poet would accord timelessness to Dante, and he exists; to Shakespeare, and he exists; or to the Psalms, to Ikhnaton's sun-worshippings, to go back no further, or to others in separate lists anybody might want to make up.

Part of the fascination of the difficult championed by Yeats is in testing assertions against truth, the difficult truth which is hard to come by and may often be found in the simplest poems. Frost's "Stopping by Woods" is a true poem and seems simple, yet its implications are deep and it has been called a death-wish poem and a Communist poem, to the amusement of the author, who was nevertheless arch in not saying precisely what he intended, lest he should deny a variety of interpretations. He wanted to be subtle to any subtlety in the reader and provided anecdotes to uphold a mask of the truth. One was about the repetition of the penultimate line as the last line, which he casually stated was a mindless repetition because he had "run out of gas," or some such statement. Yet none knows, even of those who knew Frost best, whether this was a Frostian joke or ironic contribution to dialogue or whether it was actually true.

Therefore, to backtrack before going forward, I would like to speak of what I should call dross poetry. It would be possible today to espouse a dross poetry on the grounds that everything is unclear and a clear poetry only confuses the issue, darkens perception, muddies the waters, pollutes the imagination. Clarity and perfection could be marked down as a hindrance of things as they are. No poet has a right to be blind to his time and not assess the reality of the day. He could see through the reality of the day to some future, but he should not speak as if the reality of the day did not exist.

It would be an exciting possibility to write on the opposite theme to what I have chosen, plunge headlong into a study of dross poetry, or I could call it inspissated poetry, truth and vision thickened to a roughness and turbulence which might be said to be true to the heart of our times.

To give only two examples, I could choose Neruda as a mountainous, thick, and dense poet always thrashing around in the torments of his mind to throw out rough excellences like some reckless giant.

Or I could bring up Pound's Cantos as an example of manifold dross. To walk through them is to walk through a tangled wood, a dense thicket, a dark fastness. Some may be pleased to be lost in such a wood. It is interesting that the Pisan Cantos have the clearest, most lyrical passages, one notable and much quoted ("Pull down thy vanity") because when writing them Pound did not have access to books, except a few, and wrote from the self. These few pure lyrical passages have to be felt as spiky flowers in the general linguistic vastness and tortured complexity of the whole, with its unresolved showing of many languages, historical modes, and political assessments.

I have said elsewhere that the Cantos constitute a breakthrough toward a world poetry the idea of which I admire, a breadth of mind and feeling to embrace many centuries and languages, but the dross is still greater than the clarity and the whole feeling is one of roughness, thickness, density, vast intellectual ambition, with only a few single pleasures of clarity and perfection.

Perhaps the feeling we get from Dante's tripartite poem is more poetical because Dante had the framework of beliefs given in the Church of his time and could fit every idea neatly, and grandly, into a grand frame. To me, his life work is incontestably greater than Pound's attempt at a modern synthesis. The fact probably is that, since our times do not have a single world picture and structure as neat and absolute as the Catholic background of Dante, Pound's work was destined to be a large confusion and miscellany of realities only tied together by themselves. The work is complex and disorderly because our times are complex and disorderly. Pound could not impose a superior order on his chaotic manifestations because there is none available. He made an attempt at a world view, but it is a choppy sea.

Yet it is fair to argue that, since we have no total intellectual or social world view now, Pound's dross or inspissated poetry is the best because it was the best a good mind could do confronted with the twentieth century, although it hews to the vanity of the ugly. And I should have to say that a few of his early lyrics were more important in their perfection and purity than his long work, but these have to be seen in relation to it.

I have taken the pleasure of announcing other points of view, feeling like a juggler who can throw up one ball after another, keep at least three and maybe quite a few more in sight, in orderly use against the dangers of gravity, then bring them all down again at will. The juggler makes no mistake. The juggling critic hopes not to make a critical mistake.

However, for the purposes of this essay, the ball I would like to throw up now to special view in any system of multiple criticism is the globe of purity. Burke would have beauty round, smooth, and small. I assume that there is such a thing as poetic purity, and I wish to search it out selectively, not exhaustively.

In one of my earliest poems, "The Village Daily," I ended on "And every night it sets in rigid lead/ Those who are born, who marry, and who die." Eliot put it: birth and copulation and death. Between birth and death, universal terms, one can compile an arbitrary list of universals. To choose basic subjects, these could be birth, growth, hope, joy, love, suffering, despair, death. These terms comprise man's beginning, his rise, his fall.

To strengthen these, one could cut them down to birth, hope, suffering, despair, death. One could substitute joy for hope, to read birth, joy, suffering, despair, death. Some might wish to keep love in and cast out despair. A more central list might be birth, hope, love, despair, death. The point is that such terms are grand determiners of life. Under them, all experiences are had, all life endured. They make a valid framework in which to place poems. There are fewer great poems about birth than about death, of joy than of suffering, for obvious reasons. Not all poems are about these subjects. I should say that the bulk of poetry in English is outside this selective context. While Chaucer, Shakespeare, and Milton have poems that come under these rubrics, the greatness of their works extends beyond the neatness and elegance of these arbitrary categories in my context.

Pure poetry has clarity, simplicity, and universality. These are arbitrary terms and there could be others, but these are the ones I choose. What I am looking for is poetry that is clear, that is, instantly perceived, taken in, and enjoyed; poetry that is simple, that is, absolute; and poetry that is universal, that is, unrestricted, adaptable to all, for use among all. It is possible for pure poetry to make some of the greatest statements and communicate some of the deepest feelings known to poetry.

I admit that a pure poem, in my view, tends to be short and that this may be a limitation. My idea of pure poetry does not take in the epic, long dramatic poems, long narrative poems, long satirical poems, and the like. It is hard for pure poetry to keep on going that long. Therefore my thesis, as I said, cuts out much of the poetry written in English. Not to mention other languages. Would the *Testament* of Villon, recently translated by Galway Kinnell, a long but lean work, get in? It could.

I also admit that there are single lines or stanzas within whole poems which may have dazzling quality. One could say that these dazzling properties of a poem constitute the purity of it. The rest of the poem would be a kind of dross. This would be like not seeing the wood for the trees, and I reject the notion for the purposes of this paper, while holding in memory several bedazzlements by individual lines or stanzas throughout decades. Recently Mark Van Doren has pointed out that in Marvell's "The Garden" there is, in fact, just such a bedazzlement. He finds a poem within a poem here, a jewel in a casket, crucial stanzas surrounded by a shell making up the whole poem.

We should be reminded that although pure is considered an absolute term, it has its degrees and nobody could hope for an absolutely pure poem. The hope would be more nearly embodied in an eight-line poem, as for instance the "Sick Rose" of Blake, or Wordsworth on rocks, stones, and trees, than it would be in longer poems, although one could suggest Landor's four-line "I Strove with None" as exemplifying purity and perfection.

It must also be said about pure poetry that the purer it is, the less it needs commentary. At its best, it exists as a thing in itself, clear, simple, and universal, a glory of man's perception and ability to communicate, truth of nature and truth to life uttered convincingly, economically.

An example may be in order here. It may well be that Eliot's "The Waste Land" is the most famous poem of the first half of the century. Every teacher as well as every student knows of the compelling interest of the notes. "The Waste Land" is the opposite of a pure poem. It may be one of the most impure, inspissated, ambiguous, and dross-complected poems of our times. Bright students joke that, if you read the notes and the commentaries on the poem, you will not have to read the poem itself to pass the course. The poem invites so much talk about itself that the talk may overwhelm the poetic experience. By this token, it is notoriously delightful and easy to teach. Its impurities ally it with the human condition, which we find difficulty in surpassing. We wallow, more or less happily or unhappily, in our own imperfections, relish every ambiguity and obscurity and oddity of Eliot's.

Dross, inspissated poetry is easy and pleasing to teach because you have to grapple with every meaning, come to grips with obdurate material, search out the difficult truth from fastnesses and thickets of language and thought. It exerts our muscular nature, our combative faculties.

But what of the pure poem instantly perceived, absorbed, known wholly and fully in complete response, about which there is nothing that needs to be said? The teacher has a hard time with pure poetry because it practically takes away his function. The poem teaches itself. The student gets it at once. Imperfect poems are better for classroom discussions, student papers, than perfect ones. In writing a paper on a so-called perfect poem the student is called upon, in fact, to compete with the poet, and how can he say the meaning as well as the poet did in some famous, immortal, and perfect poem? He cannot, but he would be delighted to wrestle with the almost endless possibilities of the imperfect, thickened poem, which gives him leverage to overcome the dualities and complexities of his own mind.

Compared with "The Waste Land," I consider Eliot's "Ash Wednesday" a pure poem. While it requires references, its lyrical impact is pure. It moved me when it came out and still moves me with its clarity, simplicity, and universality. I consider it one of the masterful pure poems of the century.

In passing, I should say that there are obviously numerous poems which stand between purity and impurity, with elements of both. I consider Eliot's "Four Quartets" not as difficult, impure, or inspissated as "The Waste Land," but not as pure as "Ash Wednesday" and therefore, for me, not as meaningful. Unlike some critics, I do not think of "Four Quartets," prosaic as they are, except in spurts, as his best work, but a falling off from both "The Waste Land" and "Ash Wednesday."

I should like now to name three short poems that come under the category of pure poetry. Space does not permit the setting forth of an anthology of these poems. The poems I have chosen are a few from a large body of possibilities. Their quality is such that they seem timeless in their perfection.

To quote an early, anonymous poem—perhaps of the time, thought to be sixteenth century, of "O Western wind, when will thou blow"—here is:

> Who shall have my faire lady?
> Who shall have my faire lady?

Who but I, who but I, who but I?
Under the levis grene!

The fairest man
That best love can,
Dandirly, dandirly,
Dandirly, dan,
Under the levis grene.

Students of literature know Herrick's "Upon Julia's Clothes":

Whenas in silks my Julia goes,
Then, then (methinks), how sweetly flows
The liquefaction of her clothes.

Next, when I cast mine eyes and see
That brave vibration each way free;
O how that glittering taketh me!

And here is Housman, whose classical restraint is notable:

With rue my heart is laden
    For golden friends I had,
For many a rose-lipt maiden
    And many a lightfoot lad.

By brooks too broad for leaping
    The lightfoot boys are laid;
The rose-lipt girls are sleeping
    In fields where roses fade.

About these three pure poems it is not necessary to murder to dissect, but on a short Blake poem I would like to offer lucubration, if commentary may be helpful in a poem which seems simple but has certain difficulties and complexities which invite exploration.

Ah, Sun-flower

Ah, Sun-flower! weary of time,
Who countest the steps of the Sun;
Seeking after that sweet golden clime
Where the traveller's journey is done:

Where the Youth pined away with desire,
and the pale Virgin shrouded in snow
Arise from their graves, and aspire
Where my Sun-flower wishes to go.

For our purposes this is in between a direct expression of a soul or ethereal state, holding a precarious teeter between these. It has a mid-sort of balance. In its shortness it contains greatness, is ever mysterious and evocative.

Blake's Sun-flower, I suppose, is weary of time because of its natural necessity to follow the sun's face as it moves through the day with its own. It is forever so held in a powerful control. It seems to count the steps of the sun, which suggests but is not rationally limited to the upward ascent of the sun to midday, as if seeking a sweet golden clime where the traveller's journey is done, as if it wanted a finality not in nature.

Note that the first four lines end with a colon. The second stanza is a time continuance. The capitalized Youth and Virgin add to the strangeness and difficulty of this second and concluding stanza. "Where the Youth pined away with desire" is, I suppose, compressed grammar with "pined" not a direct verb but as if to say "Who is pined away with desire." The pining Youth is seemingly equated with the Sun-flower in fixed necessity, and so is the Virgin. Both unexpectedly in the seventh line arise from their graves, which is not where we should have located them in lines five and six, the presenting and stating lines. There is a doubling back here, the last line and a fraction quickly setting it. They arise from their graves, from death to life, or from death to immortality may we suppose, and aspire "Where my Sun-flower wishes to go." Is this not strange? Even if they come back to life, or even if they achieve immortality or are heavenly, they aspire where the Sun-flower wishes to go, but it is nowhere told that the Sun-flower has any hope of getting there, fixed as it is to the magnet of the sun's recurrent, unfreeing, inholding influence. We are in paradox and we are mightily pleased, moved, provoked, and infinitely, we may say, delighted with this magnificent poem, yet on analysis it presents a closed system which cannot be broken out of and sets up in us a great sadness, a sort of finite longing which yearns to some psychic state but is held down to earthly, mortal reality.

It is a poem of universal desire to exceed one's estate. The Youth, the Virgin, and the Sun-flower all wish to break their limitations in the universal aspiration of all life toward something greater than it knows.

The hope of a pure poetry is part of this universal desire, in this case the desire for perfection.

Why I Write Poetry

When asked "why I write in verse," I have a ready answer: "Because that is easier for me." Maybe I should demonstrate by writing this article in meter. Prose, however, is better for explanation. We shall see that poetry is supreme for suggestiveness.

One writes in verse because one should give oneself to a delirium of joy, which inheres between vowels, where is the ultimate mystery of language, as being the fluid river or sea pent between rigidities or monumental masses of consonants, and is an exercise of music.

Because one does not know how many summers are left to one's life, although one felt this more fiercely, perhaps at twenty to thirty, here in the height of summer where it blazes and keeps re-creative sustenance charging the detonated beach on any coast, and poetry is a great quickness over prose.

Because poetry entertains the nuances of our frailty and leads the mind between rational essences to those other electrifying essences which blaze in the most secret hour, the strangest fashions, the primordial and fiercest individuations, known to every man, unarticulated unless poetry prize them in the specific and bring them forth in happy forms.

Because prose makes you lazy but poetry makes you bright.

Because, to say the same thing over in a thousand possible, invented ways, poetry leaps to the ultimate, in an ultimate concentration of essence, and stands for the purpose of man, needing, needless to say, not the justification of this apology, whereas prose, in its log-footed measurement and dogged stance, only tells us what we knew before: poetry suggests an infinite more, a new-made best.

If you would contemplate, this summer, while time departs from

First published in *New York Times Book Review,* August 23, 1953.

you, one line so seemingly simple as "My love is like a red red rose," you might be better rewarded than if you read a thousand pages of expository prose on any subject. What will they expose?

The simple likeness of love to a rose will offer a basic enchantment. It is only a rose-jump to "To be or not to be, that is the question." And a quick turn to "Brightness falls from the air." Or thrust toward any profound poetic statement you may love.

In these the concentration is so great that they may ramify in the mind. They put you in love with life. You become part of something beyond you. You become identified with eternal relationships. A sweet religious essence may fill you, for if you think only an hour on some vague possibility of a religious nature, you will be refreshed; if you require the specific, in any cogitation, the result will be the same, if the take-off is poetry and you are contemplative.

The poetry of the line goes over into the supreme poetry of life, of every hour, of every act, of every gesture. Thus you become a part of every man; you lose your oddity. You mate with the changeless. You may do this more efficiently and more naturally through reading poetry than through reading prose. The struggle of the poet may be painful. The reader's pleasure may be relatively painless.

Nevertheless, I consider it an assault on perhaps ununderstandable compulsions to try to state why I write in verse instead of in prose. Synaptic verisimilitude? Prose and verse are the husband and wife of letters. If they have been separated they come together again. They acknowledge an instinctive dependence. Yet each has its own individuality.

So in a sense the problem is idle, while the problems are universal! I write in verse because it is natural for me to do so. The heaviest prose, the greatest novel, may try to say what Blake uttered in "O Rose, thou art sick!"

Poetry is more challenging to me than prose. In its concentration and refinement there are greater chances for error than in the longer measures of exposition, description and narration usual to prose. Subtlety of mind is enjoined to sidestep these errors, natural to man; sinuosity of intellect is invited to the tireless game of controlling error (or allowing it to sprout in interesting ways) in the invention of a possible total aesthetic satisfaction. Poetry has infinite resource and time-defying propensities.

One reads prose for knowledge, poetry for power. Power in the sense of insight, not in the sense of practical good, although this is not necessarily excluded. It is the powerful, useless, time-defying, God-inciting and Godward-looking nature of poetry, its truth-enhancement, in which there is the greater possibility and which makes one obeisant to this primitive and exalted mode.

The best poetry should not be finally understood lest we know too much and might as well have read of the matter in prose. The best poetry should evoke suggestions which please and satisfy but do not exhaust themselves on the hardness of intellect. It is too easy to be intellectually too hard.

One can never be too sensitive, on the other hand, to the mysteries of poetry, which may entice and satisfy the soul, itself a mystery which the rational mind is always trying to destroy.

How I Write Poetry

I began writing poetry when I was about fifteen as a high school boy in Austin, Minnesota. I had a native facility with words and could write many poems with ease and with the greatest pleasure. My verbal imagination seemed at odds with a mathematical one. I was from the beginning noticeably better at verse than at figures. My mother loved poetry. On our library table was a leatherbound copy of Tennyson. I still have this copy with her name in it. Tennyson was the first poet I read in depth. He became my model. I admired his almost perfect blending of sound and sense; but of course my early exercises were derivative.

However, one poem, quite un-Tennysonian, survives from my high school days. It was written when I was sixteen, entitled "Indian Pipe," discovered many years later in its small school notebook and published in 1953 when I was forty-nine. It is about the partial death of a whole race, the race of American Indians. I used to see Indian Pipes in the woods near home. Later, I was pleased to learn that Emily Dickinson particularly liked them. They were embossed on covers of her posthumous books. Its three stanzas seemed to have a classic elegance when discovered all those years later and to give off a delicate, somewhat wistful, poetic charge.

Here is the poem "Indian Pipe":

> Searching once I found a flower
> By a sluggish stream.
> Waxy white, a stealthy tower
> To an Indian's dream.
> This its life supreme.

First published in *Poets on Poetry*, ed. Howard Nemerov et al. (New York: Basic Books, 1966), pp. 17–39.

Blood red winds the sallow creek
    Draining as it flows.
Left the flower all white and sleek,
    Fainting in repose.
    Gentler than a rose.

Red man's pipe is now a ghost
    Whispering to beware.
Hinting of the savage host
    Once that travelled there.
    Perfume frail as air.

As a student at Dartmouth, I recall Housman as our favorite poet, but I in no way imitated him. We assumed something of his intellectual attitudes, however. Robert Frost was the first poet to mention a poem of mine in print, in a small book entitled *The Arts Anthology* (1925), for which he wrote an introduction. Presently, Harriet Monroe published a group of my poems in *Poetry*, "A Magazine of Verse." But it was not until my Cambridge University years, 1927–29, that I felt I was arriving at a style to command and pursue. I. A. Richards took interest in every line of mine and helped me to get my first book published. This was a long poem, *A Bravery of Earth*, on which I worked for months under the spell of Wordsworth, whose portrait by Pickersgill I sat beneath in hall at St. John's College. Cambridge poetry was lively then. William Empson, Kathleen Raine, Hugh Sykes-Davies, Ronald Bottrall, T. H. White, J. Bronowski, J. L. Sweeney, and others made it so.

Besides Wordsworth, the poet who influenced me, probably to a deeper extent, was William Blake, with whom critics for decades noticed an affinity. I was also much moved by Hopkins when I first encountered him at Cambridge. Critics noted traces of his style in mine for a few years, but this did not persist. I probably cannot claim progenitors besides Wordsworth, Blake, and Hopkins, although critics have also adduced Whitman. I had the fortune not to feel any urge to imitate Eliot, Pound, or Yeats.

I would like to tell my readers something of how I have written certain poems through three decades and longer of writing poetry. I should like to present the poems and give commentaries. It would seem reasonable to employ here poems which have been more used, known, and discussed than others of mine less noticed. There must be some significance in acceptance and use of poems over decades. The poems which are kept in the minds of readers through anthologies and textbooks must represent the taste of the times in a closer fashion than poems which may conceivably be better but, due to difficulty, to

complexity, to some impenetrable strangeness, or to some other fac-
tor, are not accepted. There is the possibility that these known and
well-used poems are absolutely better than others. It is for the critics
to bring out their absolute values. Time winnows away the bad
poems; the true grain is in poems that have a certain timeless quality,
yet this is relative. I have felt that everything about poetry is relative
rather than absolute. Coleridge's relativist statement, "Poetry gives
most pleasure when only generally and not perfectly understood,"
appeals to me as one of the truest statements about poetry, leaving as
it does room for individual differences. Yet the oldest or most nearly
timeless poems are not necessarily the best or better than the best
contemporary poems.

Two theories about the complex and ancient art of poetry have
specially impressed me. They are opposite, yet each seems true, and I
can subscribe to both. One is that poetry comes from an excess of *élan
vital*. It is an overflowing of powerful feelings from a healthy psyche.
A poet is a normal man with superabundant creative powers. The
other is that poetry comes from a sick soul and is to heal or make up for
psychic deficiencies. One can name poets in either category. I can
never find one theory or definition sufficient for all of poetry and have
felt both these points of view as realities within myself, as well as
many realities in between.

The problem of time in poetry has always fascinated me. Does a
poet mate with his times or transcend his times? What are, or can be,
his principles when writing? It would seem that a poet, even the
greatest, speaks for a few decades, maybe only one or two. I have the
idea of a time-spirit in the air which the poet seizes, mysteriously, out
of the air to give his truth to the world. Each time-spirit differs from
every other. The Twenties differed from the Thirties, the Thirties from
the Forties, the Forties from the Fifties, and so on, using decades as
arbitrary markers. A poet may be prophetic, as was Hopkins, who
mates with our times, which would have seemed an improbable
future when he was writing in the nineteenth century, his poetry
known only to a few persons.

One had to live beyond a decade to see its limitations. Poets of the
Depression years in the Thirties who wrote of contemporary events
fared less well than poets whose realities transcended the immediate.
Each poet was struggling with the real, yet only poems which had a
reality beyond the concerns of the time survive. These surviving
poems must have something of the timeless in them. "Timeless" is
itself a relative term. I suppose that, if a poem lasts for three or four
hundred years, we can call it, but not accurately, timeless. We think of

Shakespeare's sonnets as timeless. And, if a poem is read for thirty years, I suppose that it is more nearly timeless than if it is forgotten after ten years. What makes poems survive, what unique qualities poems which survive possess, are matters of the deepest interest to truth-seeking critics. In the final analysis, although there is no final analysis, the deepest things about poetry seem to me to be mysterious. They go beyond the mind into the vast reservoir and region of the spirit and appear to be not entirely accountable to reason. I cannot go so far as to say that the deepest things about poetry are irrational, but I would include irrational perception and components in my view of poetry. Poetry is a confrontation of the whole being with reality. It is a basic struggle of the soul, the mind, and the body to comprehend life; to bring order to chaos or to phenomena; and by will and insight to create communicable verbal forms for the pleasure of mankind.

Here is an early poem.

For a Lamb

I saw on a slant hill a putrid lamb,
Propped with daisies. The sleep looked deep,
The face nudged in the green pillow
But the guts were out for crows to eat.

Where's the lamb? whose tender plaint
Said all for the mute breezes.
Say he's in the wind somewhere,
Say, there's a lamb in the daisies.

"For a Lamb" was written after seeing a dead lamb among daisies in a field near Cambridge, England, in 1928. It is a metaphysical poem based on the proposition that things are not what they seem. It can be read as straight description or as a transcendental poem. Its connotations invite transcendental considerations. The ending is ambiguous.

Here is a more complex but in some ways similar poem.

The Groundhog

In June, amid the golden fields,
I saw a groundhog lying dead.
Dead lay he; my senses shook,
And mind outshot our naked frailty.
There lowly in the vigorous summer
His form began its senseless change,
And made my senses waver dim
Seeing nature ferocious in him.
Inspecting close his maggots' might
And seething cauldron of his being,

Half with loathing, half with a strange love,
I poked him with an angry stick.
The fever arose, became a flame
And Vigour circumscribed the skies,
Immense energy in the sun,
And through my frame a sunless trembling.
My stick had done nor good nor harm.
Then stood I silent in the day
Watching the object, as before;
And kept my reverence for knowledge
Trying for control, to be still,
To quell the passion of the blood;
Until I had bent down on my knees
Praying for joy in the sight of decay.
And so I left; and I returned
In Autumn strict of eye, to see
The sap gone out of the groundhog,
But the bony sodden hulk remained.
But the year had lost its meaning,
And in intellectual chains
I lost both love and loathing,
Mured up in the wall of wisdom.
Another summer took the fields again
Massive and burning, full of life,
But when I chanced upon the spot
There was only a little hair left,
And bones bleaching in the sunlight
Beautiful as architecture;
I watched them like a geometer,
And cut a walking stick from a birch.
It has been three years, now.
There is no sign of the groundhog.
I stood there in the whirling summer,
My hand capped a withered heart,
And thought of China and of Greece,
Of Alexander in his tent,
Of Montaigne in his tower,
Of Saint Theresa in her wild lament.

I wrote this poem in a high state of awareness, in a total charge and commitment of the whole being in about twenty minutes, I think in the fall of 1933 in my master's quarters, Dormitory E, at St. Mark's School, Southborough, Massachusetts. By an ironic turn of fate, the manuscript remains unfound. I remember having to change only a word or two. Of many of my manuscripts, I would like to view this one particularly to see if I could learn anything of my state of mind from the orthography.

The vision of the groundhog was had some time earlier (maybe two years earlier) at Broadwater Farm, near Phoenixville, Pennsylvania, the estate of the father of my Dartmouth friend Andrew B. Foster, who read history at St. John's College, Cambridge, when I was there. The spot where I saw the dead animal seething with maggots was a few hundred feet from the game room, in full summer.

It may have been, however, that the poem was written in late summer. I distinctly recall writing four poems that summer, all at about the same time, and thinking that they were all equally good. I could not distinguish one from another, which may say something about the purity of the creative impulse.

Only one of the others, "In a Hard Intellectual Light," has been reprinted in anthologies and is known to some readers. Yet "The Groundhog" has had an active poetical life now for thirty years. The other two poems are unused. When I had the vision of the groundhog, he seemed to have more life in his maggot-seething body than if he were alive and running along a field. It was the paradox of life in death. The poem arises to a unified view of history.

I have always been bemused by the fact that when I wrote the four poems I could not tell the difference in their value. From a creative point of view my effort was equal, yet the results were markedly different. Poems which endure must possess some universality of meaning.

The writing of "The Groundhog" is an example of a theory I have that poetry is a gift of the gods. It cannot be had only by taking thought. The process is ultimately mysterious, involving a total thrust of the whole being, some kind of magical power. When a poem is ready to be born it will be born whole, without the need to change a word, or perhaps with the need to change only a word or two. I thus go back to an ancient theory of inspiration. It must suggest strong, active memory and an instantaneous synthesizing power when the whole being, not the mind alone, or the senses or the will alone, can come to bear on life with significance. Probably more than half of my best-known poems have come to me in this way, when the being was a seemingly passive vehicle for the overwhelming dominance of the poem, which was then put down with ease, immediacy, fluency, and comprehensive order.

Here is another early poem, "If I Could Only Live at the Pitch That Is Near Madness."

If I Could Only Live at the Pitch That Is Near Madness

If I could only live at the pitch that is near madness
When everything is as it was in my childhood
Violent, vivid, and of infinite possibility:
That the sun and the moon broke over my head.

38

Then I cast time out of the trees and fields,
Then I stood immaculate in the Ego;
Then I eyed the world with all delight,
Reality was the perfection of my sight.

And time has big handles on the hands,
Fields and trees a way of being themselves.
I saw battalions of the race of mankind
Standing stolid, demanding a moral answer.

I gave the moral answer and I died
And into a realm of complexity came
Where nothing is possible but necessity
And the truth wailing there like a red babe.

This poem in retrospect epitomizes the Thirties, for me at least. It was my answer, or one answer, to the severity of the times. It was written early in the second half of the decade. Perhaps if it had not been for the breakdown in our society in the Depression this poem would not have been written. The times forced me to a deep inward look and threw me back on the past conceived as better than the present. The poem owes something to Wordsworth's "Ode on the Intimations of Immortality Recollected from Early Childhood." My poem goes back to a vision of perfection in childhood, from which we are fallen away in maturity. The poem ends by facing a complex world of mature reality in a resolution between becomingness and the become. In the title line I intend not pathological madness, but the "divine madness" of the Greeks, their famous free spirit and play of imagination at the intensest level of consciousness. This is a Platonic poem. I think of Plato's world soul as an amorphous cloud hanging in the heavens. When we are born a portion of the world soul is joined to our bodies. They stay in mysterious relationship until the body dies and the soul goes back to the world soul. It is a pre-Christian notion. Wordsworth particularized Plato's idea. My poem holds to the immaculate quality of the ego in childhood, the early perfection of life, but recognizes the changes of time, man's inevitable confrontation of complexity, with the resolution as a tension of opposites.

Here is "New Hampshire, February," a poem dating from the end of the Thirties. I was as yet unmarried and had been given a cabin in Kensington, New Hampshire, near Exeter, during the winter vacation. The only heat was from the kitchen stove. I read philosophy and wrote poetry. One day some wasps fell through the roof onto the stove. They were numb but moved toward the center, getting more lively all the time. Recognizing a threat, I pushed them to the outside, where they grew slower immediately. I first did this innocently, by instinct. However, I had early read much Schopenhauer and Hardy and soon decided to play with these creatures as the instrument of their fate, "malice prepense." I would push them toward the center of the stove. They would become lively, buzzing their wings, able to sting. Then I would immediately move them toward the outer edge of the stove, where they would quickly become gelid. I manipulated them at will. The philosophical implications of this in the relation of ourselves to God were immediately to hand, and I wrote the following poem, with changes from the above facts which you will see. For instance, I use my breath instead of my hand as agent. There is an allusion to and reminder of "God touching his finger to Adam" from Michelangelo's Sistine painting.

New Hampshire, February

Nature has made them hide in crevices,
Two wasps so cold they looked like bark.
Why I do not know, but I took them
And I put them
In a metal pan, both day and dark.

Like God touching his finger to Adam
I felt, and thought of Michelangelo,
For whenever I breathed on them,
The slightest breath,
They leaped, and preened as if to go.

My breath controlled them always quite.
More sensitive than electric sparks
They came into life
Or they withdrew to ice,
While I watched, suspending remarks.

Then one in a blind career got out,
And fell to the kitchen floor. I
Crushed him with my cold ski boot,
By accident. The other
Had not the wit to try or die.

And so the other is still my pet.
The moral of this is plain.
But I will shirk it.
You will not like it. And
God does not live to explain.

Of the several war poems I wrote during World War II, "The Fury of Aerial Bombardment" has been most studied. It was written in Dam Neck, Virginia, in the summer of 1944 while I was stationed there as a

Naval Reserve officer teaching aerial free gunnery. I taught tens of thousands of young Americans to shoot the .50-caliber Browning machine gun from aircraft. The subject was called Sighting. All too soon their names would come back in the death lists. This depressed me so much that one time I was sitting on a barracks steps at the end of the day and felt the ruthlessness and senselessness of war so acutely that I wrote the first three stanzas of the poem, which are in effect a kind of prayer. I put it away. Some time later I felt it needed something added to it. Maybe the interval was a week or two. With an analytical mind, quite removed from the passionate one of the first three stanzas, I composed the last four lines. It is said that these in relation to the others make this a particularly modern poem. Indeed, if I had not added the last stanza, perhaps the poem would remain unused. This is an example of a certain fortuitous quality determining the fate of a poem.

The Fury of Aerial Bombardment

You would think the fury of aerial bombardment
Would rouse God to relent; the infinite spaces
Are still silent. He looks on shock-pried faces.
History, even, does not know what is meant.

You would feel that after so many centuries
God would give man to repent; yet he can kill
As Cain could, but with multitudinous will,
No farther advanced than in his ancient furies.

Was man made stupid to see his own stupidity?
Is God by definition indifferent, beyond us all?
Is the eternal truth man's fighting soul
Wherein the Beast ravens in its own avidity?

Of Van Wettering I speak, and Averill,
Names on a list, whose faces I do not recall
But they are gone to early death, who late in school
Distinguished the belt feed lever from the belt holding pawl.

After the war, I was in business in Boston for six years. "The Horse Chestnut Tree" is from this time, written in 1948. The actual tree stands in the garden of my father-in-law, now deceased, at 117 Lake View Avenue, Cambridge. The poem is based on a true incident. As with many of my poems, it came not immediately upon the experience, but welled into being some time later. Sometimes the interval would be months, sometimes years. This is another case of a poem being a "gift of the gods." When it was ready to come, it was born whole, with the need to alter only one, or possibly two words, as I recall. Thus, I theorize that poetry may come into being in a state of contemplation, where memory must be operant, when the mind and being have a grasp of more than usual order and one is able to project and execute a poem easily with total authority.

Every fall a group of wild Irish boys would troop down the street and enter my father-in-law's garden to break down the horse chestnut tree with sticks and stones to get the nuts. They were about sixteen to eighteen, very hardy types. My father-in-law was getting old and could not cope with them. They had no respect for private property or for capitalism. I was feeling very strong and capable and one fall said I would take over the situation.

When the molesting boys came into the garden I felt I had the situation perfectly in hand. I knew precisely what I would do and had every right to do it. I rushed out with perfect confidence and grabbed one of the tough youths by the shoulder, whereupon he immediately yelled "Police! Police!" and I was so startled that I confess I let go and ran back into the house. Could it be that they were in cahoots with the police? O the high-spirited, undaunted Irish! (My middle name is Ghormley.) In a hundred years they had taken over Boston and would soon have a President in the White House. I had my revenge, of a sort, on the boy whose name I will never know, by writing the poem. It may be that some day the unwitting protagonist or one of his band will read it.

I perceived that these ruffians were actually Plato's lovers of the beautiful. They perceived, although they could not verbalize it, that beauty is useless. They only wanted to hold a shiny chestnut in their hands or in their pockets. They were, in effect, aestheticians and lovers of the good. I empathized with them, for I had also loved and enjoyed the shiny feel of chestnuts in my youth. When the poem came to be written, I understood certain relationships between the desires of man and his limitations, which are in the poem. A lawless act brought me to the laws and order of the poem.

The Horse Chestnut Tree

Boys in sporadic but tenacious droves
Come with sticks, as certainly as Autumn,
To assault the great horse chestnut tree.

There is a law governs their lawlessness.
Desire is in them for a shining amulet
And the best are those that are highest up.

They will not pick them easily from the ground.
With shrill arms they fling to the higher branches,
To hurry the work of nature for their pleasure.

I have seen them trooping down the street
Their pockets stuffed with chestnuts shucked, unshucked.
It is only evening keeps them from their wish.

Sometimes I run out in a kind of rage
To chase the boys away: I catch an arm,
Maybe, and laugh to think of being the lawgiver.

I was once such a young sprout myself
And fingered in my pocket the prize and trophy.
But I still moralize upon the day

And see that we, outlaws on God's property,
Fling out imagination beyond the skies,
Wishing a tangible good from the unknown.

And likewise death will drive us from the scene
With the great flowering world unbroken yet,
Which we held in idea, a little handful.

Also from this period is one of the few pieces I have written immediately upon the experience which caused the poem. This is "The Cancer Cells." I was a fatigued salesman at the end of a hot day in August and found myself in Newark, New Jersey. I took a room at the "Military Park Hotel," curiously amused at the odd name since I was so exhausted. I bought a copy of *Life* magazine. When I entered my room, fatigued, I opened the magazine accidentally to a two-page spread of the spiky shapes of cancer cells leaping out of test tubes. The vision startled me; it aroused me to an immediate perception of the hostility and beauty of these strange forms, the lethal and the beautiful simultaneously understood, death in life. I am sure the vision would not have struck me so hard if I had not been so tired. I happened to have a pencil and an envelope in my coat pocket and wrote the poem immediately on the back of a letter just as it stands. The form of poems seems to be natural corollary to what is being said.

The Cancer Cells

Today I saw a picture of the cancer cells,
Sinister shapes with menacing attitudes.
They looked like art itself, like the artist's mind,
Sinister shapes with menacing attitudes,
Into a world beyond, a virulent laughing gang.
They looked like art itself, like the artist's mind,

Powerful shaker, and the taker of new forms.
Some are revulsed to see these spiky shapes;
It is the world of the future too come to.
Nothing could be more vivid than their language,
Lethal, sparkling and irregular stars,
The murderous design of the universe,
The hectic dance of the passionate cancer cells.
O just phenomena to the calculating eye,
Originals of imagination. I flew
With them in a piled exuberance of time,
My own malignance in their racy, beautiful gestures
Quick and lean: and in their riot too
I saw the stance of the artist's make,
The fixed form in the massive fluxion.
I think Leonardo would have in his disinterest
Enjoyed them precisely with a sharp pencil.

After World War II we went every summer to Cape Rosier on the coast of Maine. The sea gave me several poems. One is called "Seals, Terns, Time." When I had the experience of it I was not thinking of poetry. This is an example of a poem being born when ready long after the event, probably half a year later. In a contemplative state, in winter, in my study, memory and imagination arose to the consciousness from which came literary execution.

The facts were these. I was alone in a skiff a mile offshore at midday in high summer at the westward end of Pond Island, facing Green Ledges, which has a flashing light. The boat had an outboard but I was using oars. I was lolling in a large, still pool of water. Seals would come up around the boat, curious and playful, but they would never get closer than about twenty feet. By remaining as still as possible they could be coaxed quite near. Perhaps there were a dozen seals in this pack. Their great eyes reminded me of Hart Crane's line "The seal's wide spindrift gaze toward Paradise."

If I had only seen the seals I do not think there would have been a poem. Suddenly overhead, as if a silk scarf were drawn swiftly across the heavens, there flashed by, only a couple of hundred feet up, a flight of fork-tailed terns, curveting and flashing, close together, the sun catching their underbodies in a breathless vision as they wheeled from sight.

If I had seen only the terns that day I do not think there would have been a poem.

Usually when we have experiences these seem to be self-sufficient. They are part of the phenomena of life. I had no idea of "making anything" of the experience of the seals, and sufficient unto the terns was the glory of their instantaneous, unexpected vision. One lived in nature and was part of nature.

When the poem came, relationships were seen which I had not felt when enjoying the raw, disparate experiences of the poem. The significance of the events was held in the imagination and synthesized into a comprehensive view; control was laid on experience; life was ordered to a whole view of truth, within the limits of the experience and of the poem.

Man was seen (not thought of when I was sitting in the boat) as "A gauze and spindrift of the world," a delicately balanced creature on a frail integument, the boat a cockle shell on the vastness of the ocean, man a precarious creature of short duration seen against the vastness of time and eternity. In the poem man is posed as a balanced object on the sea, under him the seals, symbols of our animal nature going back to the beginning of evolution, over him the wheeling birds, symbols of our spiritual nature. The birds are enticing us to "the release of the sky." Man is in between flesh and spirit, partaking of both. He is related to both in his short duration "balanced on the sea" of meaning.

Seals, Terns, Time

The seals at play off Western Isle
In the loose flowing of the summer tide
And burden of our strange estate—

Resting on the oar and lolling on the sea,
I saw their curious images,
Hypnotic, sympathetic eyes

As the deep elapses of the soul.
O ancient blood, O blurred kind forms
That rise and peer from elemental water:

I loll upon the oar, I think upon the day,
Drawn by strong, by the animal soft bonds
Back to a dim pre-history;

While off the point of Jagged Light
In hundreds, gracefully, the fork-tailed terns
Draw swift esprits across the sky.

Their aspirations dip in mine,
The quick order of their changing spirit,
More freedom than the eye can see.

Resting lightly on the oarlocks,
Pondering, and balanced on the sea,
A gauze and spindrift of the world,

I am in compulsion hid and thwarted,

45

> Pulled back in the mammal water,
> Enticed to the release of the sky.

Another poem of about the same time came while we were driving across the country to Seattle in 1952 and stopped to see Cousin Florence, a woman of powerful mind and character, then over ninety, in the hospital. She had broken her hip but was undaunted in spirit. Again, I was not thinking of a poem during our visit. During our conversation she opened a drawer, took out a hand-sized piece of marble, and handed it to me. She said, "Richard, I want you to have this. It is a piece of the Parthenon. I got it when I was young. One picked up souvenirs in those days when there were no police around." It wasn't until long afterward, quite a few months I seem to recall, and, as it happened, after her death, that the poem grew in the imagination and was set down. I perceived the analogy of the laying on of hands, the handing down of religious traditions in the church, and the transferring of her cultural realizations from her generation to mine through the symbol of the marble.

My admiration for her was so great that in this poem character is recognized as superior to art, although we often think of art as superior to character and nature, as lasting longer than the flesh. This poem, though, holds that life itself, live acts of love, are preferable to art. The spirit is even deeper than beautiful works of "leaping marble." It is a belief not popular (accredited) in these times.

Cousin Florence

> There it is, a block of leaping marble
> Given to me by an ancestor.
> The hands that passed it held down ninety years.
> She got it in the love-time of Swinburne.
>
> This woman with her stalwart mien,
> More like a Roman than a Greek,
> Fumbled among old bags of rubble
> For something indomitable that she could seek.
>
> She saw the light of ancient days around her,
> Calling in the hip-cracked hospital.
> She chose at last. Then the clear light
> Of reason stood up strong and tall.
>
> With a pure, commanding grace
> She handed me a piece of the Parthenon,
> Saying, this I broke with my own hands,
> And gave me the imagination of the Greeks.
>
> I thought the spirit of this woman

> The tallest that I had ever seen,
> Stronger than the marble that I have,
> Who was herself imagination's dream
>
> By the moment of such sacrament,
> A pure force transmitting love,
> Endurance, steadfastness, her calm,
> Her Roman heart, to mine, of dream.
>
> I would rather keep her noble acts,
> The blood of her powerful character, a mind
> As good as any of her time, than search
> My upward years for such a stone that leaps.

Another poem from the coast of Maine, from the mid-Fifties, is "A Ship Burning/And a Comet All in One Day." This was based on a real experience. The first boat we ever had larger than a skiff, when it was laid up one fall, elicited the statement from its caretaker that we were lucky to be alive: he could put his fist through the side. We placed the hulk on Grandma's lawn before the sea, put flowers in it, and offered it to the children to play in.

Grandma's brother, now in his seventies, had been in the Naval Academy. He argued that just as we would not leave a corpse above ground and just as men love boats—as is seen in their giving them the names of women—we should give the boat decent burial. We should burn the vessel. A family argument ensued all winter. Our Annapolis relative won and the following August we had an ancient ceremony.

Timothy Rhodes, from Beach Island several miles down Penobscot Bay, determined when the tide would be at dead low. About sixty persons from surrounding cottages came in the late afternoon. About six of the men pulled the old hulk with a long line off the bank, down the shingle, to the edge of the sea. There was a sense of excitement and ceremony. The notion of a ship burning fires the imagination, taking us back to ancient Greece or perhaps to similar ceremonies in the time of Beowulf. Somebody brought red glass cups to the spectators and these were heaped with spirits—actually whiskey I am delighted to report.

A helper poured kerosene fore and aft. As the flames began I stepped amidships and raised a toast to the vessel. I remember becoming so enthusiastic and elated that I made up a spontaneous prayer, inventing on the spot a phrase which got into the poem when I consigned her "to immortal transubstantiation."

When the vessel was consumed down to the last debris, the ending of the poem actually happened, strange as it may seem. It was like a benediction. A great comet appeared in the sky, but stranger still, at the end of its long tail, in the middle, a star was set, making the whole appearance jewel-like and marvelous.

A Ship Burning
And a Comet All in One Day

When the tide was out
And the sea was quiet,
We hauled the boat to the edge,
On a fair day in August,
As who, all believing,
Would give decent burial
To the life of a used boat,
Not leave a corpse above ground.

And some, setting fires
On the old and broken deck,
Poured on the kerosene
With a stately quietude,
Measuring out departure,
And others brought libations
In red glasses to the sea's edge,
And all held one in hand.

Then the Captain arose
And poured spirit over the prow
And the sparks flew upward
And consigned her with fierce
Cry and fervent prayer
To immortal transubstantiation.
And the pure nature of air
Received her grace and charm.

And evening came on the sea
As the whole company
Sat upon the harsh rocks
Watching the tide come in
And take the last debris,
And when it became dark
A great comet appeared in the sky
With a star in its nether tail.

A poem from the mid-Fifties which, like "The Cancer Cells," was written immediately upon having the experience which resulted in the poem, is "On a Squirrel Crossing the Road/In Autumn, in New England." I was alone in my car when a squirrel dashed out and apparently ran under it. I pulled immediately to the right and came to a stop in a ditch. I saw I had not hit the squirrel. Then I experienced a few minutes of high nervous awareness during which I felt clairvoyant. I felt I knew every relationship between the small creature, myself as a slightly larger animal, and the immense idea of God. I was an instrument of fate. I pulled out an envelope and a pencil and wrote down the poem just as it is.

The wit of the last half-line increases the meaning of the poem by affording connotations which otherwise would not obtain. My British publishers suggested that I leave the irregular last half-line out. I said I would entertain the notion in proof, knowing full well that this ending was crucial to the poem.

On a Squirrel Crossing the Road
In Autumn, in New England

It is what he does not know,
Crossing the road under the elm trees,
About the mechanism of my car,
About the Commonwealth of Massachusetts,
About Mozart, India, Arcturus,

That wins my praise. I engage
At once in whirling squirrel-praise.

He obeys the orders of nature
Without knowing them.
It is what he does not know
That makes him beautiful.
Such a knot of little purposeful nature!

I who can see him as he cannot see himself
Repose in the ignorance that is his blessing.

It is what man does not know of God
Composes the visible poem of the world.

. . Just missed him!

The last poem I should like to discuss is "Am I My Neighbor's Keeper?" written January 5, 1962. The poem was begun after reading a newspaper account of a murder which occurred several years ago in the part of New England in which I live. The murderer or murderers were never discovered or brought to trial. All the powers of the law were of no avail to bring about justice.

Whereas I believe in a theory of inspiration and think that some of my best poems have come spontaneously, this poem was written by the rational use of the will. Perhaps Keats's Negative Capability was at work. If Positive Capability would be purposive action impinging on

49

the world, Negative Capability could stand for a surrogate for positive action, pen or pencil on paper creating a work of art.

I began with Keats's first line from "On the Grasshopper and Cricket," dated December 30, 1816, "The poetry of earth is never dead." This line had stayed with me all my life. I wanted something sterner, not only pleasant, and emended it to read "The poetry of tragedy is never dead."

When I began the poem I did not know it was going to be a sonnet, but this form soon developed, although I wrote two spaced quatrains before fixing on the form. These present generalizations, abstract realizations of the matter at hand. The sestet particularizes, giving graphic details of a tragedy in real life. The poem suggests that the deepest things in life are ultimately mysterious. In this case, the murder is irremediable, unsolved, and unredeemed. The statement at the end, which secretes a pun on the word "damn," not only announces the final bleakness of the tragic situation but has an overtone, perhaps, that if the murdered man could speak he would do so, although he could only do so now in the mute form of a corpse. The poem suggests universal guilt. The irony here is that society protected the definitely guilty from coming to justice.

Am I My Neighbor's Keeper?

The poetry of tragedy is never dead.
If it were not so I would not dream
On principles so deep they have no ending,
Nor on the ambiguity of what things ever seem.
The truth is hid and shaped in veils of error
Rich, unanswerable, the profound caught in plain air.
Centuries after tragedy sought out Socrates
Its inexplicable essence visits us in our lair,

Say here, on a remote New Hampshire farm.
The taciturn farmer disappeared in pre-dawn.
He had beaten his handyman, but no great harm.
Light spoke vengeance and bloodstains on the lawn.
His trussed corpse later under the dam
Gives to this day no answer, says I am.

While this poem is an example of the rational use of the intellect, as I view the writing of my own poetry since my youth, roughly over a period of forty years, I admire Plato's idea in the *Ion* when he says, "For the poet is a light and winged and holy thing, and there is no invention in him until he has been inspired and is out of his senses, and the mind is no longer in him: when he has not attained to this state, he is powerless and is unable to utter his oracles." I respect this theory of inspiration because it is beyond and above conscious will. A poem composed as the reception of a "gift of the gods" would seem to be of a higher origin and nature than a poem composed by taking thought and then by taking care.

Some of my poems which I think of as coming under this theory of creation are "Now Is the World Made of Chiming Bells," "If I Could Only Live at the Pitch That Is Near Madness," "1934," "Go to the Shine That's on a Tree," "Only in the Dream," and possibly also, but less purely, poems like "Maze," "For a Lamb," "The Groundhog," "In a Hard Intellectual Light," "In Prisons of Established Craze," "Light from Above," and "Vast Light."

On the other hand, a poem like "Am I My Neighbor's Keeper?" has the impurity, as does most poetry in comparison with Plato's ideal, of the whole warring and loving human nature of man.

The Poet as Teacher

I was sitting in a business office in Boston five years ago when I received a call. It is sometimes said that men receive a call. Life elects them to go one way. This call asked if I would come to the University of Washington in Seattle and be poet in residence.

At that time I had the notion that poetry cannot be taught, that its mysterious essence eludes explication, defies analysis. I thought that poetry could not be taught by poets. I had no doubt that it could be taught by professors. Had I not learned from them, at Dartmouth, at Cambridge, at Harvard?

Then I thought of it as a challenge. Why should one close one's mind on the notions one already has? Why not experiment with life in the act of teaching poetry? Why should not a poet, in fact, be best suited to teach poetry? So with a burgeoning sense of adventure we crossed the country to Seattle.

It should be said for the record, and before trying to come to the nub of some problems of the poet as teacher or the teacher as poet, that the call I mentioned above was, surprisingly enough, followed by four others in four succeeding years. To recapitulate, there were two large state universities, with their special and lively problems: the University of Washington and the University of Connecticut. Then there was a call to be the first incumbent in a new visiting professorship at Wheaton College (Norton, Mass.), a century-old college of attractive young ladies. Then there was Princeton, with its preceptorial system, where in addition to teaching poetry I gave a series of Christian Gauss lectures. And now there is Dartmouth, a homecoming after being out in the world thirty years. Marianne Moore has as the title of one of her books "What Are Years?" The longer one lives, the more poignant this question becomes.

First published in *Dartmouth Alumni Magazine*, November, 1956, pp. 20–23.

Actually, I received my first call to poetry when I was about fifteen.

Poetry is being rediscovered. History is swinging back to its ancient magic. And there comes into action the idea that poets can teach it. There is felt to be a need for integration between poetry as an intellectual discipline, a mode of feeling, an intuition of the mysterious meaning of life, and the so-called real events of the real world. This action has set within our universities and colleges a dozen or more poets as poets in residence, professors, or lecturers, producing an interesting American phenomenon.

By analogy, this present feeling for the need of integration has occasioned the expenditure of money on the part of businesses and foundations to return to colleges and universities, in California, in Pennsylvania, and this past summer at Dartmouth, business executives to learn from humanistic studies what at forty-odd they may not have been able to learn at twenty. Or to see things in a different perspective. And to see that business, for instance, is poverty stricken if it is not understood as an integral part of the cultural life of the nation. Business and culture were poles apart thirty years ago. Now it is seen that each depends upon the other and that they have mutual responsibilities. How fine it would be if our universities and colleges could pay back the compliment and send college teachers into business offices and factories to enlarge their horizons.

Recently I came across an old notebook containing early Dartmouth or post-Dartmouth poems. On one page appears this sentence, probably written shortly after my graduation in 1926: "Life should be lived expending energy in ideas and movements rather than on people." I have copied it just as I found it. First, a word of criticism. There is an ambiguity in "and movements," which suggests some sort of social action, but I apparently intended it in strict apposition to "ideas" and meant intellectual life for its own sake.

May I pay my respects to the Dartmouth of my time in quoting this sentence? I derived the highest respect for intellectual things from my professors. At the peak of a lust for learning was almost a limitless aesthetic delight. But note the sentence. It stands solitary in the little notebook, as if I had tried to put down the essence of a college education. It is significant that before the Crash, before the Depression, before World War II, Americans were secure. One felt no compulsion to expend energy on the people. By now we have a deeper and truer sense of democracy. Perhaps a graduate of last year's class would write that sentence almost in reverse. If you put a new electric washer in your house it will not go (I can attest to this) unless a workman properly connects and adapts it. What would happen in one month if the garbage man and the trash man did not come? Society is an integrated continuum of events, and these last mentioned members of it are as important as college professors or bank presidents. It took me at least twenty years to learn this.

Poetry fits into the picture too.

But while I am reminiscing let me recall to your memories a phrase from President Emeritus Hopkins which in my day became a veritable slogan. It was "An aristocracy of brains." Intellectual values were held before us and as young men we were to go forth to conquer the world by intelligence. It was an arresting phrase and it fired us with vague but powerful ambitions. It appears now to belong to its time as aptly as certain national slogans, such as the New Deal and the Fair Deal belonged to theirs. The movement of historical processes is complex and mysterious. It seems certain that man does not live by brainpower alone, and this observation leads me back to poetry.

Poetry is in the center of life, and if I had had the wit long ago I should have used a term which has been employed during the past two decades in schools of criticism. I should have asked for "An aristocracy of sensibility." That would bring to bear the whole personality, its total, potentially rich integration with the world. It would account for varieties of experience and contain the boundaries of both ambivalence and didacticism as modes of thought and conduct.

Now, in my own field, a real and troublesome problem exists. Is poetry aristocratic or democratic?

I wish to deal with this problem and to follow some considerations of it with the entertainment of another major problem, the relation of poetry and science.

Is poetry aristocratic or democratic?

By this I mean to ask, does the poet, that is, the great poet, or a group of leading poets, dominate the age and bring culture up to the level of the poet or poets, which may be said of Eliot in the first half of this century, or of any leading group you may name, if you agree with the proposition; or is poetry democratic in that it is judged finally by all readers through time and is actually thus an expression of the will of the people, a democratic enactment?

Let me elaborate a bit. I want to have some answers to this problem as it has troubled me for years. Is it chiefly university-bred poets and readers who keep up the standards of poetry? Can one make so large a generalization with effect? If this is so, it must follow that poetry is an aristocratic matter, since few minds in the masses of society are sufficiently trained to write or to comprehend the best poetry.

I would like now to take a position for the sake of argument. It is not a matter of total belief. The higher the mind and the greater the poetry, the more esoteric it becomes. Gerard Manley Hopkins is a case in point. He had only three poems of his published during his lifetime, which ended in 1889 at the age of 44. After the publication of his work in 1918 by his friend Robert Bridges, his value was perceived, and there followed for over twenty years an outpouring of books about him. Now the outpouring of books and articles about Hopkins has subsided. He speaks to this century closely, who could not reach the ear of the last.

I love his poetry intensely, along with that of Blake. Yet I recognize that even now, although Hopkins is large in textbooks and critical estimation, he is read by probably only a happy number of thousands of readers. He is thus, in my argument, an aristocratic poet. He appeals to trained readers, to sophisticated personalities. Is this a limitation in him, or is it a limitation in a society which is so democratic as not to care for what he has to say?

Take another example. Carl Sandburg had a great flair during the Twenties. He seemed to speak directly for perhaps a majority of Americans and to exist at the heart of our democratic culture. Sandburg represents an opposite pole from Eliot. He is not read with conviction in the universities or commented upon by the learned because he is too simple, not exciting to the imagination, and because his language is flat. We adore instead the late Wallace Stevens, who incidentally was a vice-president of the Hartford Accident and Indemnity Insurance Company. Now if you grant the premise that Sandburg is truly democratic and that we have a democratic culture in America, would you not have to elevate Sandburg and his like, the practitioners of popular art, to a place they do not at present hold?

The opposite has happened. The amorphous, scintillant, radiant, difficult, and subtle imagination of Stevens has held many minds in fascination. The subtle and difficult poets have won the recent day, but taste, as we know, is a seesaw, and change is inevitable.

I do not remove the posed question, but disallow a limitation to an either-or dichotomy. I speak instead for a vigorous pantheon of poets, which we possess in this country, and for a catholicity of taste which embraces widely divergent ideas and styles with discrimination.

Another concern is the relation of poetry, as an example of the arts, and science. They seem opposite. It seems as if science has made our world what it is and that science controls it. Science makes things happen. It seems, oppositely, that poetry "makes nothing happen," to quote Auden, that it ends in contemplation, often perhaps a beautiful, disinterested contemplation, and seems to be inferior to science.

Art, or let us retain the word "poetry," expresses the nature of a time. One does not understand much about the nineteenth century by going to books to find out how many soldiers were lined up against each other at the battle of Balaclava. One may read Keats, Blake, Tennyson, Whitman, Emerson to derive a feeling of the century. We do not understand the Civil War in terms of logistics, but through, for instance, Stephen Crane's *The Red Badge of Courage,* in which its main characteristics are revealed. This is a story written by a man who read about the war but did not fight in it. His imagination has preserved in art a significance of that war.

There is no question of inferior or superior in relating art and science. These terms need not be applied. Ultimately they represent the same use of the intelligence, that is, imagination.

In a current book, *Christianity and the Existentialists,* edited by Carl Michalson, I read on page 61 that Einstein "assures us that science can deal only with the function and interaction of matter, but can never know or penetrate into the nature of matter." He also said somewhere that in inventing a new theory of the universe the mind "jumps a gap." At some fine point his mind jumped a gap from what was then known to something new. He saw things in a new way and produced his relativity and field theory. It seems easy now to conceive of time as a fourth dimension. Not one of our grandfathers could think of it in that way. This was essentially poetic imagination.

Mr. Eliot, when he wrote *The Waste Land,* which was published in 1922, in effect threw over the nineteenth century. He invented a new type of poem, he saw things in a new way.

Thus, at their peaks, scientific and poetic imagination are equated as uses of intelligence—sensibility too, if you will. They are branches of the same tree, they have the universal roots of our common humanity.

Science is based on reason; it is limited to measurement. Poetry is often based on intuition, which has a deep, ancient resource yet has its own limitation inasmuch as it depends on a predilection whether one feels that it creates a world view and whether this world view engages one. Many intelligent people have got from birth to death without art at all.

I have given only two problems which a teacher of poetry could deal with. If an undergraduate could study, to the limit of his imagination, applying all the agility of a youthful mind, and could satisfactorily answer, with a battery of scholarly arguments, such questions as these, he might not only enjoy himself immensely but he might also move toward one end of education, which is self-knowledge.

A formulation above does not quite satisfy me. One wishes to avoid special pleading, yet allow me a confessional stance. Auden said recently somewhere something to the effect that when he is in the presence of scientists he feels inferior. He feels out of place in the presence of these rulers of the world. It is an intelligent attitude, but there is a whimsical, crafty undertone in the sentence, as if he did not mean it. If science is responsible, through reason alone, for the twentieth century, with two wars and a depression in only half of it, and with cobalt bombs prepared to spring back at them, and on all of us, scientists ought to feel primal guilt. No doubt some of them do, but they are helpless before their feelings.

In the presence of scientists I feel instinctively superior as a poet. I have announced their limitations in quoting Einstein. I have said above in all fairness that there is no argument between science and art, that imagination works equally in both; yet I feel compelled to say that most poets exalt mankind (sometimes even when condemning it, or satirizing it, or holding it up to ridicule—one may think of Baudelaire, of Swift), that poetry which lasts has perforce moral value, is for the good of man, and that its situation in the depths of consciousness allies it with religious intuitions, and that its ability to speak for the heart as well as for the head gives it a limitless potential power for the shaping of truth.

Men who have lost this vision are beginning to see it again. Man cannot live by the bread of executive gain alone, by the bread of factual control over matter, by the proudest boasts of materialism. He must live by inner compulsions, by deep natural drives, by sensitive intuitions, by spiritual realities, by concern with the ineffable, by devotion, by prayer, by humility, by all those dynamic forces which keep the soul alive in struggle and pierce the veil of illusion. Much of this reality may be imbedded in the subconscious. It is from these reaches that art is born and here I am talking of only one art, poetry.

I cannot see that the study of poetry, a serious and a glorious thing from the time of Shakespeare to the time of Dylan Thomas, can harm man, and I can see that its moral power can enrich the quality of his life. I thus think that it is valid to study it and to teach it. One writes it if one must.

I ought to end these generalizations on a note about criticism. It may be that the *apercu*, the unschematized, personal intuition is as good a type as any, maybe better than most or than any.

Students tend to rebel, for instance, at Yeats's hard-won schematization in *A Vision* which, although fascinating, fails to satisfy due to arbitrariness and straining. Few really love it. Many can admire its conic elaborations, but it somehow does not take in all of life while pretending to do so. They give it admiration, along with understanding, but they do not give it love, which it does not invite. It may be that the relatively few, somewhat undisciplined, but thoroughly human and cogent asides, chance perceptions, and penetrating remarks made by Robert Frost, whose abundant genius I praise, represent the best criticism about poetry—a criticism not of a school, also not eccentric, but wise flashes of truth thrown off easily, if sparingly, down the decades.

Last spring at Princeton, as an example, Frost said abruptly, "All science is domestic science." That jumped a gap; we relish it. This illuminates one of the above arguments. With marked wit and deep wisdom, that is, with a sublime love of truth, he related the disinterested men of science, the atom-cobalt dreamers, the earth-shakers, to the man in the street who is the woman in the kitchen and showed that scientists are, after all, only trying as best they may to domesticate the universe. It was a witty, pithy, most humane and lovable statement, at which the crowded house chuckled, and then roared.

We use doing as a kind of escape from being. The scientists are the doers. Businessmen are doers. What I am really concerned with is being. Poetry is concerned with being. It erects states of being. It is a search for a way to be. We are all trying to be. Science through doing has made us afraid of being. Poetry, as well as the other arts, encourages us in being. Let us not be so burdened with doing that we neglect to see that "Even the thorn bush by the wayside is aflame with the glory of God."

Will and Psyche in Poetry

I wish to examine the relation of Will and Psyche to poetry. I conceive these terms as opposite poles of a modern dichotomy, but they may lie at the root of the mind itself and go back to the beginning of thought. I choose them because they have impinged upon my consciousness for years. It would be possible to attempt a reduction of the reality of poetry under a multiple aegis, or to accept a unitarian principle. However, it is natural to me to think in terms of dualism; if it is too neat to cast everything into either black or white, it is also orderly, and forces an arbitrary, though not conclusive, order on what is discovered.

The presumption of poetic criticism is intellectual authority. By thinking about poetry one can make certain determinations. This is the play of the mind, a pleasurable exercise. I do not say that truth is to be found, nor that what authority one comes by is not itself subject to the sway of time. What I affirm is the relativity of truth within absolute limits and the normalcy of a dichotomous look at poetry. There is a certain modesty in my approach. One does not wish absolutism, but a relative sagacity. After reading criticism for thirty years, it is necessary to wipe the slate clean, and speak freely with all one's impurities upon one. There is a vast body of historical poetry, to which accretions are always being made. It may be of interest to look at certain types of poetry, certain poems under an arbitrary canon. I shall study poetry from the creative, or poet's, point of view rather than from the presumptions of a reader who is not a poet and has no desire to write poetry. Maybe the line between creative reading and creative writing

First published in *A Celebration of Poets*, ed. Don Cameron Allen (Baltimore: Johns Hopkins University Press, 1967), pp. 152–76.

is thin. Maybe the approach of a dualism here is mythical. In any case, my remarks shall be, I hope, exploratory rather than dogmatic.

In thinking of Will and Psyche, a battery of descriptive terms comes at once to mind. Will is of the body; Psyche, or Soul, is of or beyond the mind. Will is flesh; Psyche spirit: Will is active; Psyche passive. Will makes something happen, or wishes to make something happen; Psyche makes nothing happen. Will is impure; Psyche is pure. Will represents struggle and effort; Psyche represents an uncontaminated grace. Will is the body of this world; Psyche is the elusive, passive, imaginative quality of or toward another. Will is interested; Psyche is disinterested. Will goes back to some basic power in the cell, an animal exercise. The cell has an excess of energy over its power to maintain itself.

Psyche is at once mysterious and eludes the simplest opposition to what I have just said. I suppose it depends upon a cellular structure, for none of us living can feel what it is to be dead, and only by imagination, by intuitive leaps, can we dream beyond death. Here many ideas about Psyche appear. If one equates it with soul, then we may say it is the soul; but nobody knows what the soul is. I have touched my flesh for years trying to find my soul. I have still not seen it. But there are ancient, persistent ideas about the soul. There is, for instance, the Platonic world soul, envisaged as a vast amorphous cloud hanging in the heavens. When we are born a portion of the world soul is attached to our body, where it lives while we live; when we die, it ascends, or departs, depicted in old paintings always up-wards, back to the mother lode or static whole of the world soul. There are all the variations of Eastern philosophy, thought, and religion about the soul and the afterlife. However, to write the last few sentences I must be corporeal; it is easy to insist upon this! Therefore, by reason we may say that we do not know whether we have a soul, but without an undue amount of sympathetic projection we may assume that we have a soul, a Psyche, somewhere about us.

In a short space and time the easy absolutes mentioned above have broken open into what may be seen at once to verge upon massive speculations. This is part of the fascination of the problem. We start by saying that Will and Psyche enforce a real dichotomy, but almost at once it is seen that these terms exfoliate and proliferate; that there may, maybe must, be some Psyche in Will, for how could it be so base a thrust as by strong nature not to possess some qualities of the divine? And how could Psyche be so pure as not to possess some qualities of base human nature? They may not be white and black as we suppose. Indeed, it may be that some of the greatest poetry lies between them, partaking of both, giving the critic a complex pleasure of discovery and evaluation. It may be, depending upon the nature of the critic's piercing look, that Will poetry and Psyche poetry represent only a small part of the whole, to be enjoined by special pleading, but loved when found. I admit this as a possibility.

Of the two components in our dichotomy, Psyche appears to be more elusive, to ramify into the more interesting complexities, to be the harder to grasp since its pleasing quality resides in its ungraspable part, and by the notion of some kind of grace, whereby the mind does not wish to probe, nor the intellect to meddle, but the whole being to accept, when in the grip of Psyche poetry, thus immediately ceasing to be a critic. But enjoyment may be had either way; there are as many ways of enjoying poetry as there are ways of living. And I do not say that Psyche poetry is better than Will poetry. I say that it is more subtle, more elusive, more delicate, essentially I suspect more over-whelming by its virtue to take us in against our will, leave us sus-pended in delicious realms of ambiguity, unresolved conjurations, passive pleasure. It works partially through a religious attitude.

I have a short poem which appeared in *Reading the Spirit* in 1937 but which was written I think while I was at Cambridge, between 1927 and 1929. It was written to the world at large, to nobody in particular, and was entitled "The Critic." I wish to turn this poem upon myself. It goes as follows:

> The Critic with his pained eye
> Cannot my source espy
> For truly and purely to eye it
> He would have as critic to die.
>
> I with joyful vision see,
> I cannot his purpose acquire.
> For if the Critic were truly free
> He would love, and not be a liar.

It may be interesting to quote first a poem which is neither purely of Will nor of Psyche, but which contains admixtures of both. I no doubt thought of myself as both poet and critic. I was under the eye of I. A. Richards, and was aware of his early belief that all that modern poetry can do is to make pseudo statements, in fact, tell lies. His psychologi-cal point of departure was that in the modern world the scientist alone demonstrates truth; this is the truth of putting one thing to another and calling it, logically enough, two. This is the truth of physical experiment where, given certain facts, certain results must follow. There is rigidity and absolutism. William James enounced this reasonable world in his essay on pragmatism. A thing was good if it worked, which was analogous to the one-to-one conclusions of the experimental scientists. Americans allowed only what worked and now we were becoming great. The assumption was that this was good.

Let us see what my short poem said. It posited in the first line a pained eye for the critic. This is an arbitrary choice of a word, meaningful and setting the mood when quickly followed by the notion that the pained eye of the critic cannot espy or find out the source from which the poet writes. It sets up a dichotomy between poetry and criticism; one is supposed immediately to sympathize with the poet and believe what he says is true. The first stanza ends on the extended notion that the critic would have to die in order to see the source of the poet, or see into it.

The second stanza begins by saying that the poet sees with joyful vision; the assumption is, simply, that the critic does not. In the swiftness of the poem this is supposed to be taken unchallenged. But it is not, of course, necessarily true. The critic is not directly attacked, but the emphasis is placed on the difference of the poet, who cannot "his purpose acquire." Here is a difference, upon contemplation of the poem, that may not at first appear. The critic, in stanza one, might achieve the source of the poet were he to die as critic. The poem does not specify the methods for this dying, nor indeed state what kind of dying it is, psychological or imaginative. But in line two of the second stanza the poet, because he sees with joyful vision, cannot acquire the purpose of the critic. This is, in fact, dogmatic assertion and pleads specially for the poet. It seems to understand instinctively that creation is first and criticism second, and that this is the natural and just order of things. The poem may in fact be hostile to criticism because of the latter's power, recognized, but not stated, to be injurious, even deadly to the creation of poetry. It may therefore arbitrarily assume that the critic has no joyful vision, which in cold reason nobody would allow, while the poet has a superior hold on ultimate value. The last two lines cap off or clinch the central idea of the poem. They say that if the critic were truly free he would love, and not be a liar. What gives the poem its life is the terseness and economy of the expression. Words like "truly" and "purely" are placed, instantaneously, to work efficiently, without the mind having to stop to ponder them. At the end there is a tacit boon extended to the critic; in fact, the antilegislation of the first quatrain is taken back in the "if" proposition which assumes that maybe the critic can be regenerated. It is not to say that he cannot. If then in fact he were truly free, he would love, and not be a liar. The word "love" at the end runs back to the beginning and ties in the idea of love as intimate to the act of creation, in poetry here, as well as in fact in nature. Close association is made between love with its joyful poetic vision and truth. If the critic were truly free, he would not be divorced from the nature of poetry, and he would not have to tell lies about it, which is his professional business, but by loving he would tell the truth.

The immediate tone of the poem impresses the obvious dichotomy upon the sensibility; but with reflection and in reading it carefully, it will be seen to be a rather hopeful poem. This ultimately hopeful quality is the Psyche part of the poem, while its thrust and somewhat belligerent immediacy is its Will part. There is the elusive notion that there is something sacrosanct in the source of the poet, which is we may say his Psyche; and, still turning it around, if the critic will exercise Will he may find through love the truth. It seems to me to be a true poem neither of Will nor of Psyche, but to live and persuade with elements of both.

Before going into old definitions of Will and Psyche, let me propose two short poems which exemplify some of their characteristics. There is a famous four-line poem, supposed to be sixteenth century, which many know, an anonymous piece entitled "The Lover in Winter Plaineth for the Spring." It is a poem of the Will.

> O Western wind, when wilt thou blow
>   That the small rain down can rain?
> Christ, that my love were in my arms
>   And I in my bed again!

This is simple, direct, evocative, a cry from the heart. It is a poem of wish fulfillment as good now as when it was written. It has a positive, strong emotional force. In the death of winter, loveless, the poet longs for spring, which represents love. The ejaculative utterance of the last two lines is powerful. Physical love is celebrated as an absolute good. There is no doubt about it. Calling upon Christ is a brilliant thrust. The renouncer of the world is called upon to bring the world most closely home to the heart. Although exceedingly short, this is a whole poem written in the fullness of humanity, with ardent belief in life and in love. It is a direct poem of the Will.

A poem which comes to mind when thinking of Psyche is Poe's "To Helen," wherein Psyche is named. This is a good example of Psyche poetry in a pure, or almost pure form. There is practically no Will in it. If we tend to equate Will poetry with Romanticism and Psyche poetry with Classicism, this poem in its form, its balance and poise, is classical. Poe's emendation of his lines in the second stanza, to come on "To the glory that was Greece / And the grandeur that was Rome," is a famous example of improvement by taking thought. If these words were written as a prose phrase they would not seem remarkable; they might pass as journalism. Set as they are, with three major *g*'s neatly muted by five minor *r*'s, they become memorable.

The poem reads as follows:

To Helen

Helen, thy beauty is to me
  Like those Nicean barks of yore,
That gently, o'er a perfumed sea,
  The weary, way-worn wanderer bore
To his own native shore.

On desperate seas long wont to roam,
  Thy hyacinth hair, thy classic face,
Thy Naiad airs have brought me home
  To the glory that was Greece
And the grandeur that was Rome.

Lo! in yon brilliant window-niche
  How statue-like I see thee stand,
  The agate lamp within thy hand!
Ah! Psyche, from the regions which
  Are Holy Land!

Where you feel in our anonymous lover of the sixteenth century his loss of the loved object, and are in no doubt about the strength of his conviction that it would be good to have his love in his arms again, in bed, the reader feels no such strong pull toward its object in this poem. It is a much subtler, finer matter entirely. The poem ends in a sigh, a sort of wistfulness, a recognition that Psyche is so far removed from ordinary affairs that one can only dream about her from afar, not clasp her. She is way off in the improbable distance where her capture would be the remotest possibility. The notion of Psyche as soul is thus intrinsically honored by the poet. This is a magical poem, an object of contemplation, having little to do with action.

For all its famed simplicity the poem has a good many ambiguities and subtleties. We are supposed to think of Helen of Troy at once, yet some readers, primitively blessed, may think only of some other Helen. I read this poem for years without knowing what a "Nicean bark" was, and have again by this time forgotten, but this ignorance does not destroy the poem. The main sense is clear. The phrase "weary way-worn wanderer" always struck me as effeminate in the nineteenth-century sense, Swinburnian or late Tennysonian; I have never seen the most fatigued sailor who would fit this description. A plural number is suggested because of the plurality of barks. If they were actually weary and way-worn they would stop wandering, quit, give up, and go home. This is a romantic notion of an improbable kind of sailor, to put you in a mood of dream. We have encountered the notions of gentleness and perfume already. The barks and the men have actually got home, due to the persuasion of the beauty of Helen, which draws or pulls slowly but inevitably as a tide.

In the second stanza "desperate" is a well-chosen oppositional word and is the only one in the poem that suggests violence of action. The reader has to put up with certain nineteenth-century locutions in the poem, such as "barks of yore," "o'er" as elided, and "wont to roam." These are easily taken in. The first line of the second stanza, "On desperate seas long wont to roam," mounts an ambiguity which is probably not recognized at once by the reader; Helen may be thought to have roamed long on desperate seas as the prize of the Trojan wars, or it may be the poet-reader-adventurer who has done this, the Ulysses spirit. A suspension of meanings involves us in a smooth syllabic flow while we do not have to entertain its underlying mechanisms.

It is obvious that if Poe had transposed "glory" and "grandeur," the poem would not be great. If he had said the "grandeur that was Greece," which would after all have been possible, "and the glory that was Rome," he would have made a political mistake. The word "glory" has been used for Rome, just as we have our "Glorious Fourth," yet it is elementary that Poe, and probably a lesser poet than Poe would have done the same, perceived "glory" as specially pertaining to Greece, "grandeur" as specially pertaining to Rome. The homing notion of the first stanza is reiterated in a different way. The "hyacinth hair," "classic face," and "Naiad airs" are here the home-bringers, not now just to a native shore, but to the magnitude of spiritual and worldly dynasties.

In the first stanza we do not see Helen; it is not a photograph. It is an intellectual idea. In the third stanza we have a masterful placement, a dichotomy one part of which is a standard conception of a statue in a window-niche, an art object with a certain plastic reality to it, holding aloft an agate lamp, while almost at once this is controverted by Helen turning into Psyche, "from the regions which/ Are Holy Land." There is a great deal of magic cleverly dealt here. First, Helen-Psyche is only "like" a statue, she is "statue-like," so we are in the midst of poetry as a reality shot through with simultaneously held possibilities. Second, we are invited into a never-never land which takes us unawares, as it were, in the last two lines. They are so finely woven, as is the entire piece, that we accept at once, without the necessity for analysis. The words of the last stanza enforce, in a subtle, gentle way, a mood. The whole poem breathes a mood of gentleness and opens on far contemplations.

For instance, "Lo!," an antique word which we take in stride, is followed by "in yon brilliant window-niche." We do not have to notice the "yon" much, but it is as if a finger were pointing to an actual place, yet poetic vagueness is subsumed, we see no real building; we do not have indication of the architecture if Poe had any in mind; we do not know the material size or the shape of the window-niche. Poe as magician casually uses the word "brilliant," but this has intellectual implications with regard to the lamp and the meaning of Psyche's light.

"Ah! Psyche" involves us in the ultimate tone of the poem. Psyche, or soul, is from regions which are holy land. The sighing tone of this realization has in it tenderness and longing, yet there is no hint that this sacrosanct reality may be dealt with outright. That is the beauty of the poem. It is Psyche poetry, beyond the will of man. An ultimate reality is addressed. This reality, the soul, is admitted and placed in a true position beyond action. It is a matter almost of religious devotion, at least of religious affinity. Note that in stanza one there was a homecoming, in stanza two that there was a further type of homecoming, and I had meant to mention the ambiguity of "brought me home," which may refer back to the weary mariners or exist merely as a cant phrase, whereas in the last stanza, as if to progress to the highest spiritual plane of contemplation, there is no action at all, only a serene, ultimate sight to be seen and contemplated, beyond possession and beyond use. "Holy Land" obviously may refer to the Holy Land, and I suppose this sense is to some extent in most readers, intellectually inviting us to impose Jerusalem upon Greece and Rome. One wonders whether Poe intended this. I do not think so. The stress is on "regions." I think as magician-poet he is using valid poetic means, where words taken in usual connotation have overtones of other connotations which may be brought into focus in the mind, or left as a vaguely felt pleasure. He is having his cake and eating it too, to use "holy land" here as the very end of the poem.

The main thing to say about this satisfying poem is that there is a holy land but that we may not get to it. We may contemplate Helen but we may not touch her. If it were a Will poem there could be some anguish because of this fact. Because it is a Psyche poem there is no anguish; the poet is beyond this and the reader is beyond it too. Psyche is the region beyond strife and, as Helen, it is mythical and fabulous. A light is held on the world. We may contemplate this beauty, which is ultimately impersonal, spiritual, and ineffable.

Sometimes one mumbles certain phrases or lines of a poem in a sort of somnambulistic rite. Sometimes one does this for years. Many poems in English are great because of only a line or a phrase, or a few lines. Almost every schoolboy has learned "Helen, thy beauty is to me," and if as a man this phrase alone should persist as more memorable than another, it would perhaps be because of his will to violate the poem and possess Helen! If you say "Helen, thy beauty is to me" and stop there, you have paid a debt to Poe as poet, and as anarchic individualist you have thought to do the impossible, to possess Psyche itself. With that we leave Poe, Helen, and Psyche to the ages. They all age beautifully.

Let me now tell the traditional story of Psyche. It is interesting that the concept of Will has exercised the minds of great thinkers to a great extent, and that there is a vast amount of lore on the subject. It is equally interesting, and instructive for our own definitions and distinctions, that encyclopedic notions of Psyche are limited in scope, that there is no vast amount of lore, and that the meanings tend by the nature of the subject to be cast into story, fable, or allegory.

The tale of Cupid and Psyche, in the *Metamorphoses* of Apuleius, is interesting as the only ancient fairy tale which is told as such. In it Psyche, the youngest daughter of a king, arouses the jealousy of Venus, who orders Cupid to inspire her with love for the most despicable of men. "Cupid," continues the *Encyclopaedia Britannica*,

however, falls in love with her and carries her off to a secluded spot, where he visits her by night, unseen and unrecognized by her. Persuaded by her sisters that her companion is a hideous monster, and forgetful of his warning, she lights a lamp to look upon him while he is asleep; in her ecstasy at his beauty she lets fall a drop of burning oil upon the face of Cupid, who awakes and disappears. Wandering over the earth in search of him, Psyche falls into the hands of Venus, who forces her to undertake the most difficult of tasks. The last and most dangerous of these is to fetch from the world below the box containing the ointment of beauty. She secures the box, but on the way back opens it and is stupefied by the vapour. She is only restored to her senses by Cupid at whose entreaty Jupiter makes her immortal and bestows her in marriage upon her lover.

The Greeks were lucky in living on two planes at once as if there were no contradiction, no dichotomy. They lived in the reality of the earth and in the reality of the heavens. Thus, they were able to invent

67

a pantheon of gods and talk about them as if they were quite like themselves, yet giving them simultaneously the devotions of a different species. Psyche stands for the soul, is a term for the soul, and it is not strange that the Greeks should have told of Psyche in terms of a love story. So the soul and love are intimately allied. And this soul and this love are not so far from immediate concerns as not to have, in the story, all manner of worldly and painful trials, commissions of error, whims of fate; yet the fact remains that the story has a happy ending. The last sentences of the story, as charmingly told by Edith Hamilton (*Mythology,* p. 100), read, "So all came to a most happy end. Love and the Soul (for that is what Psyche means) had sought and, after sore trials, found each other; and that union could never be broken." If we say also that poetry is love, we have a *raison d'être* for the great amount of Psyche poetry there is in literature. And sometimes, in a plausible moment of illumination, we see things in a clear, fresh way as if for the first time and know that a fairy story with a happy ending is equal to any other interpretation of the world, acceptable as real. Then the obscurity and burden of our minds settles down into our perpetual modern cynical or doubting consciousness.

The fundamental distinction in all the ratiocination of the philosophers about Will is the primary one that it is always stewing in its own juice, is always hoist with its own petard, is always there in the meshes of the flesh, a bestial or an intellectual thing; whereas the primary qualities of Psyche are harmony, reconciliation, beauty, peace, a timeless at-oneness with some ultimate value, a fairy story with a happy ending which is possible only because the idea of Psyche is the most elusive, the most delicate, the most ephemeral and thus, paradoxically, the strongest and most complete repository of mortal awareness. Psyche becomes a myth, just as does the Virgin in Christianity. She is love, as the story was told above, and the fairytale-maker had the penetration to see that his lightness of touch really embraced and went beyond all the ponderous effects of the willing animal man. It is possible to take a fairy tale with the deepest seriousness, it is so wonderful and playful and ultimately meaningful. But in our time we do not often do so. We think of ourselves as too realistic.

In our short Will poem about the lover who beseeches Christ to bring his love to his arms again, we are not concerned with any part of Psyche. It is physical love that he wants, a total involvement of flesh and manhood. There is nothing against this, it is itself a kind of noble charm. But it presupposes that the lover will be completely joined to him in the kind of love union he wishes. But in the Psyche story love goes beyond itself to an airy and ethereal truth, subtle and deep.

There is the suggestion of the danger of looking too deeply into nature in the lamplight vigil of Psyche over Cupid. The burning oil is a sort of fatal flaw which makes the loved object disappear. But Cupid represents forgiveness at the end of the story, and we note that Psyche is made immortal by a god. This is all beyond the proper realm of reason. It is unreasonable. It pays implicit homage to the idea of mystery in human affairs, just as it is true that in marriage one never knows one's mate and that an elusive reality is an essence of marriage although it may be practiced for twenty or forty years. With this background, let us return to Will and, while holding judgment in abeyance, throw out some notions of what it is.

There is something about Will which is eternally youthful. The Will, progressing through the flesh with time, a gift of life in its deepest resources of power, has in it all that is wild, free, eager, joyful, the giver and taker of dangers, superior to, while being enmeshed in, all sorts of evils. Will is fresh and lean. Will works beneath the intellect while seeming not to and drives the personality to new action. Will is behind all aggressiveness, all savage deportment. It is there in the subduing of forests, the erecting of cities, the building of armies, acts of war. It gives off death as quickly as it shows forth enlightenment. Brain power is sometimes largely will power. Will is a torment of abuse and the search for perfection. It is a gift of nature. Its symbol could be the impassioned rider spurring the horse. It can dream of universal brotherhood but also of atomic destruction. Cunning, craft, malice, intellect; aspiration, desire, plan, thrust, perseverance, control; faculty, persuasion, peculiarity—these are all willful and are absolutes dominated by the blood drench, the flow in the veins, the strong life sense, the urgency to dominate, the pleasure of action, the health of a death-violating eye, freedom, and joy.

Freedom and joy! How little freedom and joy there are in the world. They must be made anew, forged in an active principle of blood, in a causative art. This necessity was recognized by Blake, Hopkins, and Lawrence. It is Will that will create the world anew; Will that will make something happen; Will that will make happen the compulsive poems. This also Whitman knew. The Will poet writes with the whole personality in a full thrust; he is totally engaged in the strength of his realization. A dynamic urgency burns in him; he is alive with vitality, love and aspiration and malice and scorn. I think of Crane writing *The Bridge*.

Now we come to a major problem of poetry. Does it conduce to action? Does it exert a cause from which there must be an effect? Is it offensive, distasteful, and does it make one wince? Does it fire one to

perhaps even patriotic action? Who would nowadays think of Longfellow as a revolutionary poet? Yet was not "Paul Revere's Ride" a
revolutionary poem, and did not Americans respond to his "The Ship
of State?" Would not the latter make them ready to die for their
country, that is, long ago? Yeats at one point wanted his poems to
spur Irishmen to militant action.

The Will conduces to the action of the poet in writing the poem. All
poems attempt to persuade in some way. We now arrive at the
problem of communication. And we may as well go back to our
anonymous sixteenth-century short poem of the poet calling for his
love to be in his arms again. I should say that this sort of successful
short poem creates an immediate state of identification in the reader.
The reader has no difficulty in placing himself in the position of the
poet so that he too is bereft of his lover and with equal passion wishes
for the fulfillment cried out for. The poem is universally valid for the
majority of mankind. The reader thus identifies himself with the
material of the poem. It has made something happen in that it has
made the reader feel exactly as the poet felt. We have to add that the
full sway of this poem does not necessarily bring on the desired result.
There is something comical about a despairing lover. The poem does
not say that the desired result is achieved. It is instead a strong
wish-fulfillment; but I suppose we could hold, without loss of dignity,
that if the poet willed strongly enough he would actually find a
solution to his difficulties. The poetry has made love happen. Love is
the purity of his concern. The problem seems fairly clear in so simple
an example. On the other hand, in a Psyche poem like Poe's "To
Helen" we have ultimate ambiguity and fluidity, as if the poem lived
in a perpetual continuum of unresolved possibilities, whose best
communicability is its tempting, fascinating, and endless ability not to
give up its secret, not perfectly to communicate, but to float in a
magical dew and timeless sight of something seen but not touched,
imagined but not possessed, aspired to but not achieved, so that the
residue of feeling from this poem is like the feelings about the soul
itself. It is a poetic mechanism for preponderating the soul.

Let us retrace our steps. The problem of Will and Psyche was
announced as a dichotomy, but had hardly so been stipulated than the
neatness of this dichotomy was seen to have blurred edges. A search
through literature may discover pure poems of Will, as defined, and
pure poems of Psyche, as defined; yet the definitions may not be
exhaustive, and there is a peril that any poem adduced may not be as
pure as it seems. The Western Wind poem, about the immediacy of

the desire for love, physical love, seems purely of the Will; indeed, it may be quibbling not to think it so. And yet there is the speculation, as one of a problematical number of final connotations (in this case, few) that a reservation should be supplied to the intention of the poem; the mind can conceive that it does not go far enough, for nothing is said about the nature or quality or meaning of the love that is cried for in the lover's arms and in bed. We are supposed to blind ourselves to any raveling out of thought. The success of the poem primarily keeps us within bounds; its strong, willful force binds it into a self-contained breathing machine. Except for the critic. The critic may play with these four lines, ranging over them discursive claims. What if the positive thrust of the poem has negative, even disastrous results? There is much love that brings on grief, endless trouble, every form of madness, even suicide, and may give rise to tragic literature. Only a critic would think that there is a lack in the poem because some ultimate result of the predicament is not specified or intimated. Could as great, or as enduring, a poem have been composed, which would also be of the will, if the old Elizabethan had cried out, let us say, in an excess of the kind of manliness that found its exercise and reward in seafaring, new world discovery, or hand-to-hand combat:

> Christ, that my love were never in my arms
> And I in my bed again!

I doubt if the poem would have lasted so long. Yet in the actual poem there is a frustration in the writer which makes it come into being: in my emendation there would also be a frustration, only a different kind of frustration, a modern one. If he were in his bed without his lover, wanting none, but wishing the spring and the rain, he might have recourse to extensive dreams, he might in fact be a performer in the realm of Psyche poetry.

But this gives a comic touch and may perhaps show the limits of criticism. It is not, in a sense, fair to go so far. It is uncalled for. It is not reasonable. Criticism must be based on logic and reason, on scope and judgment. The poem would seem therefore to suggest its own circumference for discussion. If one goes beyond that circle, one is committing bad taste. Bad taste must be excess beyond the facts, that is, sentimentality, and it must be fundamentally wrong headed. I have produced the above out-of-focus locution to attempt to show that criticism ought to stick to the main course, to look directly at the words and sensible connotations of a poem, not to go off into brainful asides which destroy the cogency and neatness of the suggested poetical system. But I also give it as a warning that the difficulties of criticism are many, and extreme, and that poetry is an unruly horse not easily ridden with elegance.

We then had an example of so-called pure Psyche poetry. Poe's "To Helen" has a restraint, an elegance, a fairness of proportion which does not invite destruction by easy opposition to make it a willful thing. It stands as an example of enduring, mood-producing, elusive poetry, and the only comment I have finally to make on it in the context of our subject is that, however tender and wistful and suggestive its ultimate feeling may be, Poe yet had the will to write it. So the problem is still there. If he had only daydreamed the poem, not composed it by strict, calculating, and masterful art, we should be the losers by his lack of will.

It is possible to think simply and clearly. Perhaps the great thinkers have done so. It is also possible, and just as human, to think unclearly and in a profusion of confusions, jumping this way and that, going off on tangents, trying to grasp meanings out of the air, so to speak, and great thinkers have done this. Life is complex; a famous apology for complexity in modern poetry is that it is so because modern life is complex. There is a sort of tenacity in the mind to resist conclusion. To conclude is to arrive beyond Will at stasis and finality. It is the Romantic point that to strive is better than to arrive; the struggle toward definition is more rewarding than whatever may be gained from final conclusion. Hell is more interesting than heaven; evil more provocative than good. But I suppose it depends upon the age, the age's characteristics. The eighteenth century provided a static society, a well-ordered and neat outlook on life; thus came didacticism in Pope and Dryden. The nineteenth century brought on the hidden beast in the machine, so we had the rumblings and exalted strikes-through of Romantic, assertive individualism. The twentieth century brought to flower in its first half a monstrous bloom of societal chaos, so we have a great poem like "The Waste Land" in a nonassertive revolution of intentions which penetrated into the surrounding chaos itself and brought forth chaotic resolutions.

What is a Psyche state in poetry? I would wish to continue without definition, dwelling in an ambience of vagueness, willfully shirking the duty of defining heaven. I would like to have my Psychic cake and eat it too, and not tell what it is made of! I would like to advance the cause of subtlety, mystery, and the ineffable. However, one cannot talk to no purpose, thinking runs to conclusion, and it is a pleasure to don the mantle of a sometime critic, from which I state, simply, that a Psyche state in poetry pertains to, exemplifies, or takes off from peace, quiet, calm, security, harmony, proportion, concord, tranquillity, freedom as from something (war, for instance), serenity, stillness, and silence. Now to give Will its same and simple due. Will is wish, desire, inclination, pleasure, appetite, passion, purpose, determination, choice, intention, entreaty, command, decree, power, arbitrary disposal, self-control as in a man of strong will, zeal, volition.

I wish it to be clearly understood in this paper that my dichotomy is arbitrary, existing as a framework for the discussion of works of poetry fitted more or less arbitrarily into my scheme because of my love of the poems chosen. I make no claim as a philosopher to any new original concept about Will and am in fact in awe of all the heavy ratiocination about this term in the history of philosophy. Likewise of Psyche; I do not write a new story of Psyche to equal the Greek. On both of these terms I have levied my own definitions, but I like to resist conclusions because there can be no real conclusion to literary criticism. It is a living, breathing, continuing thing.

Then also I want to make it clear, at the risk of repeating, that literary criticism is not a science, cannot be accurate in the way that a physical experiment may be accurate, and has its pleasures in a humane attitude to what is at hand. Ambiguity is one of the charms of modern poetical criticism. I entered these delighting reaches early. While I was at Cambridge, my classmate William Empson was writing, as a man in his early twenties, that seminal book *Seven Types of Ambiguity*. I want to conclude, very shortly, with an anecdote of what happened to a Roman poet who wrote an ambiguous line under Caius Caligula.

But we have to deal with literary criticism. Therefore it seems sensible in this paper to give you some added notions about it. Of the types of poetical criticism, the evaluative is best. It represents a lofty attitude. When practiced by a judicious, not a prejudiced mind, the results may be salutary. When practiced by prejudiced minds, the criticism is thrown down into the arena of politics. Politics is the low view, moiled in human error. Political criticism has little or low value. It does not aim at the truth, or at justice, but at chance, distraction, and temporality. This is not to say that political criticism should be outlawed. We must suffer it along with the greatest. It is part of the stability of democracy to entertain it. But the intention is impure.

The intention of evaluative criticism, in a judicious mind, is high. It strives to seek the truth about a work of art and to communicate this truth to the reader. All manner of subtleties of perceptions are available to this type of criticism. It does not rule out a priori scaffolding, which accounts in part for Dr. Johnson; nor does it rule out elusive intellectual concretions, which specify, sometimes, Coleridge. It does not say that the New Criticism necessarily has the last word in any ramifying arguments, neither does it allow that the neo-Aristotelians have the last word. Evaluative criticism in an honest and perceptive mind seeks to establish life-giving relationships within the art and between art and society. It wishes neither to overpraise nor to underrate. It may propose unwitting prejudices in the very structure of mind, in that mind is always idiosyncratic; the reader allows for this, and in reading Empson, for instance, much of the fun is in acceptance of his peculiarities of temperament which illuminate the liveliness of his sometimes farfetched presentations. Yet few would say that, totally speaking, he was not devoted to finding out the truth about a literary work. It takes some wit to appreciate wit.

I have no objection to categorical criticism, and assume we have yet to see a totally categorical criticism mastering the entire aesthetic intentions of the West; the field is so vast and wide that none has yet had the arbitrary ability to contain it. Dante in his *Commedia* wrote the best criticism of the medieval time, but in a sense it seems too easy: his world was unified. Goethe had a harder task and did less well. Eliot in our time leaned upon modern Christianity and seemed to take in not the whole, but parts. His view has the feel of the limited. It beguiled us for decades but, as Mr. Blackmur perceptively remarked, we tend to read "Four Quartets" instead of the Bible. We get the Bible through modern religious poetry. There is something very wrong about this. Dante's work was so happily integrated with the total religious integration of his times that one has no feeling of this sort of substitution when reading the *Commedia*. Perhaps this was a lucky and happy fall of historical events, that is all.

Too much criticism is a noose around the neck of creation. Each reader should be his own critic, should be strong to hold in abeyance final judgment on any criticism, lest he lose his soul. I propose abeyance criticism. It points up enjoyment, tones down tomb-cold finalities. Let us keep the doors of perception open.

Now we know the bold outlines of our dichotomy and we see that much pleasure of poetry resides in ambiguity, that Will and Psyche conjoin to destroy any simple black-and-white approach to them, and we will find, perhaps, a great difficulty in ever getting beyond the idea that ambiguity is a prime source of pleasure in the art of poetry; that vagueness and irresolution are values leading to possibilities of prolonged enjoyment; and that nothing ultimate about poetry can be scientifically clear.

Yet in ancient Rome a poet lost his life because of ambiguity. It is in a somewhat facetious mood that I conclude by presenting the Emperor

Caius Caligula as critic, absolute and mad. This wild man lived twenty-nine years (A.D. 12–41) but fortunately ruled only three years, ten months, and eight days, according to Suetonius. Our historian says, "He burned a writer of Atellan farces alive in the middle of the arena of the amphitheater, because of a humorous line of double meaning. When a Roman knight on being thrown to the wild beasts loudly protested his innocence, he took him out, cut off his tongue, and put him back again."

May our American critics be never as fierce as Caligula, and may I not have the will to cut off anybody's tongue in my criticism.

The Theory of Poetry

Poetically I do not have an established system of beliefs or practices. That is, I am not primarily a religious poet, a socialistic, a metaphysical, or a nature poet, and I am certainly not a popular one. You might say, then, that the relative is my absolute, but that this point was reached a long time ago, and I had thought that after a while I would achieve a synthesis of beliefs or dogmas. But no, I have no predetermined system. In spite of changes in style, attitude, convictions, and beliefs, however, I have been told that my works cohere, that they make some sort of unity. If that is so, it must be because one cannot escape oneself and in a profound sense one writes as one must. It is impossible not to write like what you are, over any length of time.

I hope I do fall into the illogic now of presenting a definite category of what I stand for, but please take the following remarks in the light of a generally catholic, relativist, and open attitude through the years and in many attempts to penetrate meaning and to re-create valuable states of mind in the varying forms of poems.

If I have a theory of poetry, it is that poetry is a gift, a gift of the gods if you will, or a gift of nature, but at any rate it is not something that can be achieved by the utmost of study. In other words, I believe in extraordinary states of being, that these extraordinary states are states of extreme intuition, and that they descend upon one unannounced. (Although perhaps they can be induced to some extent by certain conditions, an obvious one of which for me is contemplation in solitude and quietude—but recall that Crane could only write with the gramophone going full blast—and that another but less obvious one, which may or may not be induced, but usually not, is that in fatigue

Annual Poetry Lecture at Mills College, Oakland, California, April, 1946; first published in *Pacific* (Mills College) 2 (April, 1947): 18–26.

intuitions may be released where in an active state of full rest they may not be available. Yeats attempted physiological settings to induce certain states of trance or hypnosis; I have not arrived at such a point of experimentation.)

I have concluded over many years that the state of mind, or of feeling, or of intuition in which one writes poetry is a mysterious state, with the utmost difficulty or perhaps not at all subject to rational explanation, although it is liable to objective analysis of the reasoning faculty. Months go by without the incentive to write a poem; then, sometimes with the utmost suddenness, and at the least expected moment, the mysterious power will have informed the mind and one will be writing words on paper. This matter is complex and difficult to explain. I believe, then, in some sort of demonic or angelic possession; that the poet in such a state is a kind of seer; that in these periods of elevation meanings are revealed which are incapable of sight to the ordinary eye in the ordinary light of day; and that when writing a poem one has no knowledge whether it will turn out to be good or bad. This state of mind, furthermore, is in a sense blissful, although it may be characterized also as negative rather than positive; the poet is possessed (he is the medium); it is as if he were almost literally out of his mind, or say rather that his best mind is ascendant, while the ordinary mind is held in abeyance. In these heightened states of extreme awareness there is no sense of time, although they actually do not last more than perhaps an hour.

In these states one is conscious of a dualism in the personality: you can see the table, the chair, the room, you know that you are the man who half an hour ago came into the room, or that you have to make out your income tax tomorrow, or that dinner may be called at any moment, but these matters are submerged and insignificant. It seems to me, then, that the state in which one writes poetry, and in this discussion I am talking only as these matters pertain to me, is one in which the particulars of experience (and who knows how far back in time or with what ramifications of shades of subtleties), the particulars of experience come together in a harmonious relationship, in some sort of intellectual or spiritual design in the mind, and that this inhering harmony makes possible the poem.

The poem is an objective matter of words on paper; it is presumed that all the knowledge of craft gained perhaps since childhood stands in readiness at this moment to be used. To return to the question of hard work, there is no denying that the hardest work with the cold and rational intellect may and must be done on every phase of poetry in preparation for the informing spirit of intuition. Yet the knowledge of craft is secondary; poems built up studiously by an objective will to produce a poem usually turn out to be wooden, to be lifeless. The intuitive center of consciousness, which as I say is a gift of the gods, or of nature, is the heart of creation. It is a turbulent essence, a living grace, entirely potential. It is from this stuff, this mysterious essence, that a poem is created. I know of no other way to state it in the utmost simplicity than to repeat that the state of mind of poetry is a light which illuminates experience. The actual poems that come from this light, from these illuminations, are strange at the start, but when witnessed a day later, or a year later, they must be studied in the coldest glare of the critical intellect, and be compared with the best poetry of the world. When so compared, one has doubts whether any word written by him can stand for ten years, let alone a hundred, and if it were that poetry was merely an exercise, he would stop at once from having anything to do with it, but, as I said above, one is the vehicle of intuitive essences and will write when the fire strikes.

The matter of changing poems once they are written is complex. Sometimes the mechanic hand can improve a line or a word, or recompose whole stanzas, but I must remain noncommittal on this point. In general I do not believe my poems are improved by changing them after they are performed.

The subject of value in poetry is a huge one. Now that I have said something about how my poems are composed, I must attack the problem of the poem as a communicated entity. To write by an ultimately mysterious compulsion is one thing, but to have your poems communicate satisfactorily to a reader is quite another matter. The poem once on paper no longer belongs to the writer but is the property of the reader. The poet must then look at his work objectively and try to see it from the point of view of a reader not himself. This in itself is an art. The poet must rigidly reject all writing which he conceives from another's point of view not to be up to the best standards he, the poet, has set for himself. Here the general readers of a poet's work come in. In colleges, in schools, in critical circles of universities, in learned magazines, and in the press at large a poet's reputation is proposed. It is easily to be seen that a poet should not pay jealous attention to what is known as fame. It may be that he is better off in total or comparative obscurity, for it is not essential to good poetry that it be recognized at once. This statement goes against one generally held. I. A. Richards told me once that every good poet, or every great poet, makes his mark on the world during his lifetime. We have the knowledge that Hopkins could only get a very few of his poems accepted for publication in his lifetime, whose quality shines

richly in these days. A poet should not pay so much attention to his
reputation, to sustaining a career, as to perfecting his works as things
in themselves. It is equally possible to say that a poem is in the reading
of it, that poets must be heard, that a poet will dry up from inanition if
not read, discussed, and enjoyed. And as to what is value, who can
tell? The best critics are the best tellers. One summer I wrote I think
four poems at about the same time. They appeared in *Reading the
Spirit*. I never thought that one of them would come to be judged
considerably better than the others. The poem in question is "The
Groundhog." Why that poem should have been winnowed by an-
thologists and printed more often than certain others remains partially mysterious to me.

My poetry has been caused by serious compulsions; perhaps only a
little part of it could be said to possess what is called a light touch and
perhaps that only in a few satirical pieces. Everything to do with "The
Groundhog" was serious, a perception, or series of perceptions,
which resulted in an even flow of communicable ideas, communicated in a tone of harmony. Actually, I could not tell you how this
poem was written. Surely I could not have sat down in cold blood and
produced it. Say rather that it was the very being of my mind in a
certain state of awareness, my mind limited to a certain area of experience, the resulting art perhaps suggestive of shoots of further contemplation in a passionate reader. But one thing is odd. Poetry is fate
no less on the page than in the heart. I have been credited with
prophecy in this poem. Some critics considered its ending quite in
keeping with contemporary events:

> I thought of China and of Greece,
> Of Alexander in his tent,
> Of Montaigne in his tower,
> Of St. Theresa in her wild lament.

But for the fact that I did not, I might have thought of Japan and of
Germany. The poem was composed without the slightest reference to
a political situation. If at that time I had been thinking of Germany and
Japan, I daresay the poem would not have found its way into an
anthology. Because I thought of China and of Greece, certain critics
were sure I was rooting for the right side! Such is the hazard of poetry
which strives for the universal. A poem may soon be contorted from
the shape you had it in, but I repeat that once in print it belongs to the
reader and there is little the poet can do about the reader's use of it.
Some may hold that what is said is inevitable.

I have already maintained that I write poetry in an elevated state of mind comparable to what the Greeks called the divine frenzy. I must qualify by saying that not all of my poems are composed under such influence. It could not be so. Poetry is also craft; I shall try to show later how poems can be built up by meticulous and rational method, as they were in the eighteenth century. Also, the voltage of the so-called divine, or rather a most human frenzy, or maybe not a frenzy, but excitation due to looseness and tolerance in the synapses, varies. Production of work in fatigue becomes an inversion of the frenzied state. There is no way of measuring the voltage. Actually, a torrential state of passionate anger at the stupidities of mankind may produce very bad verse; it would seem more likely to do so than not, for a brute force would be imposed upon the poem and thus upon the reader, who would recoil from such treatment. The Elizabethan purity ended in the wordy, lurid, proliferous verse of late Elizabethans like Webster and Tourneur; they were magnificent, but sick, and killed off the parent strain.

In opposition, the best artistry may well be the most impersonal, the least evidence of direct passion. Subtlety may well achieve what is lost by force. The greatest intelligence may express the greatest delicacy in the least intrusive way. I think of Hopkins at once in this regard. You will recall the line: "There lives the dearest freshness deep down things." And: "But like this sleek and seeing ball/But a prick will make no eye at all." Or: "Aftercomers cannot guess the beauty been." His is a most studied art; the richness of the versification allows full play of your own sensibilities upon it. The poem will have inexhaustible meanings as you change in the knowledge of it year after year. In our times, poets like Wallace Stevens and Marianne Moore represent this theory. They extrude frostworks, they evoke lattices, they perform upon sensitive textures of subtle sound and sense. The oblique view, rather than the direct statement, intrigues as a flirtation with the absolute embedded in the texture. They prize the reader and misprize themselves. It is the artistry of the impersonal, the sophistication of sometime irrelevance causing direct perception through it of the ultimately relevant.

But let us return, now, to further of my own theories. I believe that poetry comes out of suffering. It is an ancient conception. As in every one of the infinitely fascinating topics connected with poetry, you can choose your own company of sufferers. Against these you can align non-sufferers, and play a game of choice towards some conclusions you may happily never reach. The old truisms hold, the old opposites: pain is the gateway to pleasure; it is not pleasure without knowledge of its opposite. Blake plumbed the depths of innocence and experience, so similar, yet so dissimilar. Experience cannot be achieved without innocence, yet there is a final innocence to the whole experience of life, we may say. Your first experience of the death of a loved one will teach you the bitterness but the holy clarity of truth.

In the game of opposites you will have to consider physical versus spiritual suffering. Some poets have suffered physically, as Pope, or Cowper, or Smart. Some have suffered from watching the physical sufferings of others, as Whitman did in visiting the hospitals. But spiritual suffering is the wellspring of much of art.

Why must anyone suffer spiritually? It is not necessary to live long to sense the abysmal depths of despair. Prolonged and problematical illness, the pain of wrecked bodies in war, the deep eyes of those justly accused of crime, the awesome spectacle of mental imbalance, or death itself, thrust themselves upon us all too soon. Young Buddha, the beautiful prince who had a wife, a child, and extreme wealth, all that he could desire, walked one night in his gardens. He saw an old man, a sick man, and a dead man. He fell to meditating that time had, inescapably, all of these in store for him. Creeping into his chamber in the middle of night, he kissed his wife and child without waking them and went forth to meditate under the Bo tree, never to return. For twenty years he preached that desire is evil, that you must lose the desire of things and appetites, must renounce the flesh which will be old, and maimed, and dead, must arrive as far away as possible from desire, seek the Nirvana of selflessness, passivity, purity of spirit, lack of action, for action leads ultimately to killing others; is as nothing compared with the devotions of selfless contemplation.

Poets suffer in the imagination. It is impossible to conceive of great poetry being written without a knowledge of suffering. But you see there are pitfalls in all talk about poetry. Shakespeare does not seem to have suffered much, so far as we know. So you must evaluate as you will any postulates made in this paper, or in any critical writing you will read on the subject of poetry.

I have three divisions to this paper. The first was the announcement of the general type of poet I am, that is, one who has written under a dynamic compulsion since about the age of seventeen. The second point was that poetry is somehow allied to suffering. Of course, not all poetry seems to be so convolved. Again there is the fascination of opposites. Herrick does us pretty well still, or Herbert, or Vaughan, or Donne, and none of these seems to be the type of the suffering man in a simple sense. Yet to suffer in the imagination is worst of all.

To speak a little of my life, at Dartmouth I had my first encouragement in print from Robert Frost. Harriet Monroe published me, as she did many beginners. At Cambridge I was precisely helped by Richards, and owe to him the grave debt of his studious criticism of every line as I wrote them, for two years. Empson was there, the most brilliant young man I ever knew. "It is the pain, it is the pain, endures," he wrote, a line that has stayed with me for fifteen years. One sat to Quiller-Couch once a week in the evening before a great English fireplace, in a high-paneled room, having been handed a cigar and a glass of port by a peevish butler, while the mild old gentleman in evening clothes spent a discursive and charming hour reading, but mostly discussing in a rambling, engaging way, one paragraph of the Greek of Aristotle's *Poetics*. One had Leavis and Tillyard for lectures; one heard Shaw, Chesterton, or Belloc at the Union; one could drop in on A. E. Housman in his classroom, although I never did. To Cambridge I owe the meticulous and thorough study of poetry. Her dons were informed with a spirit I can only classify as human in the deepest sense.

Those were the days when one would travel in the middle of winter to walk all day alone upon the ramparts of Carcassonne; when one went to the Balearic Isles to see the shaft of sunlight through the great rose window at the cathedral of Palma; when one spent repeated and enchanted hours walking amid the gargoyles on the roof of Chartres; when one bicycled along the wild west coast of Ireland, and drank Irish whiskey with James Stephens in Dublin. At AE's you got no whiskey, but on Sunday evenings at his house he might toward the end of the evening bring out his paintings of fairy-like figures, white and wraith-like, suspended in postures of dance or supplication amidst improbable, ineffable greens. And once, at Oliver St. John Gogarty's house, I was the young American poet dinner guest, a fourth to Gogarty, AE, and Yeats. I sat all evening beside Yeats. He drew a somewhat languid hand through his long strands of gray hair every now and then. Sometimes they spoke in Latin, which impressed me. AE's curved pipe nested in his beard, buried in it to the top. He would often strike a huge wooden match and apply it to the pipe. I suffered against the possibility of his incandescence. At midnight I walked abroad with Yeats. It was a dark and gloomy night. He was deep in his thoughts and said nothing. After six blocks or so I knew that I must turn off down a side street. In utter self-consciousness in the darkness, walking beside the great man, for blocks I wondered whether I should say anything, decided not. I wheeled off, leaving him headed on darkly through the Dublin night. I knew that he would go on to eternity and that I would never see him again, as I did not.

What I have said here tells you little of what I suggested as imaginative suffering, but perhaps when one comes to the end of one's life one can pierce back to the secret springs of one's spirit.

I wish to show, arbitrarily, three types of writing. There could, of course, be other categories, and indeed the ones I choose may not be the best ones.

The first type of verse is relatively simple; it is also metaphysical in my case. The second type is made under the aegis of the demon intellect which erects a barrier of difficulties through which you may wander for years, seeking a spiritual goad, but lost like Scott and his party among blizzards of ice crystals, crevices, and interminable sastrugi. The third type may attempt to speak out instead of in, or at least the third type may speak more directly than the others, after further years of experience, and now after the war years just passed. I trust there is no finality in this last type, and that experimentation will not end. Of type one there are "Cover Me Over, Clover," and "Rumination." Later in composition, but belonging to this metaphysical category, is "Imagining How It Would Be to Be Dead."

Although you can take this latter poem apart and study it word by word, I don't know how you would put it together, unless you grant the validity of my first point. This particular poem was not written, as must be dictated by its subject and its tone, in what I specified as a kind of frenzy, but it was assuredly written in a state of heightened awareness, and not in any state that holds you in the writing of prose. In the time of composition, the ideas were somehow joined together and forged into the poem; as if one could see several ways at once, hold all ways at once together, yet resolve them instantaneously too.

From the second type, under the aegis of the demon intellect, there is one poem this evening. It is a built-up poem. It was studied in advance before composition. It was considered over years to the last syllable. It is an intellectual poem. It is an experimental poem. And it goes as far as I have gone, perhaps, away from the theory of spontaneous inspiration or intuition. I wanted to write a poem about the whole of life, so I called it "The Human Being as Exercises for a Recorder." This signifies a certain modesty in attempting the whole of life, and the word "recorder" enjoins a calculated ambiguity. The suggestion is of neat little tunes played on the recorder, an instrument to which I am addicted. But there is the suggestion that all the actions of life are exercises for a Recorder, the Judge of Mankind. Thus, arbitrarily, I broke man down to five organs of sensibility, a stanza for each. First, about fingers, with which we do much. Second, eyes, sight; third, ears, hearing; fourth, kinaesthesia through feet;

lastly the mouth, which becomes the mouth of Christ. The grammar of the poem depends upon a framework of alliteration, possibly too intrusive.

The last type has more easily communicated poems such as war poems like "Dam Neck, Virginia," "The Fury of Aerial Bombardment," "The Hell-diver Gunner," and "At the End of War."

Now, since my whole endeavor in writing poetry is to seek out the truth, I would like to close with a poem about the truth, entitled "Of Truth":

> O the wicked, winking incidence of truth!
> The wicked wink and incidents of truth;
> The wink, the flicker, the flight, the snicker, the flare,
> The raging actor flying, baring bodkin.
> When I fetch it, it is gone; where leave it,
> Find it. Unruly, leonine, most unruly substance!
> Substance? It haunts me like all shadows. All shades
> Of meaning whipping in and out are there.
> This torturer is a great lover of professors,
> Psychiatrists, chaplains, sits on their faces' skin
> But when I look at them it's on my own,
> Then flies to another place, leaves me in arrears.
> King bat! He leaps out of the ink of the sages;
> He is the blood-dressed ghost walking all battlefields,
> I sense his uncanny wing in the air of the age.
> Mysterious essence! to be so wary-vaporish,
> That cannot be found honestly anywhere,
> Refusing with absolute sublimity
> Satisfaction to the adept at adding up.
> The learned doctor has got him in his indices?
> The lecturer has him in his leaves? The leaves
> Have him in their lectures? The lawyers have him
> In legalism? The President has got him in his speeches?
> Has the astronomer caught him in the starlight?
> The epileptic, paling, in a jagged flash? The hirsute
> Pommeler in a left to the jaw, and a right
> To the jaw? The pilot seeing the icing wing?
> The janitors banding together to strike at Yale?
> Or does he reside in beddings of cold terror
> In the root and remorseless heart of cancer?
> Does he dwell in the realm of sleety accident
> Where he rides with death at the automobile wheel?
> Devil or angel, child or seer or both,
> The absolute in the relative, the relative in
> The absolute, the Bible, or the yelping babe,
> He comes at me but I cannot come at him.

As the spectacular is suspect, but passivity
Is a means often given undue prominence,
Truth is I avow a vast middle quality,
Not voided, although it never will be known.

Poetry and Politics

I want to begin by stating that I do not consider myself a dogmatist, nor to have overriding ideas as rigid as a stake to beat you with. I am a relativist and am given to entertaining multifarious ideas from a speculative and contemplative point of view, and I am not averse to changing my mind.

In this question I am on the side of poetry and against the side of politics. In my country almost all of our blacks are part white. There was a white man lurking back there somewhere on the plantation. Many white men have black souls, many black women and men are angelic. In mixing reality and metaphor I indicate the complexity of the problem. I think it comes down to temperament which side you are on. I can imagine standing here and making convincing literary arguments in favor of political poetry, but I shall not do so, because my main feeling is that the best poetry is non-political.

But we are moving too fast. What does the title mean? Are we talking about politics in the state? Politics is the science of the possible, whereas poetry is the art of the ideal. That is, what is the connection between poetry and politics as practiced in Washington, London, Moscow, Peking? Or are we talking about the politics of poetry, how poetry is conducted, how reputations are made and sustained, what you do within the art to protect and fulfill your visions, all that? I take it we are not talking about this subjective and heavy matter. We are talking about politics in the outside world.

I begin by denying that poetry changes the course of national events. Hundreds of anti-war poems have been written in recent time against the Vietnam war, of which mine are to be included, yet all of them put together, or not one of them, had power to make Johnson or

First published as "No News Is Good Muse," London *Guardian*, June 29, 1973.

Nixon desist from dropping even one bomb, let alone ending the killing. The poets of World War I did not stop World War I (Owen said all poets could do was to warn); the poets of World War II did not stop World War II (Eberhart asked why God has made us as we are).

Poetry may not change the fate of nations, but poets should and do speak from their consciences against every kind of tyranny and evil. They defend the best parts of man and sustain cultural values in a society.

Somewhat recently, while the war was on, I was asked to lead off a week of poetry readings at the University of Massachusetts in Amherst. I said I could not come on Monday but would come later in the week, which I did. They asked Denise Levertov, who was born on your island, to begin the session. She said she would and all was arranged when suddenly she wrote, demanding that her statement be printed in the local press, that a week of poetry readings by many and whichever poets was idle, unproductive, and useless in the face of the gross realities of the war, and she refused to come to the poetry week either to read her own poetry, anti-war or not, or to listen to the poetry of her colleagues.

I mention this instance as bearing on our topic in that here was an admired poet who thought politics was so much more important than poetry, at a certain time, that poetry itself was useless and everybody ought to get out and take direct action against a sea of troubles. Poets could write anti-war poetry if they wished, but it would not matter. What mattered was political action. May I remark that the week's poetry readings were wide ranging as to subjects and emphases, and may I remark that for me the best of Denise Levertov's poetry has nothing to do with politics.

I should now say that there have been pro-war poems through the ages. "The Thermopylae Ode" by Simonides (556–467 B.C.) holds that the best thing that can happen to a young man is to die fighting for his country, whether right or wrong. To give one other example, Pound's "Sestina: Altaforte" speaks for Bertrand de Born (ca. 1200), "I have no life save when the swords clash." He continues that, when the broad fields are crimson, "Then howls my heart nigh mad with rejoicing." I assume the audience knows many of the anti-war poems of our language, so I shall mention only Hardy's poem about love and labor going on though dynasties pass. I might add that Milton's "On the Late Massacre in Piedmont" is a humane poem.

We have nationalist poems like "The Star-Spangled Banner" and "The Battle Hymn of the Republic," but nobody considers them among the best American poems. I remember Yeats saying somewhere, I cannot recall where, that at one point in his career he wanted poetry to inspire Irishmen to fight.

As I said above, one could argue in favor of political poetry and pro-war poetry, but my temperament leans in the opposite direction. I suppose some of Byron's Cantos were political; Shelley was ousted from Oxford for politics; Blake, Wordsworth, and many other poets had something to say about politics; but I feel that the best poetry of these and of most poets in English has dealt not with politics, but with other conditions of man.

We do not know what the personal politics of Shakespeare may have been, but I cannot feel that we are the worse off for this. Milton's *Paradise Lost*, some might say, was a vast political affair, but for me the poetry means more than the politics, if you admit any. Wordsworth's lyrics are unpolitical, as are the lyrics of Blake. The only political fault I find with Hopkins is that he was concerned only with the five Franciscan nuns drowned, in whose happy memory he wrote "The Wreck of the Deutschland," and not with the others. The poem overcomes this fault, yet listen to this: (*Poems*, 3rd ed. [1948], p. 220*n*): "Sudden, unexpected disaster overtook the Deutschland, with her emigrants and exiles bound for America. A hurricane of wind and snow drove her on to a sandbank. For a whole night without succour, the passengers and crew of the crippled and settling ship were buffeted by the elements: many were drowned." Hopkins did not concern himself with these others.

Auden understood man as political in his early plays, but he stood above the issues, depicting these. His political poem, "Spain," is not one of his best poems. Spender's political views have been known for decades, but I would sacrifice his political writings for "I think continually of those who were truly great," itself a truly great poem. I do not care about Marvell's critical opinion, but in the "Coy Mistress" and "The Garden" he has two time-defying poems. Dylan Thomas's "Fern Hill," unpolitical, will last a long time, at the center of his youthful spirit. In America we had many political poets in the Thirties, but none or few of their political poems have come down to the present.

I hold that the main strength of poetry in English, in the most numerous examples, and these of the highest quality, from Chaucer to today, is in the realm of non-political poetry. This vast body of realization applies to the essence of man, man's heart, man's suffering, his hopes and despairs, his being.

Literary Death

Death was first mystical anguish. It was passionate realization at the elaborating point reaching to infinity. Then it became the great individualist. After a while it took turns as master dictator, infidel clown. Then it became a howling success and reaped candidates by the dozens, the good, the bad, the soft, the hard, the crushed and the uncrushed, believing atheists, disbelieving religious.

Then death became a bore. It was too boring for words and I gave it none. Still mystical, individualist, dictator, clown, success, it was a bore the likes of which shows no comparison in the world. By becoming boring it can only raise our interest by screaming. It keeps us from reacting to the right things. It makes us write about itself instead of writing about life. It has partially seduced me in this way for over forty years.

When Hardy died I heard the bells toll in Cambridge. They tolled for me. I was always involved in some way, but varyingly. Three days before Yeats died R. P. Blackmur, Tessa, Philip Horton, and I read his late poems in a building outside Harvard Yard which is now a Gulf station. The gulf was about to be widened.

Later on they came thick and fast by decades. Jack Wheelwright was killed at dawn at the corner of Massachusetts Avenue and Beacon Street, a few blocks from his parental home, which the bachelor radical never had left.

When Ted Spenser died, as his casket was hoisted by six in Christ Church, Cambridge, and passed out of the ancient door, a few flakes of snow descended elegantly onto the black box. When F. O. Matthiessen jumped out the window of the thirteenth-storey of the Manger Hotel, it was April 1, the cruelest month. He left his wristwatch

First published in *Granite*, no. 6 (Autumn, 1973): 152–54.

and ring neatly on the window sill. The bachelor critic desired to be buried beside his mother. He was known so little actually that in the morning I was called up to see if I should be a pallbearer. I did not know him that well, declined.

Jeffers brought no tears, his poems were as hard as mountains. Several years before his death he came out, old and blind in one eye, from his house, pulled by a massive bulldog on a huge chain, to greet us. After a while he became friendly, gave us tea in the kitchen and finally took us over the house and talked of poetry in his study.

One gets mixed up in the order of death just as life is a mixed order.

When Cummings died it seemed too early. I remember bringing a bottle of milk and the Sunday *New York Times* to him in Patchin Place in the Thirties. After his death a passionately devoted late friend, a Greek, told me how well he spoke of my work. Had I known this I would have gone to see him in the last decade of his life. We live in ignorance.

Several months before the death of Wallace Stevens we were writing letters. He was monumental, his death seemed another monument along his way. Only one literary person went to his funeral. When Bill Williams died it was not unexpected. He died piecemeal, one stroke after another, but to the last wrote poems, letters, and inscriptions, in an almost indecipherable hand.

Oscar Williams spoke on the phone from the hospital with a rasping voice, gallant of spirit, saying, "One was faced with birth, every man must face his death." It burned in me like a clarion call.

We should have expected Blackmur's death, but it is always a shock. Ten years before he could only walk a hundred steps, then would have to rest on the sidewalk as we talked further about Plato, in Princeton.

When Dylan Thomas died it seemed nerve-shattering, a world-shaking event. The wildness of it brought tears gushing for days.

In his last January I phoned Frost to tell him of his winning the Bollingen Prize and introduced every member of the committee in turn. He talked in a strong voice from his hospital bed, made a joke about what to do with the money, was friendly, alert, and keen. Two weeks later he was dead, followed by expected pomp and funeral circumstances. I thought it unFrostian for so earthy a man to be cremated. For Shelley, yes; for Frost, no.

When Ted Roethke died it was a shock, unexpected, a muffling of drums. He used to shake his hands like a wrestler, as if he wanted to get rid of them. Once in a bar in Saratoga he threatened the bartender from our table because he did not bring him his drink quickly enough. We had to restrain him by talk. I felt that if he had gone up and accosted the bartender he might have got his block knocked off. He often lived in fantasy, where he felt power.

When Dame Edith Sitwell died it was like Christ's blood streaming in the firmament. She loomed large in our land, unique. She said to meet her at White River Junction with a wheelchair. She had slipped on a floor in her palace in Italy, injuring her toe. While being introduced in 105 Dartmouth she stayed out of earshot in the wings. Professor Harp and I each took an arm, escorting her slowly, dramatically to the stage before a hushed audience. She complained of a cold but after drinking water and starting she was splendid. We could not get her a berth on the train at one in the morning. She was too big to fit into our berths anyway, had to sit up all night going back to New York, but took the inconvenience with good grace and charm.

When Eliot died he had laid down so many words that it seemed a natural transition to further words and considerations. The death of Hart Crane was so far back that it seems a fable, but it seemed a fable then.

When Randall Jarrell died it was a shock, but I had only met him four or five times. In 1962, at the Library of Congress sessions commemorating the fiftieth anniversary of the founding of *Poetry* by Harriet Monroe (whose death was romantic, on a far-off South American mountain top long ago), I introduced him to Robert Frost at a party Frost gave at his hotel, accompanied by Helga Sandburg. When I was retiring the day after his death in Robert Penn and Eleanor Warren's house in their guest room, I pulled down a magazine by chance. It fell open by chance to a review of four new books of poetry in a *Hudson Review* of 1948. My eye hit his name simultaneously with the title, in capitals, *Losses*. Stunned, I recovered to read a bit. The critic flayed the young poet. What is the meaning of such coincidence?

On Thursday, January 29, 1970, at the Academy I talked quite a while with Louise Bogan and John Hall Wheelock. A bit later I enjoyed seeing them sitting together on a settee. As I was handed a drink at the bar, nearby I heard a crash and turned around to see a glass broken on the floor, a man already moving to clean up the drink and at the same time I saw Louise fallen to the floor. I was about ten feet away and quickly moved and lifted her up onto the settee. She was dazed for a while but regained her composure. I went to Boulder. Following my lecture and reading I was taken up into the mountains where about ten colleagues and friends were having a relaxed time in subdued light around a red table. One mentioned the death of Louise the day before in New York. The shock of it ruined my evening. Only eight days before I had had no thought that her death was so near.

A Haphazard Poetry Collecting

Last year at Smith my wife and I heard a paper of impeccable and fascinating professionalism by Philip Hofer about important books and difficult acquisitions, psychological methods of obtaining books or manuscripts from implacable characters in fortress Britannia. I listened in strict attention and was well rewarded to learn much in one hour about a subject little known to me from a man who conveyed his findings with wit, enthusiasm, and compassion.

When asked to talk this year about collecting I was at once flattered and dismayed. I was flattered because I must have been thought to be able to follow in the professional footsteps of Mr. Hofer but was instantly dismayed that I could surely have nothing to say on collecting, being a random and amateurish collector and this only by happenstance, not by design, or, to go back to my beginnings, to the most rudimentary designs of a young poet who loved the look and feel of books of poetry as they appeared, their make and feel as aesthetic objects as well as the contents of their pages, and even enjoyed when perceptible the arch delicacies of the smell of printer's ink. I used from college days to buy the books of poets with a view to collecting them throughout the years of the life of the author. *Tulips and Chimneys!* How well I recall the look and feel of early Cummings, mud-luscious and puddle-wonderful! And Millay, with what intensity I attended to her pages, trying to fathom her personality from her poetry.

As introduction, then, I should say that I know nothing professionally about book collecting. I have never, or seldom, bought books on the market. I have never gone to great book auctions where notable items would be purveyed. I have never sold my own books for lucre, although in 1970 I was told I could and should crop my library of

First published in *Chicago Review* 24, no. 4 (Spring, 1973): 57–70.

duplicates and triplicates up to 7 percent of the total, which could be done without violating the integrity of the collection.

I have to talk about only one part of literature, poetry, for I never collected prose except in a desultory fashion, although of course I have many books of criticism and essays along with the upbuildings of poetry. And I have to limit my unpremeditated collecting mainly to the decades of my writing life, which began in the Twenties and continues now, something short of half a century.

Let me make a remark about collecting prose. When I was in college the Nonesuch Edition of the Bible came out (I believe the year was 1925) in four magnificent volumes bound in strong pale hide, with excellent type and title page, somewhat ornate, adorned with pictorial and other devices, a veritable treasure to behold and to hold.

I loved the books aesthetically, but cannot one love a book too much, collect it, so to speak, too hard? I did not read these books, except a little, but I treasured them so much that, as if their message had not already bestridden the centuries, I wrapped them up in what I hoped was imperishable heavy wrapping paper, put them in a trunk at the very bottom for utmost safekeeping and, whatever the vicissitudes of my life, did not look at them again for forty years.

I adduce this activity of mine, this secret love, as an example of collecting gone too far, without the slightest worldly use. However, in attenuation, I must say that when I retrieved the books somewhere around 1965, unwrapped them and looked at them, they had a pristine glory and look of the year 1925, that of their birth. The stalwart wrapping papers, somewhat dry-stained by time, preserved the volumes themselves as each was wrapped separately before all were wrapped and tied with a strong cord. They looked as sumptuous (yet now I was forty years older, in my sixties) as when I laid them down with love. I fancied I had the same zest for my treasured Nonesuch volumes of the Bible, including the Apocrypha, number four, as I felt as a young, enthusiastic man. My face was different but their face was the same. Mine showed use. Theirs showed uselessness, timelessness. The purpose of collecting could be said to be the daring of a beautiful moment which might blazon with splendor in some impossible, guessed future when, opening the treasure hoard before you in a miracle moment, would stand unblemished, unspoiled by time, the great object and symbol of your love.

Let me return, after this prose excursion, to the main road of my paper.

It is said that if you will look at a man's library you can tell something, even a great deal, about the man. This is palpably true. There must be still in this country ostentatious libraries of false-front books in so-called great houses where the fraud is covered up by fake buckram but you know the owner never read a book in his life for disinterested pleasure. In my early years the Eliot five-foot shelf of books, real though uniform, was the subject of ridicule among my colleagues. Anyone who had such a set of books, although the name smacked of all Harvard behind them, was judged to be a boor and was promptly dismissed as of no account.

I must say that when the first waves and battalions of paperbacks came over the fields of vision, there was a similar, but less sure presumption that paperback books were somehow a sham, were shamful, a cheapening of good hard-cover reality, but in a few years they won the battle by the millions and now nobody is considered inferior to read a work in paperback rather than in hard cover, although it will fall apart. In fact, paperbacks seem to predominate, especially among the young and in universities. One is reminded that it took America a long time to copy the excellent paper formats of the French.

But here is a crucial point to talk about. The bare fact is that paperback books do not last long, relative to hard-cover ones, and that it is much more rewarding to collect poets you like in hard cover than their duplicate pages in paper. Ten years later the paper will look sorry, if it lasts that long; certainly twenty years will pretty much use up a paperback book of poems, unless somehow kept under severe conditions against the ruck of time, whereas I have hard-cover poetry books which look spruce and inviting forty years after purchase.

Of course there is a snobbery about all this, but the fact remains that a first edition of a book of poems bought in the Twenties or Thirties seems infinitely preferable to a second or *nth* edition of the same words. It is the splendor of the newness that counts.

But here I must put in a sour note, for after forty or fifty years of gathering in loved first editions of books of poetry, one comes to the hopeless philosophical conclusion that after a certain age, what is the point of buying new books of poetry? Your poet friend and other friends, some of them, will be dead. Your library will have become so unwieldy that you groan to think of adding even one more book to the shelves. And what then? The whole times they are a-changing. The young poets and their works are new fables. Indeed, you do not have to read them if you do not want to, whereas when you were a young poet the reading of all the poets was a matter of life or death, actually of your spiritual life or death.

While I have made the above point, somewhat to my astonishment,

I want the reader to understand that it is not my total point of view and to take it somewhat lightly. I still cannot resist buying new books of poems by new and older poets. Their old irresistibility obtains still.

I now wish to make a diatribe against the quality of American life in general, and of ours at the present time in particular, although we are supposed to be having the best kind of time on our phase-out winter term off from Dartmouth. The times and our present kind of life are not bookish. Everything about the realistic, existentialistic current scene militates against reading books or taking thought, even writing these pages. We are so much with the times, with the objective realities of every day, that we are not with thoughts of the significance or value of action as recorded and embedded in books.

It may well be said that a certain lack of character obtains, a certain lack of will, else I should be living in books at this time instead of among people, places, and things. I readily agree, but insist that the American scene is not conducive to a bookish life. One must fight for such a life, demand it, sacrifice for it in order to realize it. One must make the basic assumption that a bookish life is one's deepest, best life and demand total devotion to that life, which is easier to say than to do. Ten minutes later one is on the way to the supermarket to buy groceries.

Mr. McLuhan's prophecy that books will be outmoded by the year 2000 is an extension of the notion that we live too fast now. Our nervosity extends to electrifications which effect instantaneous communications. TV images are bounced off satellites and may be seen at the same time in widely separated parts of the world. The realities of the battlefields in Vietnam may be brought as they happen into living rooms in Bangor or El Paso, except that man still, with all this power, desists considerably from showing the worst parts of his nature in maimings, mutilations, and killings. A censor still exists.

Should we preserve old TV documentaries as well as books by which, in the future, to read the past? No doubt we will. Old Charlie Chaplin black-and-white movies are delightful to see a quarter of a century and more since they were made. But books are more valuable and give a greater depth to the qualities of life depicted, as well as allowing aesthetic pleasures which are unique.

Let me emphasize the random nature of my poetry collection. I did not start it with any conception of what it would be forty years later. I was not systematic in acquiring books. The collecting was a rambling exercise in sporadic love. Also, I had no idea what monetary evaluation would be put on my literary estate in 1970. It was just that I cherished certain books of poetry and wished to keep them.

Of course when a poet would come to our house I would have him or her sign my books, as for instance Robert Graves or Marianne Moore, but to show the true low key of my collecting, on several important occasions I forgot to ask the poets to sign and felt remorse later. If they came back years later I would make up for the deficiency. I remember Allen Tate with his then wife, Isabella Gardner, coming and going, slipping through my noose, as it were, forgetting that I had a signing intent. And I. A. Richards, my old mentor, many of whose books I had. I was appalled once fairly recently to see how many of his I had unsigned, so the next time Ivor and Dorothea came to walk, as they loved to do, into the open air to build a fire in snow, making tea in their "billie," and enjoy a winter day, I would proffer him quite a number, going back decades, which he would sign with true warmth and feeling.

I recall one of the most extreme examples of what I shall call partial fulfillment. In Robert Lowell's first year at Harvard, he then having issued from the long, exciting association I had with him and Frank Parker at St. Mark's for several years, Cal gave his first poetry reading. I cannot recall all the details, but I had just met Phelps Putnam, who looked like a minor version of Baudelaire, a sour-looking and decayed American dandy who dressed and looked the part of a frayed Parisian intellectual. I admired his work in part. Whether he asked to see me or how I got onto him I forget, but he was sitting in one of the joints off Harvard Square, I think off Massachusetts Avenue. We had both gone to hear young Lowell read. We were in a booth drinking and in came Cal. The old poet to my astonishment and equally to my embarrassment drew out a handful of what used to be called dirty postcards or filthy pictures and thrust them across the table at his new friends. While this might have been hilarious or comical it was calculated to be shocking, which to me it was, which shows how far I was in my rigorous mind from taking immediate delight in obscene revelations.

But this episode passed and what we talked about I cannot recall. Putnam agreed to come to our place on Lake View Avenue and we repaired thither. I recall how much I enjoyed the nature of Phelps Putnam, now much forgotten, and at one point in his visit I remembered to ask him to sign his books, which numbered two. Always being of a quick-moving and impulsive nature I recall moving hurriedly to the bookshelves and immediately pulling down *Trinc*, which he nicely signed. As impulsively I looked for his other book but it did not show so I soon gave up the search and returned to the conversation. The meeting ended. With incredible swiftness, in a matter of weeks, his death came. I always regretted the lack of his signature on the other volume, which I found with a little patience after his visit but did not have the impetus to ask him to come back, nor to go over to his house just to have him sign it. I remember when he was there I told him I owned his other book but he did not rise to an instantaneous search.

Sometimes after death I received books which mean a great deal to me. Dame Edith Sitwell, whom with Sir Osbert we had thoroughly enjoyed on their literary excursions to our shores, directed a book from her library to be sent to me. Writing here in Arizona I cannot recall its title, although research could make the determination, but I shall not forget the act of friendship.

Some books collected were positively thrilling to see, to handle, and to know. Of these I think especially of the four or five hand-printed and bound books of her brother's work sent me by Elizabeth Yeats from the Cuala Press. I could hardly have cherished books more than I cherished these thin books on heavy paper with strong type of works of Yeats in either poetry or prose. I have written elsewhere of my meetings with Oliver St. John Gogarty, James Stephens, AE, and Yeats in Dublin during a summer vacation from Cambridge, also with Miss McNie, the cartoonist of Yeats and AE passing opposite to each other before a Georgian house, heads haughtily inclined, in a state of amusing mutual disdain, the copy of which I found in my library only three months ago in its pristine and signed state. This was a bicycle trip in Ireland in August, I think, of 1928, during summer vacation from St. John's, Cambridge, from Limerick, where I tried to find some of my ancestors' gravestones, or living Ghormleys, but failed, to Bantry Bay and back across country to Dublin. But thereafter for years in the Thirties Elizabeth Yeats would remember to send me the latest imprints from the Cuala Press.

One of my books which took the longest ride was a small book about four by three, or five by four, with a red jacket, by I. A. Richards, entitled *Science and Poetry*. Already his admirer, who was soon to be known at Cambridge, I purchased this book in Manila in 1927 on my tramp freighter trip around the world, or largely around it, prior to entering Cambridge University. I read this book with avidity. I loved it and so cherished it that I kept it secretly at the bottom of my one suitcase, wishing to preserve it from harm throughout the vicissitudes of harsh ocean tramp freighter passages. When I met the Richardses at Cambridge I showed it to them with pride, how I had preserved it all the way across the Indian Ocean while I was sweating in the hold of the boiler room at 120 degrees Fahrenheit. The book is neatly inscribed, mentioning the "spring goddess" I brought to them at graduation in 1929, and exists to this day.

While I am mentioning the Richardses I may as well detail the fate of another book. I was devoted to the poetry of Hopkins, who after Wordsworth and Blake affected me most as a young man. I·possessed a first edition of his poems, every page of which was known intimately. Indeed, I could not exaggerate the love I had and still have for this volume, now rare. Time passed and the Richardses were going to China, where Ivor was to write, among other things, *Mencius on the Mind*. They asked if they could borrow my Hopkins as they did not have one. I lent my prized copy to them and thought nothing more about it.

Time passed. The next episode in the story is unexpected and painful. While in China in Peking there was a flood in the temple where they were living, which destroyed the Richards's effects in the basement, among which was my first edition of the poetry of Gerard Manley Hopkins.

Imagine my shock and disappointment at this news, along with my gratitude for their care and consideration when, upon their return from China, they took the trouble to secure the same volume, but perforce now in a second edition, which was faithfully inscribed "This substitute," in memory of the original.

Skipping a great many years, another special book-signing comes to mind. I bought Robert Frost's *In the Clearing*, his last book, and consider one poem in it, "Away," one of his best, written when he was in his eighties. Elsewhere I have criticized this poem as blasphemous but will not go into my considerations in this regard here. My point is to remark that I signed my name on the flyleaf. The next time Robert came to our house he wrote over my name, actually atop and below it, "To the poet of Dartmouth and the USA, Robert Frost." He then named November his last fall. The ascription is particularly meaningful to me because two months later he was dead.

I might make a diversion while speaking of Frost to mention a lightning flash of recognition I had even closer to his death. I was on the Bollingen board meeting at Yale in January, 1963. With books for consideration on the table, either for a year, or the prize could be given for a lifework, it suddenly struck me, amazingly without premeditation, why do we not give it to Frost? The Bollingen is our highest prize. Frost never won the Nobel, although many openly wondered why not. I had my own reason which was that he exhibited a kind of chauvinism and was not close enough to the people. I noted that the Nobel often went to a candidate far to the left. It was significant that

Steinbeck won it for one book depicting the raw state of America. While Frost wrote simple poems, in some instances, enjoyed as it were by everybody, he had not the people's touch of Sandburg and later in life wooed the universities, intellectuals, and critics.

The suggestion met with immediate response. My suggestion was a *fait accompli* in no time. We notified the Librarian and as I seemed to know Frost best of our group I was elected to phone him bearing the good news. He was in the hospital in Boston. His voice was strong and he was cheerful. He accepted the prize with gratitude and, showing how deeply ingrained in him was a sense of humor, asked what would he do with the money? As was the custom on other elections, each member of the judging board then spoke with the winner. John Hall Wheelock asked to be last as he was the only one among us, although he was elderly, who oddly enough had not met Frost.

It was a gesture for the record which I thought was right, as did my colleagues. The gesture gained added significance when Frost died about two weeks later.

Pursuing the random nature of these considerations I may as well memorize a few events from my Consultantship in Poetry at the Library of Congress. The first will be visual, the second nonliterary, the last two literary.

The first two anecdotes come under the part of my title denoted "haphazard," but do not have to do with book collecting. I hope you will not mind two memory collectings.

I remember the young King of Thailand with his young wife, a woman of extreme beauty, entering the Library of Congress to give gifts from his country to ours. After the ceremonies and a tour their Majesties left the building. Drawn up was a modest fleet of gleaming cars, into one of which stepped the Queen. The King noticed countrymen of his a hundred feet away, beyond the foundation, on a greensward in positions of abjection and humility. In fact, they were kneeling on the grass, and some may have been prostrated. I happened to be standing by. The King walked cautiously and alone toward his subjects. In the big, crass materialism of our country it was deeply moving to behold the wordless spectacle I witnessed. There was the sense of total, selfless devotion of the Thai subjects to their King, the sense of the enormous difference between their state and his, yet a union and living confidence stretching back thousands of years in the mutual respect of subjects and ruler.

Perhaps there were only thirty or so Thais gathered unofficially on the lawn. They were good looking and most were young. They probably never imagined that their King would approach them. He walked maybe twenty paces, came within ten or twenty feet of them, and stood before them with an absolute immobility and calm. It was a profound and mysterious moment. Nothing was said. There was silence and no motion. The mood, in the open air, was of enormous dignity and seriousness. He made no gesture. His features were impassive, a deep Oriental quality imposed there. After a while, with an American-type arm-waving or acclamation of goodbye, though silent, the King turned slowly and walked back from his adoring subjects to the waiting cars. It was a strange, impressive moment in history.

The second memory is when His Majesty the King of Nepal came to the Library. My wife and I stood inside the doors. There was a procession of State and other officials, superficial greetings or nod-dings at the start of a tour of the Library leading to a high room far back in the building where there was displayed a large collection of literary and religious Nepalese works going back many centuries. I had been tipped off that His Majesty was a poet. My reason for being there was because of my poetic position in the Library. At one point, in the display room, His Majesty seemed free. The swirl of official people had momentarily swirled away. He stood alone with nobody within ten feet of him. It was my cue. I moved in, introduced myself, and said in friendly inquiry, "I am told that you write poetry?" He looked at me without expression and answered, "Sometimes." Wishing to be so-ciable, I asked something like do you write much poetry or often? With an impersonal look he vouchsafed again the one word, "Some-times." But this time I was baffled by His Majesty's imperturbability but was determined, as his part-host and American well-wisher, to ease the situation. I tried a third time with some other, similar locu-tion. It was not that he was hostile, it may be that he did not under-stand me, but on the third try all I could get out of the King of Nepal was "Sometimes" to stand for his entire life as a poet. The swirling crowd swirled back, surrounded him in a sea of voices and faces as I retreated from him.

No books were involved in these two encounters.

Mikhail Sholokhov came to town and the Library wanted to enter-tain the Russian novelist appropriately. Through the Russian Em-bassy an official roundtable meeting was planned. I had read Sholokhov hurriedly in English translation some weeks before his appearance, having read little of him before that. I have some kind of built-in empathy with writers of about my own age.

There were probably a dozen persons around the table, one young Harvard man who knew Russian as interpreter. There were people from State and from the press. Somebody would ask a question. It would have to be passed through the head of an interpreter to Sholokhov. He would reply, sometimes slowly, with pause for linguistic identifications, the reply being relayed, as had always to be the somewhat painful case, through the head of the interpreter to our ears.

When it came my turn I said something to the effect that I thought he did not give in-depth representations of character in comparison with Dostoevsky or Tolstoy, who treated not only objective reality but subjective realizations as well, and I asked him whether he was aware of this difference and whether as an artist he elected to write as he did.

He replied, "I give the beefsteak not the hamburger."

This was startling and provoked a hush in the audience. There was something so humorous about this that everybody seemed bemused. We were dealing with the difficulties of translation through the heads of linguistic interpreters and I thought immediately that he had not understood my question. If he had understood my question how could he have given a reply totally opposite to what was expected and which I and, I gathered, others thought was totally wrong? Silence ensued due to frustration of communication and the remark passed without further debate.

Let me reiterate. I held that his work was pictorial-narrative and objective in the sense of leaving out inner realizations while depicting only exterior events, in comparison with Dostoevsky and Tolstoy, who presented psychological, subjective realities as well as narrating a story. To use his metaphor I should have thought and indeed been certain that he gave us hamburger, a chopped-up meat, not beefsteak. He held, however, that his work represented the beefsteak, the central fare of literature, not cut-up bits of reality. I leave you to ponder this question. I suppose I shall never know whether he truly heard or understood my question, whether his reply was because he heard and understood it and did not like the implications put by my question, and so defended his work as truly depicting the depth of the Russian soul and actions; or whether the interpreter had somehow mangled my point through misinterpretation and given Mr. Sholokhov a wrong cue.

The final phase of the meeting, an after phase, was unexpected and startling. Usually when persons entered my office I was warned by secretaries. However, in a day or two the doors flew open and in walked briskly a blond Russian about thirty from the Russian Embassy bearing an almost square box wrapped in plain brown wrapping paper. He advanced briskly, somewhat militarily. I had the impression it might be a bomb, a notion which instantly seized my imagination along with the thought: This is It, I am about to be blown up but I will die serving my country. The blond, lithe Russian spoke no word but walked straight to my desk. I think I may have even said, somewhat hilariously, What is this, a bomb? He said no word but deposited the package before me, turned abruptly, and left the room.

Assuming that the bomb was not going off I gingerly unwrapped the package and found, to my delight, a splendid present from Mikhail Sholokhov. It was a boxed, four-volume set of *And Quiet Flows the Don* printed in English in Moscow. It was signed to me in Russian which I do not know. The small, thick volumes varied from six hundred to eight hundred and sixty pages, had pictures on the jackets, were bound in red imitation leather, and looked something like late nineteenth century American novels of the time of Bret Harte. I admired the Russians for publishing their major novelists in English in Moscow and wondered where were our counterparts of major American novels published in Russian in New York.

My last memory of Library of Congress days which I wish to present is an encounter with Yevtushenko and Voznesensky. I wrote an article about the evening they spent in our house in Georgetown but as I do not have this to hand I will try to tell it again. Do not forget that ten years or so ago we were all much younger, the Russians especially. Vozne, as he was called, was in his early twenties, a small, amiable but intense short man of dark complexion who knew perhaps fifty words of English but was dauntless in trying them on us, all hopelessly mispronounced and misused. Efty, if I may so style him, was in his late twenties or thereabouts, positively impressive in his great blond height, his unlined and handsome face, and his strange Russian clothes with red tie and red socks. He radiated youthful vigor and friendliness, a positive force of wonderful goodwill to which I cottoned with such enthusiasm that we were soon talking in a most compulsive manner, always slowed down, however, by the needs of a language interpreter. We seemed to see eye to eye on many things. I thought of Efty as if he were or could have been a blond American from the farms of Iowa or Nebraska. He had a youthful energy and charm which reminded me of such big young Americans from the midwest from which I had myself sprung. It seemed at once as if true friendship could exist between poets of our two different countries. There were eight or ten in our modest living room, a man from State, an interpreter, the dancer Mary-Averett Seelye and a friend or two of hers and one or two of ours. It was an enchanted and a high-spirited time. Efty knew no English at all at that time, if my memory is correct.

Whenever we would seem to be getting too friendly or communicating too enthusiastically on a one-to-one basis there was a commissar in his mid-thirties whom the embassy had brought along who would invariably break in and take over the conversation, subduing it by giving a long-winded lecture on Russian politics or literature. His job apparently was to keep the young Russian poets in line and bring them back into line if they said anything which might be construed to be too democratic. They acceded to these break-in forays, and indeed the whole evening was conducted in an exemplary, friendly manner.

It came about because the poets wanted to meet me, but this had to be handled through their embassy and ours, which took a day or two of rather frantic planning. My wife and I wanted them to see a high form of American art, a dance hour by Mary-Averett Seelye during which she dances poetry. That is, using her tall and elegant body as an extension of her voice, she has developed remarkable interpretations of modern poems by Sitwell, Cummings, MacLeish, Eliot, and others. We thought the Russians would like to see her sophisticated performance. But their embassy thought otherwise on the night in question. They thought their young poets, in line with Communist ideology, ought to see an example of what they thought was the most democratic form of our arts and charged them with seeing a movie of Marilyn Monroe. It was agreed that following the movie they would come over to our house, skipping the Seelye dances, but she would be there and we would all meet together. They came in around ten o'clock and stayed as I recall until about one.

I remember a few things especially. They did not like our whiskey, which was too strong, and settled for beer or water. I had not had the wit to supply vodka. A Yale Series record of my poetry had just arrived that day so I showed it to them. I recall Yevtushenko's taking up the record and examining it on both sides, marveling at its make. This surprised me. He noted carefully the grooves, the sheen, the patina, the label. Of course he could not have understood the words and there was no move to play the record. It struck me as a wonderful naïveté in the young Russian to admire the excellent American make of a poetry record, as if his people could not but envy us the mechanical virtue of manufacturing so fine an object. I knew that these popular young poets were the wonder of their world and drew audiences in Moscow beyond ten thousand; that their books of poetry were state printed, sold for what would be less than a quarter here, and were disseminated in the tens, even the hundreds of thousands, poetry among the Russians pleasing the people in part as a kind of religious rite, formal religion being largely denied them. Imagine my surprise and delight when Efty and then Vozne, both of them, took out of their pockets their latest volumes of verse, of small format, and writing in these books handed them to me as presents. Again I was embarrassed not to be able to read what they wrote in their inscriptions, but I was to have these translated later.

It was a wonderful, exciting evening and I thought it would be the beginning of real friendships, which we mutually protested; but as fate had it, living as I do in New Hampshire, I never saw either poet again in the several times they came to our shores in subsequent years, but they naturally gravitated to New York and made friends with poet friends of mine there. A few years ago we did try to get Vozne to come to Dartmouth but after much haggling about the price Moscow would not let him out to come.

I have an amusing anecdote about the commissar, of whom I have spoken as an official intruder whenever the young poets should deviate from what I suppose was the proper line of talk from his point of view. When they went to New York from Washington an old Cambridge classmate of mine, George Reavey, one of their translators, had them in tow and took them to some restaurant in New York, perhaps in the Village. The omnipresent official commissar was along too. The room was crowded and only a few could sit at the table and it was a happy chance for Reavey that the commissar, with maybe a minion or two, was forced to sit apart, maybe forty feet away, allowing no overhearing of the conversations of the poets and Reavey and his party. They thus for a while had the Russians quite to themselves and could speak freely of anything in the world without the constant monitoring of the commissar. This was considered a happy triumph of circumstance. Not of course that they would be saying anything that they would not have wanted anybody to hear.

I recall that in the article I wrote about the meeting at our house I detailed some of the intellectual ideas presented. For instance, in one of his butt-in lectures, the commissar said that Aristotle's notions of tragedy, all Greek tragedy and Shakespeare's as well, were bogus, outmoded, without value. The idea of catharsis was based on a high view of a high individual falling by inner flaw to a low estate, but this was now an absurd notion since in Russia and in Communism every man was as important as every other man in the society; no one was high so no one could fall; and men only lived to work for the state, their common good, so incidentally there could be no individualism in literature but only "socialist realism," of which we have heard *ad nauseam* in the debate between Russian poets and those of the open Western world. The time may yet come when Russia may realize that she should not hamstring and shackle the spirits of her poets and dictate to them how and what they should write.

It is now time to end my ramble and these notes written in various parts of the continent at different recent times. I am back in my study looking at the books I have collected through the years. As our children grow up and depart from us, though they are always in our minds, our books stay on the shelves and we outgrow them, although their influence is built into us too. As our children go outward into the world, our personal libraries are likely to go inward into a larger library, there to collect whatever meanings of their time may pertain to them. As it is better to have a child than a book, the fact remains that we know not what a child may become, whereas a book is what it is and it is the same book of poems, in my case and in my library in 1971, as when it was acquired, maybe forty years earlier.

We do not know how we influence our children, in the profoundest sense, but then neither do we know ultimately what certain books of poetry did to us. Science may be able to measure the world but in the world of poetry feelings rule and there is no measuring rod subtle enough to mark the stages of love of parents, spouse, children, nature, or God. Great poems are at the center of life. We feel their truth and they abide with us. I would end on the note of love and say that the love of collecting books of poetry through the years is part of the love of life, our inexplicable master, part of our attempt to grasp the mystery of life in which we find ourselves, bound as we are to time with time running out, and that poetry, like religion, embraces our deepest feelings as we embrace it in turn with the unique feelings which it engenders, which can be expressed in no other way but in the poem itself.

As between poetry or other book collections years ago and now, I would like to say that formerly a poetry collection would go to the children or family of the poet, yet nowadays the young are not sufficiently established early in life to keep and tend a thousand or two thousand books, so these tend to go to libraries. They may even be sold and help to support a poet in his later years, an idea which may never have occurred to him when he was collecting each volume as a loved and rewarding thing in itself.

I recall a remarkable occasion a few years ago in the nearby village of Etna, New Hampshire, when we visited friends who had lying about, almost in full sight but actually in a large cardboard box brought in from another room, remarkable literary effects. These consisted of original, unlisted and uncataloged letters written by nineteenth-century authors to ancestors of the family. I recall a haul of over a dozen letters of Theodore Parker, some from William Lloyd Garrison, and a charming letter from Hawthorne, I do not know whether the only one, giving the following news: Hawthorne was to sit for his portrait in miniature at, say, eleven o'clock on a Wednesday morning but wrote to say that his wife had just had a baby and he could not make the appointment.

There has always been a lively argument in our house as to the disposal of literary materials, whether letters or books. My wife is a New Englander and comes down from persons having the notion of letters or signed contemporary books as a real part of life, as real as anything, so that it would not seem extreme or unnatural to have a letter lying around, easily to hand if wanted, from Emerson or Phillips Brooks or whomever. There should be no will to canonize these by incarcerating them in a library. They would give off their spirit of life as real objects still real in the household, although written long ago.

As a Midwesterner I always held the opposite view, that such letters or books from or by important literary personages should be viewed and felt as sacred objects and should be carefully preserved in a library against fire or the plain destruction of time. Which is the better notion in regard to literary effects? As I have collected my books of poetry with an eye to their time-defying properties, it is to be announced that I belong to the sacred-object school and would like to keep signed books of first editions faithfully preserved in a suitable library.

However, nothing is absolute, everything is relative, and it was with pleasure that I passed on my Nonesuch Bible volumes, which began this paper, to our son Rick on his twenty-first birthday. I began by saying I did not read much in these, the assumption being that one had read the Bible before, but since our son is a graduate student at the Pacific School of Religion at Berkeley, I hope our young theologian may read them explicitly, and subjectively, as the years go by. I hope to give a comparable gift to our daughter Gretchen on her twenty-first birthday.

A last word. Order struggles against disorder in the world. If you enter my poetry library, the shelves look more or less orderly, but actually there exists a kind of erupting chaos of disorder. As a blind man may feel to see, I intuitively grasp for a book here or there, knowing the size and look of it, although it may have been long ousted from an alphabetical context. Often with dismay I have to fight through hundreds of backs of books in the hope of finding what I am looking for. Often it is hopeless. One simply cannot find the volume in the welter of conglomerate acquisitions. But I like to think that my random collecting of poetry books through decades, the collecting of books loved for themselves, represents a kind of order, however imperfect, not a riot of disorder, not spasms of interest, but sustained devotion to poetry, and to the ordering power of poetry.

PART TWO

Empson's Poetry

"Delicate goose-step of penned scorpions"

Coincidence dictated that I should be up at Cambridge coterminously with Empson, hence that I should be intimately aware of his poetic career from its inception. At twenty-one Empson was, with Hugh Sykes-Davies, editing *Experiment,* the livelier of the two literary magazines which mushroomed among the undergraduates, and was also contributing to the other, *New Venture.*

In the first number of *Experiment* appeared three of Empson's poems: "Letter," beginning "You were amused to find you too could fear/ 'The external silence of the infinite spaces'" (entitled "Letter I" in the 1935 edition of his first *Poems,* from Chatto and Windus); the amusing, startling "Part of Mandevil's Travels" (likewise republished in the book); and "Disillusion with Metaphysics" (later printed as "Dissatisfaction with Metaphysics" with variations in two lines). George Reavey, J. Bronowski, E. E. Phare, Hugh Sykes, and T. H. White were other original contributors. (Miss Phare, who was later to write one of the first books on Hopkins, here contributed an article on Valéry and Hopkins.)

The second number of *Experiment* contained two other Empson poems, "Camping Out," a brain-tickler which exercised many hours of drawing-room discussion in Cambridge, and withheld its ultimate ambiguous secrets for years, and "The Earth Has Shrunk in the Wash." The same issue offered the prose "Ambiguity in Shakespeare's Sonnet XVI," which began those extraordinary microscopic and expanding views of grammatical context in poetry which were elaborated to make *Seven Types of Ambiguity.* The pupil of I. A.

First published in *Accent* 4, no. 4 (Summer, 1944).

Richards inflamed the imagination of his master: Richards understood instantly Empson's value. Although the chief indebtedness in the association of the two Magdalene men since 1927 has been that of Empson to Richards—the prefatory note to *Seven Types* includes the author's statement that Richards "told me to write this essay"—the master exploited the fineness of mind of the pupil, wise to see in Empson's beginning criticism a nice adjunct to and a different end from his own. And as late as 1940, he wrote an appreciation of Empson in *Furioso*. In this same second number of *Experiment* appeared my "Request for Offering." I, too, in a less direct manner, was to fall under the spell of the master; to him I owed, and owe, heady allegiance for the sensitivity he evinced in every manifestation of poetry one exhibited.

Experiment began in November, 1928, and ended in October, 1930, with its sixth number. Empson made contributions to all the remaining numbers: prose on Herbert's "The Sacrifice" and on T. S. Eliot, and five additional poems, all of which have reappeared in his later volumes of verse, some with alterations. Empson also published a good many poems at this time in *The Cambridge Review*.

The scholar may enjoy noting how Empson worked alterations as I quote first the periodical version (1928) of "Relativity," then the 1935 book version with its new title, "The World's End":

Relativity

"Fly to the world's end, dear.
Plumb space through stars.
Let final chasm, topless cliffs, appear;
What tyrant there our variance debars?

Live there, your back freezing to All's Wall,
Or brinked by chasm that all chasms bounds;
There, with two times at choice, all plots forestall,
Or, no time backing you, what force surrounds?"

Alas, now hope for freedom, no bars bend;
Space is like earth, rounded, a padded cell.
Plumb the stars' depth, your head bumps you behind;
Blind Satan's voice rattled the whole of Hell.

On air, on cushions, what's a file worth
To pierce that chasm lies so snugly curled?
Each tangent plain touches one top of earth;
Each point in one direction ends the world.

Apple of knowledge and forgetful mere
From Tantalus too differential bend;

The world's end is here.
This place's curvature precludes its end.

The World's End

"Fly with me then to all's and the world's end
And plumb for safety down the gap of stars;
Let the last gulf or topless cliff befriend,
What tyrant there our variance debars?"

Alas, how hope for freedom, no bars bind;
Space is like earth, rounded, a padded cell;
Plumb the stars' depth, your lead bumps you behind;
Blind Satan's voice rattled the whole of Hell.

On cushioned air what is such metal worth
To pierce to the gulf that lies so snugly curled?
Each tangent plain touches one top of earth,
Each point in one direction ends the world.

Apple of knowledge and forgetful mere
From Tantalus too differential bend.
The shadow clings. The world's end is here.
This place's curvature precludes its end.

It has always seemed a pity to me that several excellent poems, of the profusion of work Empson produced in a relatively short time, have been omitted from his books. Three poems in particular deserve to be more available than they are in the files of *The Cambridge Review* and in the anthology *Cambridge Poetry 1929*. Conditions are such that I am unable to credit *The Cambridge Review* with thanks for the liberty of quotation, but it is hoped that the editors would have no objection to my quoting these three poems at this time.

The first poem, "Une Brioche pour Cerbere," employs Empson's sly wit, the first four lines reminding one in tone of "Rolling the Lawn," with its unforgettable "Holding the Holy Roller at the slope/ (The English symbol, not the Texas Pope)":

Une Brioche pour Cerbere

Tom nods. No senior angels see or grapple.
Tom enters Eden, nodding, the back way.
Borrows from Adam, and then eats, the Apple.
"Thank you so much for a delightful stay."

If it works, it works. Nod to the man at the door.
Nor heed what gulfs, nor how much the earth between.
If radio light, from the last sphere before
Outer dark, reflects you, you are seen.

So can the poles look in each other's eyes.
Within that charmed last vacuate of air
Who is my neighbor, and who safe from spies?
Earth sees me nod. No, nothing to declare.

Porter, report not my heart contraband.
Of you, you primitive culture, stored flame,
I scotophile, friend by short cut, had planned
To view the rites, no high priest first to tame.

My dear, my earth how offer me your halls?
Grant me your Eden, I see Eden Station,
Whence stationed gauge you whose full scale appalls
And all whose porters would ask explanation?

The next poem shows a spirit of gaiety even then characteristic of
the author: unbridled, but well reined, gaiety of word play:

New World Bistres

The darkest is near dawn, we almost butter.
The churning is fixed now; we have "gone to sleep"
In body, and become a living pat;
It is then that the arm churning it aches most
And dares least pause against the ceaseless turning.
I am sure he will soon stumble upon the gift,
Maypole his membranes, Ciro be his eyes,
A secret order, assumptive, distillation;
Fitting together it will be won and seem nothing.
    Oh socketed too deep, Oh more than tears,
Than any faint unhurrying resurrection,
That ever rain, manna (the manner born,
The man born of the manor, and that bourne
Turn Cardinal Bourne. The Palace, Washing Day.
Lux and her cherub, here is a nymph handy.)
Those glacial, dried soap film, shacken packets,
That rain of hushing, elixir-centred sequins,
Falling through space, gracious, a feather swaying.
    Rising, triumphant, hooter, whine, mosquito,
The separator, pausing by violent movement
Stands at the even not skimming of stood cream.
Moss can be grown on tops. Gyroscopes
Holed with grim jewels set in resounding brass
Rector and tractor of earth's vertiges,
Claw, widely patented, pierce, sinking,
Armoured resentience their lead fathom line.

The third poem, in loaded gear, follows:

114

Insomnia

Satan when ultimate chaos he would fly
battered at random by hot dry wet cold
(Probably nor Probability
his view the total cauldron of a sky
Milton nor Brownian hesitance foretold)
One purposed whirlwind helpless whole hours could hold.

> From Bottomless Pit's bottom originally
> who durst his sail-broad vans unfold
> thence till (God's help the rival gust came by)
> Hell seemed as Heaven undistinguishedly high
> Through pudding still unstirred of Anarch Old
> had sunk yet, down for ever, by one blast controlled.

So to the baked Chaos that am I,
Potion whose cooling boat grates crystal shoaled
gears on a mixed bank allotropically
untempered patchwork to the naked eye,
one hour the snow's one pattern, and I bold,
gale knew its point all night, though nine through compass rolled.

> Though large charged carpet units insulately
> alone processed, each from the former's mould,
> each further angle could new shades supply,
> roads every earlier opposite to tie
> in single type Hell's very warders scrolled,
> Nine intersterile species nightmare's full Nine were foaled.

There is another early poem, never reprinted since its appearance in *Experiment* No. 4 (November, 1929) which has stuck in my mind and calls for comment now:

UFA Nightmare

Gramophony. Telephony. Photophony.
The mighty handles and persensate dials
That rule my liner multi-implicate
Ring round, Stonehenge, a wide cold concrete room.
(I run the row from A to O, and so
—To and fro; periscope, radio—
We know which way we go)
        "If we can reach the point
Before the tide, there is another style.
I shall checkmate, given the whole board;
Juggling the very tittles in the air
Shall counterblast the dreadnought machiner."

> (Scamper, scamper, scamper.
> Huge elbows tumble towards chaos.
> Lurch, sag, and hesitation of the dials.)
>   A tiny figure, seated in the engine,
>   Weevil clicking in a hollow oak,
>   Pedals, parched with the fear of solitude.

Here was a remarkable poem, timely then as it still is. Its title, wickedly foreign, excused its oddity, let one wander in the dream, yet there was something scientifically precise about it. It had wit; originality in every line; very subtle music; drama; lines that strode across the years, summing up the age; and, as in most of Empson's poetry, a strange quality of hiding the meanings, hoarding its strength, elusively secreting delicacies of perception.

The first line was novel. One had not heard a poem start that way. The license, however, was not excessive: something balanced about the three terms, which you never knew whether you were pronouncing properly, a fact giving the more pleasure—you wondered whether the author calculated even on that, or whether it was merely your stupidity—and there was the other level of meaning in the sound of "phony." Line two went off with a great swish, quite released from the first, or even a Miltonic dignity. One had the tendency in Empson to enjoy single successful lines, savoring them as they were, out of context with their grammatical relation to previous or succeeding lines; and this was one. What his "liner" was one did not yet know; "multi-implicate" was new; "Stonehenge" was thrown up in your face. You finally derived pleasure from using this last as a verb, certainly a novel notion, but you could take it as a noun singly, giving a different and yet quite similar suggestion to "wide cold concrete room." Contrast of the static with the dynamic, ancient simplicity with modern complexity. Then the musical lilt of the next three parenthetical lines, how accurately the music controlled! I recall a vague feeling of similarity with Hart Crane here, the only place in Empson, quite evanescent, probably wrong. "We know which way we go" struck me as masterful, for I never knew in those years which way I was going—would have loved to know—but that is going out of context again.

Now supposedly the technician is speaking. Something dramatic and opulent in the first two lines. Switch to a chess image; odd, but provocative, keeping it from being too nautical. "Juggling the very tittles in the air" was a ravishing line. It was what the greatest critical insight always did: it lifted you up high into the rarified air of exquisite contemplation. I always thought of it as what Empson as poet and critic was doing. Again that nice contrast between two lines, in the heavier consonantal values of the "counterblast." "Juggling the very tittles in the air" was delicious! Juggling them, all most delicate thought or perception would finally overcome the heavy opposing weight of world or matter, put all in order.

The scamper motif was transitional, referred back to the first line. The huge elbows tumbling toward chaos went on telling the story, commenting on machinery. "Lurch, sag, and hesitation of the dials" was another line which stuck in my head. As a single line it was magnificent. You could take it all together, or you could draw it out. The line following, "A tiny figure, seated in the engine," stuck, too, became for me universal, a universal picture of modern man. The ensuing shift to the weevil "clicking" (strange relation to mechanics) in the hollow oak (even the weevil endowed with some mechanical similarity to man) was justified in the same way the chess image had been. And then the poem ended subtly with another change of tone, stress, grammar, seemingly awkwardly, and you could take it more ways than one. The whole poem was a compact piece, in which a various new world was ready to expand in the mind, baring images not violently opposed to the world as it was.

In December, 1939, when he had come to America from Japan but before he had returned to England, Empson told me that he considered his early poems in the nature of experiments, trial balloons or something of the sort. He was glad his criticism had "caught on" in this country, but was not surprised that his poetry had not. He said he had written some verse in the East, but not much. I recall prophesying that it would take America a decade to discover and estimate Empson as a poet, and I was short of the mark. It may be permissible now to discuss the nature of his contribution to poetry, in his early phase, before considering his second book.

First, let it be said that during my time at Cambridge, 1927–29, Empson was considered a startling poet by the learned. His mind had early been weighted on the mathematical and scientific side; he was rather Shelleyan in that, as he was in his exodus from Cambridge, for reasons as interesting to this century as were those of Shelley to his. Empson was brisk, quick-moving, florid. When he took the tripos in June, 1929, they had had to give him not only a first, but a starred first, a rare distinction. No American, I understand, has ever won one.

In Cambridge everybody talked about Empson's poetry. His poems challenged the mind, seemed to defy the understanding; they amused and they enchanted; and even then they afforded a kind of parlor

117

game, whiling away lively hours of puzzlement at many a dinner party. The shock and impact of this new kind of poetry were so considerable that people at that time had no way to measure its contemporary or its timeless value. They were amazed by it. Eliot was already enthroned. The "Oxford Group" had not yet got fully under way. And Cambridge was buzzing with activity.

Empson had the power to shock. Old dowagers who had known Meredith (I remember one), or young girls from Girton who knew their Hopkins, or dons who talked much but did not know where they stood, were stumped, balked, and rebuked by "Camping Out," which began: "And now she cleans her teeth into the lake." You could read the poem twenty times and not know what it meant! You could read it so many ways! You could argue about the grammar by the hour! And as for the meaning, did Richards himself know for sure? It was all so intellectual, so exciting, so very Cantabrigian.

This is not the place to dwell upon the course of the poet's activities. Had Richards not gone to China, where he was for one thing preparing his book on Mencius, it is questionable whether Empson would have gone to the East. The reserve of his mind was such that the *Poems*, his first volume, did not appear until 1935. This seems significant. Meanwhile, the "Auden gang" had raged on the world, the world was listening to them, there was a bewilderment of opinion as to the relative merits and demerits of each, they had their "little mag," their anthologies. The new signatures were on the wing. The excavations into sociological reality made by Auden constituted an enlargement of English poetry from its immediate past; one thought of the service of enlargement made earlier by Browning. (Or, better, one did not think of it; Browning was unmentionable.) I have said an enlargement, not a deepening. And if Oxford had seemed to produce something thought of at this time as a school, the Cambridge writers maintained their lack of group consciousness, their strict individuality and, in Empson's case, their austere, meticulous distance. The Oxford writers went out to woo the world; Empson, as an epitome of Cambridge attitudes, remained aloof, in a kind of scientific maze of his own words. Let the world come to his poetry when it would. His modesty coupled with his wit might have convinced him it was not a world-shake anyway. But Empson, whatever initially caused his poetry, was typically a Cambridge writer: the passion for meticulous truth, the scientific attitudes intruding on poetry to rule out anything "romantic," the care for minute perceptions communicated in a subtle way, the daring exercise of new grammatical possibilities of English, under the aegis of a master, these made for a poetry not in the old style of the humanities, but in a new, a sharper, a keener but also perhaps a less profound mode.

Some points in favor of the early poems follow. Not only did Empson load every rift with ore; he loaded them with more than one kind of substance. The compression of his images and the conscious ambiguity of his grammar, when he exercised both, were salutary in that they insured the reader against the ragged or the loose. A poem of his would not yield its meanings immediately, but one would be well paid in time: a sign of good poetry. It was a poetry of concealed riches. Another point was in the seemingly almost perfect control of the use of language. There was no excess in these poems. If they were bizarre, they did not offend; if witty, they did not degenerate into foolishness; if elaborate, they did not invite careless attention; if puzzling, they enchanted one with the answers. They expressed a certain aristocracy of intellect, but were not aloof from fundamental propositions. They constituted a microcosm of realities.

Against Empson's early poetry, charges could be leveled and were indeed applied. This poetry was not "great" because it was not "universal." There was no world view, no philosophic, inclusive view behind the poems. It was repeatedly said that they were too purely intellectual: the compliment was turned into an adverse criticism. His look was too rarified for human nature's daily food. On an old measuring rod of the simple, the sensuous, and the passionate, these poems could not rate high; they were not simple, they were not sensuous, and their passion was limited to the intellectual kind. Others held that the poems did not cohere; these found disorder who had not imagination enough to divine the niceties of a new order. Others held that when wit dominates to the extent that it did in these poems, the sign was of a certain smallness; the great poets all had a nobility, a depth, a seriousness lacking in this work. And still others believed that a religious consciousness, traditionally based, in one mode or another, such as had given Eliot "Ash Wednesday," was necessary for the scale of importance which these poems did not touch.

For perfection of form, precision of statement, and delight of language, some of Empson's early poems will last as long as any of those of his contemporaries. Richards, who may be excused the bias of a learned teacher upon a learned pupil, thinks Empson is the best of the lot. Be that as it may. It is probable that the early poems constitute minor poetry of a high order. That in itself is a very considerable achievement. Some are satisfied with a few poems of Marvell; some would be satisfied with one. Values notoriously change; a decade or two hence, those now considered major may be considered minor, and vice versa. It is conceivable that a few of Empson's poems may be read ages hence.

Some single lines which impressed themselves upon me for a decade I shall quote. They became part of the fullness of one's consciousness. "How small a chink lets in how dire a foe." "Space is like earth, rounded, a padded cell." "Blind Satan's voice rattled the whole of Hell." "Each point in one direction ends a world." "Delicate goose-step of penned scorpions." "Gods cool in turn, by the sun long outlasted." "I approve, myself, dark spaces between stars." "It is the pain, it is the pain, endures." "'Twixt devil and deep sea, man hacks his caves." "Solomon's gems, white vistas, preserved kings." "Law makes long spokes of the short stakes of men." "One daily tortures the poor Christ anew." "The laughing god born of a startling answer." "All those large dreams by which men long live well/ Are magic-lanterned on the smoke of hell." "The beam of Justice as in doubt for ever/ Hung like a Zeppelin over London river."

Before going on to consider Empson's second book, *The Gathering Storm*, we may take a poem of his from the first book, which also appeared in *New Signatures*, and work it as a good specimen of Empson's poetical powers.

This Last Pain

This last pain for the damned the Fathers found:
"They knew the bliss with which they were not crowned,"
 Such, but on earth, let me foretell,
 Is all, of heaven or of hell.

Man, as the prying housemaid of the soul,
May know her happiness by eye to hole:
 He's safe; the key is lost; he knows
 Door will not open, nor hole close.

"What is conceivable can happen too,"
Said Wittgenstein, who had not dreamt of you;
 But wisely; if we worked it long
 We should forget where it was wrong:

Those thorns are crowns which, woven into knots,
Crackle under and soon boil fool's pots;
 And no man's watching, wise and long,
 Would ever stare them into song.

Thorns burn to a consistent ash, like man;
A splendid cleanser for the frying-pan:
 And those who leap from pan to fire
 Should this brave opposite admire.

All those large dreams by which men long live well

Are magic-lanterned on the smoke of hell;
   This then is real, I have implied,
   A painted, small, transparent slide.

These the inventive can hand-paint at leisure,
Or most emporia would stock our measure;
   And feasting in their dappled shade
   We should forget how they were made.

Feign then what's by a decent tact believed
And act that state is only so conceived,
   And build an edifice of form
   For house where phantoms may keep warm.

Imagine, then, by miracle, with me,
(Ambiguous gifts, as what gods give must be)
   What could not possibly be there,
   And learn a style from a despair.

Line 1. The question to be asked about this line is: do we need to know what theology is intended? Also, do we need to know about the author's private attitude to religion to determine what he may want to suggest by Fathers?

2. Supposedly they are in hell; supposedly they knew the bliss before they were damned. Paolo and Francesca?

3. "Such" refers to the bliss. Empson would be the one to dilate on his use of "but" here. If bliss occurs on Earth, that is all there is to heaven and hell. "Let me foretell" rings ominously.

4. The comma could be left out after "all." Used, it emphasizes "all," makes it substantial, a universal, and affects a nuance in the rhythm of the line. The comma also throws a slight stress on the word "or," which it otherwise might not have, lending a slightly different connotation than if "heaven" and "hell" were equally stressed, with "or" merely as a link. Bliss we might have expected to have been all of heaven; now we are invited to the notion that it would be "all" of hell. He can be using both terms in a generic, and also in a "worldly" way, simultaneously. It may be illogical to suppose there could be any bliss in hell; yet this may be taken in the sense of the pleasures of worldly sin. The point of the quatrain is, however, that they had known bliss in this life; that was final, whatever would happen to them upon damnation after death.

The first quatrain is firm in tone, dignified, serious, controlled, stating the problem. The musical quality of the verse is apparent. Low-register rhyme words are employed for damnation, "found," "crowned." When he makes a dictum, the poet uses higher-register rhyme words, "foretell," "hell," as appropriate to the sense of bliss.

5–8. These four lines can be considered together, the sense running on. Recall "the damp souls of housemaids." Housemaids need not be prying, but are so posited for purposes of the comparison. We must expect here a kind of Empsonian wit available in other poems of his. The tone, therefore, is made lighter than in the first quatrain; a kind of metaphysical joke is supplied. But the meaning behind the levity is equal to that in the first quatrain; the basis is agnosticism, astringently intellectualized. Man may know the happiness of the soul as a prying housemaid might look through a keyhole. The use of "to hole" as an infinitive is a liberty taken with grammatical oddity which is characteristic of Empson: but it comes off. But, again, the words are ambiguous; if "hole" is taken as a noun, a less metaphysical, more straightforward possibility will pertain: you are getting somewhere. Maybe "the key *is* lost." This is all rather funny. At any rate, man is safe; he knows the door of the soul will not open, therefore he can go on looking through it; the keyhole will not close, so that he can go on contemplating. There is a smirk to the passage, which is both a criticism of and a satire upon bliss, a criticism and satire upon man contemplating his own soul.

9–12. Perhaps the key is not lost. Empson had watched Wittgenstein walk through the streets of Cambridge. The sentence (I have not looked it up in the *Tractatus*) is pompous. "But wisely" suggests the egocentric nature of the philosopher (or of the author); he may be looking through a keyhole, but certainly he is not looking at us. The rest of the quatrain speaks common sense, which is, however, too often forgotten in such matters as these: it doesn't do any good to ponder too long: you can see things at a glance with greater clarity than through prolonged study, sometimes.

13–16. These begin to bind together the foregoing information. Some changes were made in the grammar of lines 13, 14. You can play with the idea of the crown of thorns here. The negative statement is at least affirmative!

17–20. These four lines were added to the original version. The teacher is at the board with his pointer.

21–24. The first two lines are the most compelling of the poem. They weigh upon the memory. The rhythm recalls lines 13, 14 of Shakespeare's Sonnet 129:

> All this the world well knows yet none knows well,
> To shun the heaven that leads men to (this) hell.

Empson does not go so far as this last line of Shakespeare, yet he has implied a similar attitude in the poem up to this point. The large dreams are magic-lanterned on the smoke of hell. The smoke of hell may justify the boiling pot, although not only fools go to hell. "Magic-lanterned" gives a tone of artifice to the large dreams, seen as pictures (through the keyhole?) on or in smoke which itself is shifting by nature. But magical, too.

In lines 9–16 low-register rhyme words were employed; now, as in lines 3–4, when the poet offers his dictum, higher-register rhyme sounds are used. The slide, the keyhole, the membrane through which reality is perceived seems to be called the final reality, arbiter of the knower and the known.

25–28. "Most" was substituted for "all" in line 26, a musical loss, I feel. Here the will seems to be given the initiating power; else a great prince lies in prisons he did not build. Subjectivity is not easily lost. The inventive mind can make its own pictures of heaven and hell. Agnosticism again; or at least no acceptance of orthodox dogma; and at most, skepticism. Empson, or you, or I, can feast in a Marvellian dappled shade if we like, forgetful in our own wish.

29–32. This begins the resolution of the poem. Keep up the pretense for what it is worth. There is delicate self-abnegation here, grave reticence, although they may carry a strong undertone of recognition of the futility of the position—yet there is some pleasure in it.

33–36. Higher-register rhyme sounds are used to round off the whole proposition. It is the complete skeptic who can and must imagine miracles. The poem is so good that one wonders why it might not be enjoyed in 2044. But see Empson's note to the poem; a reader may read more into it than was intended. "The idea of the poem is that human nature can conceive divine states which it cannot attain."

In 1940, five years after the first volume, appeared *The Gathering Storm*, from Faber's. We might begin with the notes. Again he has supplied these, this time in greater abundance, and in themselves they constitute occasional prose of remarkable nicety. The note to "Bacchus" is reprinted intact, with one sentence tidied up: "*Glancer:* she made eyes at both opposites at once" becomes "Glancer: she looked both ways and wanted heaven as real as earth." Indeed, the total new note to "Bacchus," which goes on for about six pages, is a mine of Empsoniana. He is as good on his own poem as he can be on any poem, approaches it with as avid a disinterest, and divulges what minutiae his critical acumen deems sufficient. He does the critic's job for him. This is bound up in the notion that "many people (like myself) prefer to read poetry mixed with prose; it gives you more to go by; the conventions of poetry have been getting far off from normal life, so that to have a prose bridge makes reading poetry seem more natural." The idea gives on to a deeper apology for his poems: "But partly they are meant to be like answers to a crossword puzzle; a sort of puzzle interest is part of the pleasure that you are meant to get from the verse, and that I get myself when I go back to it." The earlier poems seem to me to come more closely under this concept than the later ones, which are not as difficult as those, excepting that "Bacchus," now stretched out to seven stanzas, remains fascinatingly difficult. His "clotted kind of poetry" does not actually have the clots of the earlier work. Nobody could improve on his notes; one could only quibble here or there. So there is nothing to say on this score, and they are recommended to the reader entire. You could read the new poems without the notes; or you could read the notes without the poems, if only to savor the exegetical Empson mind.

The poems in the second book take in a wider range of experience (China principally); they maintain his near-genius for precision; they bear the undeniable look and stamp of his other poems, are on the whole less ambiguous, become merrier and gayer in tone, and they achieve a breakdown of his style, toward the end, into what seems to be a newer style, but this is not as masterful as the old. The density of sense is the same; the poet writes with authority and charm; yet the adverse criticisms heretofore mentioned stay, and the favorable notations are given again. There has been no profound change in the nature of his thinking; this volume is a continuance of the first, rather than a new departure.

"Your Teeth Are Ivory Towers" regales us with the witty rhymes, "Ba," "Pa," and "Ha," which only Empson could achieve. He likes the three-line stanza, which he employed so successfully before. The poem is marred for me, however, by two phrases, "only the child" and "we must deliberate," which echo directly Auden in "Another Time."

"Aubade" is a telling poem. Note the plainness, the directness of it in comparison with earlier poems. He says what he says. Note also the reluctance to part with the three-line stanza, here interspersed.

"Four Legs, Two Legs, Three Legs" returns nearly to the difficulty of the early work, but is easier to comprehend than, say, "Camping Out." It seems revealing that Empson should take a "Reflection from Rochester." He would not reflect from Wordsworth (cf. the sally in "New World Bistres.") He is further revealed, dated, savored, in a "Reflection from Anita Loos."

Empson earlier dignified the villanelle form with serious import in the two excellent pieces beginning "It is the pain, it is the pain, endures" and "Twixt devil and deep sea, man hacks his caves." We are now given another equal to these, the beautiful poem entitled "Missing Dates," beginning "Slowly the poison the whole blood stream fills." In addition to this masterful line, a second of equal single power is "The waste remains, the waste remains and kills." These add to the universality of utterance I claimed for Empson above. "The fat is in the pyre, boy, waiting for the end," from "Just a Smack at Auden," in his rollicking vein, will not soon be forgotten. The cleverness of the satirical monotony with which he builds up his rhymes on the word "end" in this poem deserves mention: a cutting and a cunning imitation and devitalization.

Nothing is more characteristic of his funds of abstruse knowledge than the matter of the liver fluke in the poem "China." "That the thing can play these tricks without having any structure at all is what is so frightening; it is like demoniacal possession."

In the last poem, "Autumn on Nan-Yueh," Empson cuts loose from compression and lets his words fly with an ease and brilliancy unparalleled in his other work, although you may think the poem is not serious enough. He writes with the sheerest pleasure, making perfect strokes ("We do not fly when we are clay./ We hope to fly when we are dust." Or "And all styles can come down to noise") with rapid energy forming the most readable verse, seemingly informal and offhand, yet composed in a strict but stately measure recalling the eighteenth century. If this is the stylistic way out of his formerly tortured verse, we can ask for more, even if we reproach him a bit for confiding his matter to the architecture of an old verse form rather than beating out something new to him and new to us. Although one line, "Excuses, consequences, signs," sounds of Pope, "the heat-mists" of his vision drive the words into strongly original ways, and the pleasure of reading is the pleasure of reading the best kind of light verse, a heady pleasure. "I hope the gaiety of the thing comes through."

Pound's New Cantos

I am not interested in what was reported to be another incident in the life of Ezra Pound. I am interested in the Cantos as poetry. I am not concerned with Pound's political beliefs, nor with his social pronouncements, which have not seemed logically to cohere. To what extent one can abstract these from the total impact of his late Cantos I am not certain. An approach to the work as poetry is necessary and more rewarding, at least to me, than reading the Cantos as political, economic, or sociological manifestoes. Fifty years will remove the politics and leave the poetry. The Cantos can be read disinterestedly, which is only to pay them their due as art, and indeed in these new Cantos one would assume a task of special pleading to overestimate the political or sociological as predominantly significant.

The eleven new Cantos (74–84) carry on much in the manner as they do in the type of matter of the former Cantos. If anything, they are more lively and more lyrical than their predecessors; some might assess them as more violent in places, more nervously jumping from point to point in a kind of insistent distraction, with less cohesive order, throwing off shoots and flares of lyric. The dates come up into the last few years, imparting an interest of the immediate to the work. One wonders when the century will be reached, and what will then be able to be made of the whole work.

We are invited to compare the later work of Pound with that of Eliot. These works represent two major approaches to life, the religious and the secular; contemplation versus action; the feminine set against the masculine; the inner against the outer world; the world of spiritual timelessness against an artistic reconstruction of history.

The last quartets of Beethoven have been witnessed in regard to

First published in *Quarterly Review of Literature* 5 (1949): 174–91.

Eliot's. Beethoven's last quartets have the power to excruciate. They are excruciating. The word could not be applied to Eliot's later work. His trilling wire in the blood is a small wire, with no maddening vibration. Beethoven was straining at the bounds of sensibility. Eliot does not strain, even at the bounds of grammar; the form is placid, controlled, studied, considered, in keeping with the gentle, deep aspiration of his spiritual wish. He is not angry. He has denied such things, and that is his criticism.

It is more difficult to write good poetry of acceptance than it is to write good poetry of revolt. The *Four Quartets* do not shock us. They are to speak beyond such things. The allusions are provocative, as before. I will not point out the selection of "Erhebung," the careful admission of "smokefall," the masterful perception of the word "twittering." Nor exclaim the niceness of "where the field-mouse trots"; the newness of "haruspicate and scry"; the syllabic delicacy and nuance of "sortilege, or tea leaves"; nor the resurrection of "Behovely" ("Sin is Behovely").

I would point up some solemn comments. "human nature/ Cannot bear very much reality." We are so much of our age, and Eliot has expressed it so dominantly, that I have heard no one object to this statement. It is taken as a matter of fact, as basically acceptable or accepted truth, the truth about humankind. Yet if we look with detachment at this statement, we do not necessarily believe it. It becomes a pseudo-statement, the best poetry can do, unscientific. Actually we do not know what "reality" means, and we have no measuring rod for "very much." But even if we could be satisfied on these points, the possibility arises of transcending our times, which could mean transcending Eliot's statement, with attendant removal from the subtle intoxication of its persuasion, from the very tone, from the very texture. It would then be possible to see this statement, from some future point of view, as period writing. It would be possible to refuse it total assent as feminine, soft, weak. It would be possible to consider certain past, heroic times as perhaps having equal value, differently emphasized. Some Greek, some Elizabethan, or our present Pound could announce the opposite with telling effect. For humankind can, and has, borne, and will bear, very much reality, by whatever semantic gist. There is a core of man's humanity which Eliot's statement does not reach. Blackmur (*Sewanee Review*, Autumn, 1946) would have the statement modified by addition of "that humankind cannot *know* very much reality," and that in his inability he rushes "heartlong into the arm of authority, if not the authority of some past revelation then the nearest spatch-cock authority to hand, when it is asserted as genuine and its own. Authority is ostrich." The switch to cognition is plausible, but takes away from the feeling of having to bear what he knows, and it would not seem that man's inability to know very much reality is cause which results in his rush to authority. Eliot's emphasis on the feeling in "bear" would seem the more profound, whether or not we are concerned with the authority. But my point is that Eliot's statement remains aloof from the deepest human suffering, affronting our profound recognition of this, and does not belong with the endlessness of humility.

The positive, the masculine, and the heroic (or its inversion in satire) are in the realm of Pound. The end of Eliot's vision in the Quartets is a state of grace shining from a line Tennyson could have written: "And all shall be well and/All manner of think shall be well."

As yet we have no feeling that this state is available to Pound; nor that he would welcome it; nor that he could make poetry of it. He is the militant mind still protesting, still aggressive, dominating his forms, making an objective picture of the world out of intellect and feeling, in which there is great spirit, but in an entirely different sense from the technically religious spirit. There is a sense that man has borne very much suffering, and can bear it, but as against Eliot's statement we have the typically Poundian, individualistic, intellectual, aggressive comment (74):

> I don't know how humanity stands it
> with a painted paradise at the end of it
> without a painted paradise at the end of it.
> the dwarf morning-glory twines round the grass blade

The poetry of Eliot's statement depends from the whole structure of Christian doctrine, less a made thing than Pound's. Here the ideas stand up in their own right. The method of the make is evident. The trouble is that it is a squib. To what extent is it deeply felt in Pound's philosophy? These are four lines in a welter of lines quickly running through all sorts of ideas and sensations. Either Pound has so much to say that he hurtles us along in his hectic, headlong pursuit of his exuberant, prolific world, as if his magic would break should we stop for months to consider, say, these four lines. Or, Pound is not interested in penetrating, or cannot penetrate, the depths of life and will cast out these laconic lines, for instance, for the sake of laconicism. Either-or. The fallacy of either-or is also evident, and not final.

One is harassed by the squib-writing and can scarcely find three pages of unbroken coherence. This is probably to misunderstand, out of imperception, the niceness of musical structure, the necessity of every line and phrase being precisely where and as it is.

To return to an Eliot-Pound contrast, it could be substantiated that in his poetry Eliot has little love of individuals. The compassion, and the passion, Hopkins had for specific human beings in his poems, the deep realizations he erected of their essential humanity, as, to name one instance, Felix Randall, marks him. Where Eliot is deficient in this respect, where Hopkins applied to individuals deep love, Pound is objectively interested in all kinds and conditions of men, historical and contemporary, those in old legends, old courts, or modern states and senates, and lays about him with hatred as well as with sometime affection. This is to be expected, granting the objective, secular, history-redacting nature of the work. It also marks the poet interested in this world, the world—rather than in the soul, the after-world.

As for the polylinguality of Pound, one becomes used to it. The constant repetitions, cries, tags, pointers mingle with the plain (or rather Poundian) English of the text. One finds accountably that Pound relies more heavily in places on Italian than on other Romance languages; that his Spanish is sparse; that his German is as it were unfriendly. The Greek is always sightly, if not, as I am told, always accurate. He has a real love for old French, early English. I am not prepared to comment on the Chinese.

Instead of the English being cluttered up with foreign tongues, one would like there to be more of them, in denser proportions, which is to ask for a radical attempt to write in half a dozen languages. Joyce more nearly did this than Pound does, with radical aim of a new synthetic language. In Pound the importations, poetically, are embellishment and ornamentation, and are not organic in effect. The meaning is organic with the whole, yet the effect is often of the cymbaler, of glissando. The intellectual lie is given to the method in Pound's resistance to any method more formidable. He uses only a few languages, and these up to a certain point. He eschews Siamese, Swahili, Russian. The ordinary informed Westerner who is intrigued with Greek, Latin, or old French tags would be baffled by a more formidable system. No new language has been created, as in Joyce, but conventional languages imported into English. The effect is stimulating and pleasing, the method highly developed as Pound's own, and perhaps a more radical departure should not be desired. Polylinguality is relative, absolute polylinguality futile, partial polylinguality pleasing. It is to be noted that the heavy bulk of the work is to be understood in plain English.

Plain English in Pound is not plain English elsewhere. As we know, it is inspissated, whirled around with abbreviations, slants, grammatical oddities, capricious quirks and tricks of spacing, indentation, and repetition; time is scrambled and comes out like meaning, like history, sometimes translucent, sometimes cryptic. Pound has hem-stitched a new style, quite his own, which nobody would want to copy and would do so disastrously. It does not seem a great new direction in English verse, but a mind-like vehicle and necessity of the author. One would like to hear the Cantos declaimed by loudspeaker from the Greek theater at Taormina, or at Berkeley, preferably by Pound himself. His reading of *The Seafarer* was powerful, strident, exhilarating; the Cantos would lean to the dramatic so declaimed. But they are best enjoyed in the solitude of the study in a collation of discriminations over a long period of time.

The problem of Pound's redaction of history should be attempted. Is Pound's history true? This poses the problem of the relation of art to life. History is always changing. The imposition of his art changes the way of looking at it, not only within the framework of the Cantos, but outside that framework as well. Yet the question is not fundamentally of the validity of the method, but of the value of the work as art, as poetry.

Aristotle says,

It is not the function of the poet to relate what has happened, but what may happen,—what is possible according to the law of probability or necessity. The poet and the historian differ not by writing in verse or in prose. The work of Herodotus might be put into verse, and it would still be a species of history, with metre no less than without it. The true difference is that one relates what has happened, the other what may happen. Poetry, therefore, is a more philosophical and a higher thing than history: for poetry tends to express the universal, history the particular.

Pound creates a species of history in verse. The history is not the first consideration, but the poetry. We are challenged by him as to the universality of the poetry.

The secular nature of Pound's work and the time in which he is constrained to live work against the unification of ideology and poetic means known to Dante. It is not for nothing that we often cannot see the wood for the trees, the master plan in a Canto or number of Cantos, the totality of design in episodic content.

Universality in secular work I should judge to be more difficult of attainment than universality in a Dantesque sense, where what is given, the Church, is the very altar of absolute meaning. Pound thus, in a sense, has chosen a more difficult task for our times than Eliot;

perhaps choice is the wrong term, since each is compelled by the necessities of his own nature: choice is not pure. But Eliot, in assuming the Church (whether of England or Rome would not be radical here), has the likelihood not only of a greater unity in his performance, but of a greater potentiality of credibility in that he has penetrated to, or attempted to penetrate to the heart of Christian feelings in a Western world largely Christian.

Pound is the masculine, aggressive writer, attempting to dominate an immense secular scene and field, to wrest from many centuries, several languages, and multifarious events a pattern of significance, his own, but related to these, whereas Eliot is the feminine, passive writer (in his later period) who accepts the strictures of a predetermined way of life, in which there is paradoxically the greatest and the richest freedom, within the confines of which he is able to submit his art to values which he cannot and would not wish to supersede. Eliot can arrive at a statement of the deepest poetry in "Humility is endless." The truth of this statement is incontrovertible, granted, of course, a Christian premise. It comports with the highest type of action in a Christian society. It is a wisdom at the base of passion and thought. Eliot's given type of being and character has allowed him to arrive at this, as one conclusion, in which many can share, and have done for centuries. A pagan, however, or a Communist, or any enemy of Christianity, anyone who conceives of life without the necessity for Christianity, would not grant the premise, and to him Eliot's statement, although it still might be valid poetically, could be without deep significance. It is gratuitous to attempt to judge what would be Pound's allowance of significance to this phrase, but there is the point that in secular life, in the use of facets of history explicitly, it would be difficult to find a trope as profound as this, as indeed one is haunted all through the Cantos with the question of Pound's profundity.

How profound is Pound? Reading the Cantos hour after hour crosses the mind with the notion that they are not profound, if the bias can be permitted that secular work of this kind, being pagan, is of less value than work of the deepest Christian meaning. Reading the Cantos is like walking through a jungle in Yucatan. Not profundity, but an efflorescent spectacle. As if we in some Rousseau-super world were to view historical tags, Chinese mementoes, personal histories hung on febrile trees, lambent Soutine beasts beside, with an orator flinging imprecations, proffering hortatory truths through a screen and forest of live oaks hung with Spanish moss.

To return to Aristotle: "By the universal I mean how a person of a certain type will on occasion speak or act, according to the law of probability or necessity, and it is this universality at which poetry aims in the names she attaches to personages. The particular is—for example—what Alcibiades did or suffered." In the Cantos we hear many personages speak through Pound: the question is how fully we assent to the validity of his shiftings of emphasis and meaning, revising what seemed to be historic truth to make his own artistic truth; how credible the made artistic truth is; whether it is universal in the Aristotelian sense.

There can be no doubt about the validity of Pound's method. A poet can do anything that he can do. The assessment of values comes later. You cannot expect Beddoes to be Hardy, Webster to be Shakespeare, or Pound to be Eliot. Aristotle again: "It clearly follows that the poet or 'maker' should be the maker of plots rather than of verses; since he is a poet because he imitates, and what he imitates are actions. And even if he chances to take a historical subject [note the suspicion of unlikelihood] he is none the less a poet; for there is no reason why some events that have actually happened should not conform to the law of the probable and possible, and in virtue of that quality in them he is their poet or maker." That Pound is a maker of plots in a sense, on a vast scale and forcibly conceived, though not of course tragic-dramatic ones, is evident. Blackmur in "Masks of Ezra Pound" has given us "an exhibition of the principal subject-matters in summary form" (1935), dealing primarily with the then thirty Cantos, to a lesser extent with the following eleven. And codes for ensuing Cantos in the form of concurrent criticisms are available.

Aristotle continues: "Of all plots and actions the episodic are the worst. I call a plot 'episodic' in which the episodes or acts succeed one another without probable or necessary sequence [see *Anthony and Cleopatra*]. Bad poets compose such pieces by their own fault, good poets, to please the players; for, as they write show pieces for competition, they stretch the plot beyond its capacity, and are often forced to break the natural continuity." These remarks are not directly relevant to an epic poem, but carrying over from a play to a long poem they allow us the authority of Aristotle (we do not have to accept it) upon which to hang or fit the continuous but sometimes poorly hanging and incompletely fitting episodes of the Cantos.

While Aristotle ends by holding that Tragedy is a higher mode of imitation than Epic, he has cogent things to say of Epic before he reaches that conclusion. As regards length or scale, "The beginning and the end must be capable of being brought within a single view. This condition will be satisfied by poems on a smaller scale than the old epics, and answering in length to the group of tragedies presented at a single setting." It would seem that the Cantos are epical in dimension, but the condition will not be satisfied. This, however, for the avid will be a favor to the Cantos, rather than the reverse. He says, however, that Epic poetry has a special capacity for enlarging its dimensions, for "In Tragedy we cannot imitate several lines of action carried on at one and the same time; we must confine ourselves to the action on the stage and the part taken by the players. But in Epic poetry, owing to the narrative form, many events simultaneously transacted can be presented; and these, if relevant to the subject, add mass and dignity to the poem." In a sense, the many events of all the Cantos are simultaneously transacted and can be simultaneously held in the mind by the skilled reader, since it is part of the musical structure to move forward and backward through history. They can be held thus, not in particularity, but in their type of tactile scope, their peculiarity, giving us the weight of their mass and dignity.

Aristotle says Homer is the only poet who rightly appreciates the part he should take himself. "The poet should speak as little as possible in his own person, for it is not this that makes him an imitator." He would give Pound bad marks for the interwoven anecdotal intrusions of what "Bill Yeats" said, or "J. B.," his conversations with "Fordie," what he thought of a dinner at Hewlett's, an endless series. Yet these pertain to Pound's love, aforementioned, and endear the objects of his affections to the mind.

Things as they were or are. Things as they are said or thought to be. Things as they ought to be. Aristotle, lastly here, says a poet must of necessity imitate one of these three objects. Pound's history eschews the first. He cannot encompass the third, due perhaps to the secular nature of the intentions of the work. His tirades against banks, money, and political machinators would come under this category, but announce artistic limitations. There is no entire moral or ethical view of man in the sense that Pound is presenting the world as it ought to be. He harangues against usury, but offers no complete economic platform, only negative criticism. There is no espousal of a Gandhian agrarianism, or of a world state, or any solution theoretically posed. Indeed, it seems a rebuke and limitation that Pound, so roundly smashing idols as he thinks with negative criticism, has not been inventive enough to propose an imaginative solution to the dilemma of man. But where is there one, from a secular departure? He is much too intelligent to think that there is any. But he is not as wise as the makers of scripture. And the Cantos can be richly enjoyed as poetry.

Things as they are thought to be. Pound is the maker of his own conception of events as he thinks them to be. His conception embraces entire histories East and West, the rise and fall of civilizations, the reappearance in one country of political intrigues known in another in a different century, the evil in man cropping up everywhere, the aristocracy of art also recurrent ("to sort out the animals" 80), Chororua equated with Taishan, "The enormous tragedy of the dream in the peasant's bent shoulders" (74), but "Fear god and the stupidity of the populace" (74); "Entered the Bros Watson's store in Clinton, N.Y." (77) related to "The cakeshops of the Nevsky" (78), et sic de similibus.

Pound has a handle on the truth and carries history along with him in his case, wearing a gaudy suit of motley. As history, the Cantos are not impressive; as reconstructed history they are a vessel of wonder: as poetry, they are in their element. History, linguistics, economics, sociology, myth are all brought together documentarily, in the weaving of a rich tapestry. I think of the Cantos as a mosaic, or a tapestry, as of an intricate ancient work put together with incredible skill and patience over a long period of time, a Uccello in colored silks.

The new Cantos (74–84) are in some ways more nervous, elliptical, incoherent, lyrical than their predecessors. The lyrical quality is a boon, and the wiry liveliness is highly stimulating. One might make out a point that his later work in some way approaches surrealism, although it does not arrive there. This is odd in view of the hard, prosaic actuality of much of the past writing. Someone might study the more effusive, lyrical quality discoverable in the present Cantos in comparison with the more nearly incipient lyricism in the earlier. Also cogent would be a study of the Cantos in relation to musical structure; the present Cantos abound in melody, in melodic refrain. The subtlety of the spacing of the repetitions of phrase, and their metamorphoses, are cunningly contrived in an orchestration of sound and sense.

The art of teaching is to suggest. Pound is in one facet the frustrated teacher neurotically forced because his pupils do not know about, or enough about, or qualitatively enough about Padre Jose Elizonida, Kung, Tao, Chung, Kung futsen, Tangwan Kung, or Tsze Sze's third thesis. He wants them to know about these. He lays them out to view in a long fury of explication. He ends by stuffing them down the throats of his readers. After the *nth* reference to *x*, how many of his readers will be provoked to refer to, study, and inwardly digest that individual or datum? The error is that of explication, and of explication, of incomplete explication. And of explication, perversely that it is not evocation. Pound is all on the outside of the mind. The work is all brains, no soul. Or better, not sufficiently humane in brain, not deep enough in soul. We do not go to the Cantos for knowledge. We go to them with our own knowledge for revisions of feeling, for accretions of new feelings.

Hopkins wrote of Duns Scotus's Oxford. The implication was so profound as to move a generation of young poets. Duns Scotus became a point of entrance and departure in reference to the totality of Hopkins's mental life. There is more weight in Rilke's reference to Gaspara Stampa than in two dozen assorted references in Pound. The Cantos are a depot of references. A key is in the unselectivity, the sporadic, chaotic growths; in the fact that scarcely one of them seems to have as significant an equation with deep influence on Pound's mind as have those of Hopkins or Rilke on theirs, and where they are significant, they seem objective, exterior, secular, rather than profoundly inner, as in the others.

Eliot provoked a generation to new consideration of Webster, Dante, Dryden, Donne, Marvell, and others; he changed the times in his own fashion. It was performance, in some manner unknown to Pound, by implication, by suggestion, by evocation. How many actually go to Fenollosa because of Pound's use of him? Pound piques the scholar, but there has been no concerted movement of the contemporary mind to make his personages a part of its innermost life; they have become a part of its life, but not of its inner life. A concerted movement may or may not be of qualitative value, but in any event the value of Pound's personages and references to historical events is a poetic value.

To turn to a minor point, the four-letter language of D. H. Lawrence was used with a spiritual aspiration to cleanse the mind. His was a cathartic and a revolutionary principle. We have seen that he did not revolutionize prejudices too deeply ingrained to accept his proposed usages. Pound scatters about him four-letter words and abbreviations without a cathartic or revolutionary principle. They estimate themselves as pinpricks.

The Cantos cannot warm as Eliot's later work fully warms. One gives the Cantos respectful, purely intellectual admiration. They are unique in modern literature. One has admiration for the daring of such scope, for the amassing and reforming of such an interesting totality of matter, for the full-bodied feel of dense work in a time of partial insights. "Here error is all in the not done" (81) cannot name a perfection of all the Cantos, but "To have gathered from the air a live tradition" (81) is massive gain to modern letters. The Cantos are a marketplace. They are not a cathedral.

Let us choose now, at random, arbitrarily, from the plethoric images one set of ideas for partial explication of Pound's method and use of counterpoint. The Cantos are a music of ideas ("Some minds take pleasure in counterpoint" 81). The interweaving of melodic ideas, of rhythmic ideas, could be shown in any number or combination of tropes, the peculiarity of the linguistics residing in the evocative power of phrases in spite of their frequently explicit, objective nature, and some lines quoted hereunder will be found to have a sensuous, lyric yield as of Pound's early period.

Let us point out and up his play on Mt. Taishan, the interweaving ideas of periplum, light, clouds, wind, rain, mist, classic images, the sun, the moon. Note, in the present Cantos, how these are heavy in Canto 74, are light in 76, increase in 77, lighten again in 78, are absent in 79, echoed in 80 in a new way, begin Canto 81 but stop abruptly, die out but for one word in 82, return sonorously and fully in 83 and then die down in 84. Thus this particular set of ideas is worked in each Canto, excepting the one manuscript page of 75. The extraction of the quotations of course does violence to the meaning of an entire Canto and is intended only as an indicator of the method. Readers may wish further to note the relative placing of these quotations in the body of the text and to study the significance of the linear distances between the recurrent images. It is unfortunate that book paging cannot here be noticed, but manuscript paging may be suggestive relatively and similarly. It has seemed best to present the following quotations without comment, at the risk of partiality, and with no intention of indicating the tone of whole Cantos. The quotations are almost, but not quite, exhaustive of their subject:

Canto   Manuscript page
74.1   "the great periplum brings in the stars to our shore."
  .3   from the death cells in sight of Mt. Taishan @ Pisa
  .5   and there was a smell of mint under the tent flaps
        especially after the rain
                and a white ox on the road toward Pisa
                        as if facing the tower,
        dark sheep in the drill field and on wet days were clouds
        in the mountain as if under the guard roosts
                A lizard upheld me
                the wild birds wd not eat the white bread
                from Mt Taishan to the sunset
  .6   in tensile
        in the light of light is the *virtù*
                        "sunt lumina" said Erigena Scotus
                        as of Shun on Mt Taishan

.6   Light tensile immaculata*
            the sun's cord unspotted
    "sunt lumina" said the Oirishman to King Caroius,
          "OMNIA,
    all things that are are lights"
.7   one day were clouds banked on Taishan
        or in glory of sunset
          and tovarish blessed without aim
    wept in the rainditch at evening
          Sunt lumina
.8   -------------------------
        to the solitude of Mt. Taishan

    ----
    under the grey cliff in periplum
.10   surrounded by herds and by cohorts looked on Mt Taishan
.12   Haec sunt fastae
      Under Taishan quatorze Juillet
    with the hill ablaze north of Taishan
.14   cloud over mountain, mountain over cloud
.26 ——— under Taishan
    in sight of the tower che pende
.28   as the winds veer in periplum
.29   He said I protested too much   he wanted to start a press
    and print the greek classics . . . . . periplum
.35   How soft the wind under Taishan
          where the sea is remembered
        out of hell, the pit
        out of the dust and glare evil
        Zephyrus / Apeliota
    This liquid is certainly a
        property of the mind
76.39   : the sun in his great periplum
.44   20 years of the dream
      and the clouds near to Pisa
        are as good as any in Italy
    said the young Mozart:
.48   and the clouds over the Pisan meadows
      are indubitably as fine as any to be seen
77.55   (interlude entitled: periplum by camion)
.56   and Mt Taishan is faint as the wraith of my
        first friend
    who comes talking ceramics;

*Cf. "Confucius" (*Pharos* no. 4 [Winter, 1947]): "this unmixed/ is the tensile light, the immaculata" (p. 32).

<pre>
                        mist glaze over mountain
                     "How is it far, if you think of it?"
     .56   The Pisan clouds are undoubtedly various
                     and splendid as any I have seen since
                  @ Scudders Falls on the Schuylkill
     .57   periplum
                  (the dance is a medium)
                     "To his native mountain."
     .60   the clouds over Pisa, over the two teats of Tellus
     .66   Mist covers the breasts of Tellus-Helena and drifts up the Arno
                  came night and with night the tempest
                        "How is it far, if you think of it?"
   78.78   the shadow of the tent's peak treads on its corner peg
                  marking the hour, The moon split, no cloud nearer than Lucca.
   80.94   Whitman liked oysters
                  at least I think it was oysters
                     and the clouds have made a pseudo-Vesuvius
                           this side of Taishan
                  Nenni, Nenni, who will have the succession?
   81.124   Zeus lies in Ceres' bosom
                  Taishan is attended of loves
                           under Cythera, before sunrise
   82.137   periplum
   83.140   ————, your eyes are like clouds

                  _____
                  ————, your eyes are like the clouds over Taishan
                     When some of the rain has fallen
                     and half remains yet to fall

                  _____
   83.141   With clouds over Taishan-Chocorua
                        when the blackberry ripens
                  and now the new moon faces Taishan
                  one must count by the dawn star
                        Dryad, thy peace is like water
                  There is September sun on the pools

                  Plura diafana
                        Heliads lift the mist from the young willows
                  there is no base seen under Taishan
                        but the brightness of ————
                  the poplar tips float in brightness
                  only the stockade posts stand
    .142   the sun as a golden eye
                           between dark cloud and the mountain
    .146   clouds lift their small mountains
                        before the elder hills
                  A fat moon rises lop-sided over the mountain
</pre>

84.150   Under white clouds, cielo di Pisa
           out of all this beauty something must come,
           O moon my pin-up,
                   chronometer

Pleasure in reading these latest of Pound's Cantos can be extreme. The student is recommended to read them about six times before their flavor can diffuse through the blood: after that their structures may inhere to the delight of the mind. The readings have invited resubmission to the entire body of the work, as indeed to all Pound's poetry. It should be said that certain prejudices have been mitigated in the process, since for twenty years I have not been deeply moved by Pound—as I have been deeply moved by the spiritual depth of Eliot. I never enjoyed temperamental affinity with Pound's work, excepting certain examples of the early lyrical strain, although his excellence and value were not questioned. There is a freshness, an easy flow, a splendid orchestration in these new Cantos, flashes of lyrical intuition and powerful chance statements about life and people, which rebuke by former obtuseness; in reading the earlier Cantos by book-lengths it seems that their variability is not extreme, yet I prefer the sometime abandonment in these new Cantos. I have tried to indicate this feeling only by quotation from the Taishan motif, but assure the reader of literally scores of similar sets of notions as brilliantly woven, unwoven, rethreaded, arranged, shifted, played upon, in a most lively intellectual grasp of Pound's chosen cyclorama.

Not to be resisted, lastly, is an attempt to point out some of the rich examples of Pound's philosophy, wisdom, and wit. Note the comment on Possum-hang-whimper. "And with one day's reading a man may have the key in his hands." "and in this war were Joe Gould, Bunting and Cummings as against thickness and fatness." This is the "as if" method with a vengeance; the selectivity of art here inhumanly striking the nameless dead. "Lordly men are to earth o'ergiven." There is the anecdotal tag, Mr. Adams on teaching at Harvard. "filial, fraternal affection is the root of humaneness/ the root of the process."

I refrain from quoting the Yidd-Goyim passage, hateful deposition. One despises that attitude, but there are only a few lines of it. "every man to his own junk-shop." Flashbacks like "Until I end my song," "We who have passed over Lethe."

"no unrighteousness in meteyard or in measure (of prices)" Cf. Leviticus 19: "Ye shall do no unrighteousness in judgment, in meteyard, in weight, or in measure." Then "and there is no need for the Xtns to pretend that/ they wrote Leviticus/ chapter XIX in particular." "just getting stupider as they get older."

For long keeping: "nothing matters but the quality of the affection—/

in the end—that has carved the trace in the mind/ dove sta memoria."

> "and Gaudier's eye on the telluric mass of Miss Lowell"
> "the wind mad as Cassandra/ who was as sane as the lot of 'em"
> "theatre of war" . . ./ "theatre" is good. There are those who did
> not want/ it to come to an end." "There/ are/ no/ righteous
> wars" "can that be the papal major sweaten' it out to the bumm
> drum?" "Athene cd/ have done with more sex appeal"

The comments on Hovey, Stickney, Loring, Mr. Beddoes in re: Mr. Eliot. "Tune: kitten on the keys/ radio steam calliope/ following the battle hymn of the republic," "Les moeurs passent et la douleur reste," "Orage, Fordie, Crevel too quickly taken," "I have been hard as youth sixty years," "what thou lovest well remains, the rest is dross," "the loneliness of death came over me/ (at 3 P.M., for an instant)," "the humane man has amity with the hills."
And two superb lyrics:

> A lynx, my love, my lovely lynx,
> Keep watch over my wine pot,
> Guard close my mountain still
> Till the god come into this whiskey.
> Manitou, god of the lynxes, remember our corn.

> Ere the season die a-cold
> Borne upon a zephyr's shoulder
> I rose through the aureate sky
>
>> Lawes and Jenkyns guard thy rest
>> Dolmetsch ever be thy guest,
>
> There I heard such minstrelsy
> As mocketh man's mortality
>
>> Lawes and Jenkyns guard thy rest
>> Dolmetsch ever be thy guest

Note too the quatrain on who has passed a month in the death cells; the statement again that the Brothers Adam are our norm of spirit; what "Stef (Lincoln Steffens)" said you can (cannot) do with revolutionaries; and the last lines

> If the hoar frost grip thy tent
> Thou wilt give thanks when night is spent

NOTE: In the fall of 1946 J. Laughlin sent me the manuscript of Pound's "Pisan Cantos," asking if I would like to write something about them. In the light of subsequent controversy it should be stated that the article appears as it was then written.

Some Memories of Dylan Thomas

There was something impish about Dylan Thomas, and there should be something impish in me now to tell the truth about him. There should be such a thrust, but such a thrust would jar things, and it is not time to tell the truth. Perhaps it is never time. Perhaps the truth would be Comic when we live under a predilection that it is Tragic. The fact is that we live the truth but cannot tell the truth. Poetry is involved in the truth and is the final truth, but, by paradox, it is a parcel of myth; which is to use the word not in pejoration but in praise, and to use another word were probably better. Say then poetry is myth of sleight-of-hand-sleight-of-mind tricks to show iridescent-qualities of the soul. Is not Thomas's poetry a continuous artifice in this sense, a series of masks each paradoxically revealing the truth, or part of the truth, and is not his conscious craftsmanship itself an ability of the self to fend off reality so that reality will not be used up, a deftness to vary the conception with every poem, with every year, with every new insight, a consuming making of reality in the form of poetry, so that the total depth of life will never be exhausted?

Thus his poems, every one a struggle, were composed at once with dynamic energy springing from some genius not to be quite described or quite named and at the same time from some sly, cool, subtle, controlled intellectual craftsmanship, so that he knew, quite well, what effects he was preparing as he prepared them. He composed harmony from the fusion of these two forces.

One should talk of the impishness, if that is a good term for it, in Dylan. I should recall a blond girl living in our house when he first came to Cambridge for his first reading, and by what impishness he astounded her on the ride over from the South Station to Cambridge;

First published in *Yale Literary Magazine*, November, 1954, pp. 5–6.

how he astounded Matthiessen before the reading; how he delighted everybody in his actual performance; how he shocked and astounded everybody at the Advocate party afterward, and I should tell just what he said; how he astounded everybody later in the evening at Matty's, and I should tell just what he did, how he still astounded a late small group at Wilbur's; and how my wife and Charlee Wilbur had finally to deposit him in his Harvard guest house in the small hours, and just how they did it, how they had to do it.

I should then have to go on to reveal those startling truths of his progressions nearby, with friends, to various places for readings.

But it is not time to tell the truth; maybe it is never time. Everybody connected with him has his own adventures to remember.

I should have to tell how, on his second trip here, when he stayed at our house, my wife tried valiantly to get him to eat something, but only succeeded in four days with one piece of bacon; how I had to (and was delighted to) get him up in the morning by plugging his mouth with a bottle of beer, this wonderful baby.

I should have to recount how, just after dinner before I was to introduce him at the Brattle Theatre for his first reading of verse drama in America under the auspices of our Poets' Theater, he had not yet decided what to read, and with what instantaneous deftness and command he decided, once several of us had ransacked bookcases and thrust probable books into his hands, exactly what he wanted to read and was prepared for action on the instant. Then to leap onto the stage and give a stirring, memorable reading from Webster, Marlowe, Beddoes, Lear, and finally his own poems.

I should have to recount many charming episodes, as, that my wife, when we took him to the airport early on a cold morning to take a plane, clad in the dirty thin one suit he had brought from Florida, gave him my naval officer's raincoat, which we never saw again. Incidentally, how at the airport, amazed as always at American gadgets, he delighted in the machinery that produced Cokes, and had four before stepping onto the plane. And how, through the aid of John Brinnin a very long time later, Dylan sent the coat back from Wales, but this time it was an odd, little, tattered British affair all buttons and flaps, no bigger than he, his own coat, which I could not wear.

I should have to recount a time with Dylan and Caitlin which was to have been a half-hour at midday but which went on in talk and drink for ten hours.

One should tell the truth. One should put down all the stories before time dims their contours or presses them into some unnatural shape. In fact, the impishness I began on as a quality of his was less apparent from his second visit to these shores, and could not be made out as a permanent characteristic.

If I were more impish myself now I should relate the truth! One cannot tell the truth. It would be too harsh, too unbelievable; too rich, too deep, too wild, and too strange. The truth is more dramatic than fictions. It should be confided in this case to private papers and left to posterity. One has to defend Dylan against the total humanity of the man.

Others knew Dylan much better than I did, but I loved the man. I hope all who knew him will want to write down their impressions. He was so natural, friendly, jolly, and bright (without ostentation) that personal reminiscences of him should be preserved. Already there are critical appraisals; time will accrete more of these.

One shudders at the depths of the truth. I found myself thinking, after the shock of his death, that he had been a long-term suicide and that a drive to destruction was inextricably bound up with his genius, somehow, itself; that his high and wordy nature demanded the extreme penalty for being completely itself; that he could no more escape his death than he could his genius; and that he lived and died to exalt mankind and to express something recurrent and ineffable in the spirit of man, the strength of the imagination, the exaltation of the soul.

West Coast Rhythms

The West Coast is the liveliest spot in the country in poetry today. It is only here that there is a radical group movement of young poets. San Francisco teems with young poets.

Part of this activity is due to the establishment of the Poetry Center at San Francisco State College three years ago. Its originator and moving spirit is Ruth Witt-Diamant, who began by offering readings by local poets and progressed to importing older poets from the East. She hopes next to stimulate the writing of verse drama.

Part of the activity of the young group has been inspired by Kenneth Rexroth, whose presence in San Francisco over a long period of time, embodying his force and convictions, creates a rallying point of ideas, interest, and informal occasions. The influence of Kenneth Patchen is also felt by this group. Robinson Jeffers looms as a timeless figure down the Coast.

Some of the interest may also be attributed to the universities, colleges, and schools where an unusual number of poets teach and write. These poets are older than the youngest group, which is still in its twenties.

The second important center of poetry on the West Coast is Seattle, where the University of Washington is notable for its work in poetry. Theodore Roethke has enlivened this region for a number of years. Stanley Kunitz has been there this past year. Nelson Bentley, William H. Matchett, and Kenneth Hanson are active young poets there. Carol Hall, Caroline Kaizer, and Richard Hugo, not directly connected with the university, are also producing. Melvin LaFollette, a graduate, writes in Vancouver.

In the Bay region there are several poetry readings each week. They

First published in *New York Times Book Review*, September 2, 1956, pp. 7, 18.

may be called at the drop of a hat. A card may read "Celebrated Good Time Poetry Night. Either you go home bugged or completely enlightened. Allen Ginsberg blowing hot; Gary Snyder blowing cool; Philip Whalen puffing the laconic tuba; Mike McClure his hip highnotes; Rexroth on the big bass drum. Small collection for wine and postcards . . . abandon, noise, strange pictures on walls, oriental music, lurid poetry. Extremely serious. Town Hall theatre. One and only final appearance of this apocalypse. Admission free."

Hundreds from about sixteen to thirty may show up and engage in an enthusiastic, free-wheeling celebration of poetry, an analog of which was jazz thirty years ago. The audience participates, shouting and stamping, interrupting and applauding. Poetry here has become a tangible social force, moving and unifying its auditors, releasing the energies of the audience through spoken, even shouted verse, in a way at present unique to this region.

The Bay region group, by and large, is anti-university. Its members make a living at odd jobs. Ambiguity is despised, irony is considered weakness, the poem as a system of connotations is thrown out in favor of long-line denotative statements. Explicit cognition is enjoined. Rhyme is outlawed. Whitman is the only god worthy of emulation. These generalizations would probably not be allowed by all members of the group. They may serve, however, as indicators.

The most remarkable poem of the young group, written during the past year, is "Howl," by Allen Ginsberg, a twenty-nine-year-old poet who is the son of Louis Ginsberg, a poet known to newspaper readers in the East. Ginsberg comes from Brooklyn; he studied at Columbia; after years of apprenticeship to usual forms, he developed his brave new medium. This poem has created a furor of praise or abuse whenever read or heard. It is a powerful work, cutting through to dynamic meaning. Ginsberg thinks he is going forward by going back to the methods of Whitman.

My first reaction was that it is based on destructive violence. It is profoundly Jewish in temper. It is biblical in its repetitive grammatical build-up. It is a howl against everything in our mechanistic civilization which kills the spirit, assuming that the louder you shout the more likely you are to be heard. It lays bare the nerves of suffering and spiritual struggle. Its positive force and energy come from a redemptive quality of love, although it destructively catalogs evils of our time, from physical deprivation to madness.

In other poems, Ginsberg shows a crucial sense of humor. It shows up principally in his poem "America," which has lines "Asia is rising

145

against me./ I haven't got a Chinaman's chance." Humor is also present in "Supermarket in California." His "Sunflower Sutra" is a lyric poem marked by pathos.

Lawrence Ferlinghetti is the publisher of the Pocket Poet Series from his bookshop in San Francisco, the City Lights Pocket Bookshop. Small, inexpensive paperback books have already appeared by Rexroth, Patchen, W. C. Williams with Ginsberg, Denise Levertov and Marie Ponsot scheduled to follow. Rexroth's "Thirty Spanish Poems of Love and Exile" has efficient translations of Guillen, Alberti, Lorca, Machado, and others.

In this series Ferlinghetti's "Pictures of the Gone World" offers his own poetry in a flowing variety of open-running lines. He develops a personal, ritual anecdote as a fresh type of recognition, with acute visual perceptions. He seems to have learned something from James Laughlin. His work measures a racy young maturity of experience.

Most of the young poets have not yet published books, but two others who have should be mentioned. They are James Harmon and Paul Dreykus. Harmon's "In Praise of Eponymous Iahu" (Bern Porter) is struggling between a traditional, mellifluous type of lyric like "Song" and realistic poetry in the manner of "Hawk Inlet." "Stone and Pulse," by Dreykus (Porpoise Book Shop) has aesthetic poems like "Light on Two Canvases," about Miró, and a realistic one, "For Observation," about "An angerfleshed man."

Of the still bookless poets, Philip Whalen has somewhat Poundian poems and a highly successful refrain "Love You" in a direct and forceful poem entitled "3 Variations: All about Love." Gary Snyder's poetry is most like Rexroth's, not due so much to direct influence as to identity of sources. Both owe much to Far Eastern verse and philosophy, both are deeply bound into the natural world of stars, birds, mountains, and flowers. Michael McClure writes with grace and charm on "For the Death of 100 Whales" and "Point Lobos: Animism," striving for "The rising, the exuberance, when the mystery is unveiled."

Surrounding this young Bay region group are older poets like Josephine Miles, Yvor Winters, Robert Horan, James Schevill (whose verse drama about Roger Williams was recently produced in Providence), Anthony Ostroff, Leonard Wolf, Thomas Parkinson, Albert Cook and others.

The young group is marked naturally by volatility. It seems to be a group today, but nobody knows whether it will survive as a group and make a mark on the national poetic consciousness. Poetry being a highly individualistic expression of mind, soul, and personality, it would seem that the idea of a group at all is a misnaming. It may be so. These poets all differ one from another. It may be that one or more individualists will survive the current group manifestation.

It is certain that there is a new, vital group consciousness now among young poets in the Bay region. However unpublished they may be, many of these young poets have a numerous and enthusiastic audience. They acquire this audience by their own efforts. Through their many readings they have in some cases a larger audience than more cautiously presented poets in the East.

They are finely alive, they believe something new can be done with the art of poetry, they are hostile to gloomy critics, and the reader is invited to look into and enjoy their work as it appears. They have exuberance and a young will to kick down the doors of older consciousness and established practice in favor of what they think is vital and new.

Memory of Meeting Yeats, AE, Gogarty, James Stephens

After my first year at Cambridge I made a trip to Ireland. I went to Limerick to see if I could locate any Ghormleys. I had been given this middle name for my maternal grandmother, who had thirteen children in America. I found no Ghormleys. I walked and bicycled on the west coast. Returning to Dublin I met James Stephens and Miss MacNie, AE, Miss Sarah Purser, Gogarty, and Yeats. After a lapse of twenty-eight years I discovered a letter written upon returning from Ireland to Cambridge (October 13, 1928), apparently never sent and probably written as a diary to preserve these early literary memories. The letter follows:

"My bag was still lost, and I was staying at 84 Lower Baggot Street, wherein I was flea bitten beyond the point of tolerance, until I had a hide in motley, and it was while the flea was omnipotent that I suffered martyrdom but re-created my Valencia island afternoon and wrote a poem by candlelight to forget the jumping army.

"At Ely Place I called on Oliver St. John Gogarty. He showed me his first editions, pointed out of the window to the garden in which George Moore used to write, showed me a personal picture (and a sword) just received from the Kaiser, and when I saw a shelf of Nietzsche I rejoiced, for we had considerable in common. Gogarty asked me if I would like to meet his friend Lord Dunsany, and said he would send me to him at once, but asked if I knew his works, and when I said no, he made a jest and said it would be impossible, for odd Dunsany talks only of himself. I liked Gogarty's frankness and his wit:

First published in *The Literary Review* 1, no. 1 (1957): 51–56.

he said all Yeats needed was a mistress, that Yeats was a cult like Rossetti and (more important, I add) that Ireland's literary renaissance would die out surely, and that proud as they were, Ireland was but a part of Great Britain. Gogarty was reading Pindar. He talked intelligently about Greece and Rome. Would you like to meet Yeats? He's leaving for Rapallo soon, as he is supposed to be an invalid. Come to my house at nine o'clock Thursday, Yeats and AE will be there . . .

"At nine in the evening, Thursday, I knocked several times. The maid let me into the drawing room upstairs. A fat man was sitting in a chair, and a man with his back to me was sitting on a divan before the fire. Gogarty arose, greeted me, the gray-headed man turned, and I was introduced to Yeats. I noticed the shortness of his fingers and the soft texture of his hand when he made the polite gesture, and was struck by the height and physique of Yeats. He wore glasses, a soft blue shirt with a bow tie, his coat was open and one button of his waistcoat was unbuttoned. A magnificent head! His voice had a querulous quality in it. Sometimes he ran his hand through his long iron-gray hair, which lay back from his temples in gentle strands. Coffee was brought, and I was sitting beside Yeats on the divan. The conversation, after Yeats had asked me two civil questions about America and Cambridge, became at once animated concerning the Censorship Bill to be brought up in the Dail Eireann. The Catholics want to censor everything from birth control to 'immoral' literature, and even propose, like ostriches with their heads in the sand, to allow no printed mention to be made anywhere of venereal disease, thinking, in a most peculiarly Irish illogic, that they can do away with an evil by refusing to see any mention made of it. Senator Yeats made a jest about contraception. The party was indeed animated with serious discussion of all points of the bill. The intelligentsia of Ireland is limited to a few. These members of the Senate were the center of that group which upholds tolerance and a desire for widespread education. Yeats said that nothing about the body was evil, he pleaded for the Doric discipline, and wanted practical education. The fat man, some editor, left, and Gogarty brought a bottle of claret. There was a knock below, and Gogarty went to welcome AE.

"Yeats had been anxious for AE to come, as he wanted to get him to write some editorial apropos of the Censorship Bill in his *Irish Statesman*. It was about 9:45 and while I was alone with him he said it would do no good. Impassioned, he arose and made an impetuous gesture with his arms, yet there was ennui in it, saying he was to give his last speech in the Senate on October 10, but that it would do no good, that 'he would only make another of his impassioned speeches' and the unenlightened would rule. It was touching to realize the meaning of this. Yeats had given years to the service of his State; it was futile; he must retire to Italy and have no longer an active part either in the Government or in the Abbey Theater.

"AE came in, I retired from the divan to a proper chair farther off, Gogarty gave AE a cigar and the talk became so fervent that the tea was forgotten when it was brought. AE sat in a chair near the fireplace. I could see his right profile, and noted the fine texture of his skin, and the little depression the frame of his glasses made from ear to eye socket.

"One thing led to another, and I had been quiet until Gogarty opened up a discussion about the Chamberlain subterranean treaty note with France in the face of the Kellogg pact, and announced, almost, the next war, which will take place in twenty years between England and America. Ireland must have a port, Galway, to claim U.S.-Europe shipping, and thus would claim neutrality. England would conspire to have a break between Japan and America, then subtly would come in as the aggressor, send her fleet to our eastern shores, and it would be a battle of the air. This was so absurd, and so Irish, that I did not get excited at first, but AE said he had talked in closet with an important American educator, to be unnamed, about the same possibility, and Yeats took it in and added a word now and then, until the discussion took on such a sinister aspect that I felt as if doom were upon us and the destruction of the civilized world. I argued that our airships had the advantage of swooping off our own shores, that even if our coast cities were damaged the people could retreat inland, that Canada, South Africa, and possibly India might sever from the Empire, that England was not friends with Russia and could get no supplies, but was rebutted that England is still the gold center of the world, and that it would be an economic conflict. There was much reviewing of past civilizations, Greece, the fall of Rome, and statements that sooner or later an intolerable balance of power would be between England and America: inevitably one must fall, by war. It is significant that I heard all this talk in Ireland! And have never heard a breath of it in England!

"When the war was over, quelled by excellent tea, the conversation turned to scholarship, poetry, and the humanities. I only remember Yeats' views on two persons. Speaking of Baldwin he said he was much more intelligent than he had expected him to be; and after sincerely lauding Baldwin, he turned to Gogarty and said, 'Gogarty, he has studied politics as you and I have never studied poetry.' And about T. E. Lawrence, after lauding his self-effacement after heroism, he said, 'That act should be a great thing in history.' But these sentences appear a little absurd out of full context.

"We looked at our watches, it was near midnight, AE had gone a while before, so Gogarty helped us on with our coats, and I felt as little as possible as if I were with the poet Yeats. We walked into the night, and went the same way for a few blocks together, and there was nothing to say. Yeats was to make his last speech in the Senate, he was going from his island to Italy, and if I had thought of it, when I turned and walked into the night, I would have said, 'Sweet joy befall thee.' "

It is circumstantial to be old enough to try to psychoanalyze one's former self. I give the letter as it was written, with minor changes. Yet I know that I was afraid to express fully my feelings at the end of the Yeats episode. I remember these feelings very clearly. At that time I had not yet published a book. I had boundless belief in poetry and wanted more than anything to be a poet. I had already begun, but knew that Yeats could not know of my early, just-sprung work. I idolized Yeats, and AE, and James Stephens, all the literary men who were kind to me and were interested in me in Dublin, beyond the telling. I worshipped them. So that while I was walking a few blocks from Gogarty's house with Yeats in the dark night, I had an intense perception of his greatness and immortality. I had whirling words to say, to tell him how much I enjoyed his poetry, but this frenzy was quieted by common sense. I hated to take each step, for I knew that up the street soon he would go one way, I another. I would turn off and go alone in the dark to my own place and dispensation. He would go straight on and I knew I would never see him again, as indeed turned out to be the case. I was having high drama walking along. Yeats seemed in deep thought, heavily meditating, looking straight ahead and saying nothing. We spoke no word. How thrilling it was! I was speaking millions of words to him. I was so sensitive I wondered nervously about the common civilities. Should I say good night? Should I mutter some polite phrase? Actually, the most eloquent thing happened, an eloquence of silence. When we came, walking together in the Irish night of literary time, to the predestined corner, he did not look at me and I did not look at him. I turned off right-face on my street and we parted forever without a word.

I recall going to the literary club (its actual name escapes me) in Dublin. There were perhaps twenty men for lunch there in an old, comfortable room. What was remarkable was that James Stephens held sway for an hour or more, keeping everybody in laughter. His wit was engaging, authoritative, total. Nobody else could speak. I cannot recall a word he said, but remember the remarkable effect he had. It was electrifying. His extreme shortness was no hindrance to a Gargantuan comic sense. His wit had a staccato quality. Everybody burst out laughing again and again, abandoned to his rapier-like thrusts.

I recall another time when Stephens and I called on Miss MacNie, who drew the famous cartoon of Yeats and AE. I remember the quantities of Irish whisky Stephens consumed at her place and again the lightning quality of his wit. He had a gnome-like quality, a strong head on a short stalk.

Of the Irish poets then in Dublin I knew AE best. He used to invite me to his office, where I passed a number of unforgettable afternoons. He was then editor of the *Irish Statesman*. (About a year later it came to an end; in its last number he reviewed fully my first book.)

AE had painted the walls of his office with somewhat mystical and mystifying paintings depicting imaginary or historical Indian scenes. He would sit behind his big desk looking out over his long gray beard through thick glasses, a heavy, introspective man, and talk by the hour in the most mellifluous voice I had heard. He told endless legendary tales from Indian mythology or talked about visionary poetry. He put me into a kind of trance the likes of which I have never experienced in listening to any other poet. It was a most pleasant sensation. While I would ask questions now and then, I recall these sessions as primarily monologues. AE was content to talk on in his soft voice from deep sources of memory and imagination, creating a dream-like consciousness and atmosphere. He spoke mature wisdom, yet he was ever as gentle as a child.

On Sunday evenings he and his wife were at home at their house. I attended on several occasions. After an hour or two of literary talk there was always the question whether AE would show his paintings. After some coaxing and as a climax to these intimate evenings, he would bring forth from a back room several canvases, all of them showing variations on a white nymph or nymphs dancing in a dark wood. They all had a characteristic chiaroscuro. They all pointed to some strange, heavenly place where there was serenity, peace, and exaltation. These canvases were usually small, but they had the ethereal quality of his verse. After the paintings had been shown and explained, it was time for the guests to depart, which they always did with reluctance.

Emerson and Wallace Stevens

Emerson had a sense of humor, for all his leanness and New England dryness. He said, "Transcendentalism means, says our accomplished Mrs. B., with a wave of her hand, *a little beyond*." He put the phrase "a little beyond" in italics. Is this not witty and a pregnant saying? If one wished to be bold, one could take and leave transcendentalism as that, never worry one's head with a thousand labyrinthian pages of commentary, intellectual probings and spiritual graspings at the thinnest air.

Time is something we cannot see. Therefore, says the rational intellect, there must be something, as it were, beyond. There is something beyond this moment. There will be a moment, as far as we know, in 2063, just as there was a moment of time for Emerson one hundred years ago.

To look beyond is to transcend the present. The witty part of Emerson's remark about the lady is that she looked "a little beyond." This is a choice perception. I see in it nineteenth-century intellectual sophistication. Note that Emerson left the sentence at that. He did not go on to moralize, or to draw conclusions, as I am doing. He felt that the overtones of the statement would be immediately communicable, the references known, all the imaginings anybody could make would be implicit.

The satisfying part of this statement, one hundred years later, is just this restraint. The phrase "a little beyond" is itself an arch criticism. It casts a mild sort of derision on the notion that transcendentalism could get so far beyond mankind and man's condition as to embrace or envelop absolute Godhead. It allows for depths of spiritual vagueness. It allows for the massive, inchoate reaches of metaphysical

First published in *The Literary Review* 7 (Autumn, 1963): 51–71.

reality, a dream-like area in which one can swim and toss throughout a lifetime without coming to a conclusion.

Emerson was a Unitarian, but he was called "infidel and pagan." This little phrase "a little beyond" is at once the pride of intellect and a springing meadow where may be danced all the rites of the senses. There is the recognition that an intellectual man cannot abrogate his intellect; there is no use to throw away the million open thoughts that assail him, to sit on one conclusion; and there is the hint that a little beyond whatever he thinks and feels is a wonderful world of possibility. It is therefore a sane and witty proposition. It is critical, sprightly, and also profound. To transcend oneself a little may, in some very human way, be equated with transcending oneself a lot. There is just as much meaning in thinking you may be more effective in some small action, as there is meaning in feeling that, if you strive to your limit, some day you may understand the meaning of the universe, even delve and swim in occult seas of godhead.

One more point. This little phrase allows for the practical as well as the dreamy. It is a fusion of opposites, or a reduction of manifold possibilities into one precept. All you have to know, if you wish it direct, is that "transcendentalism means a little beyond." That's all the farther away the Soul is. The positive assumption is that one can arrive there.

Emerson's essay "The Over-Soul" is studded with ideas. There are so many quotable sentences that indeed the essay may be said to be pregnant with meaning—it gives birth to marvelous speculation. I shall pick out a few, almost at random.

He says, "Unity, that Over-Soul, within which every man's particular being is contained and made one with all other." The Over-Soul is allied and equated with unity, unity of being. The overtone is that we are all members one of another, all the living on earth. We enjoy one brotherhood of man, inescapably joined together because we all inhabit the flesh. That is a notion of the Over-Soul while it is still under the ban of the flesh. But there is a hierarchy here. Another sentence reads, "The least activity of the intellectual powers redeems us in a degree from the conditions of time." This is suggestive. Again he says, in the same vein, "Is the teaching of Christ less effective now than it was when first his mouth was opened?" When we use our minds we are joining in an invisible union with others who have used their minds, here, anywhere. . . . He says again, "The soul knows only the soul; the web of events is the flowing robe in which she is clothed." The web of events is time.

Note that there is a scale in this essay. There is the intellect and what it does, but now he is talking about the soul and what it is. "The soul answers never by words, but by the thing itself that is inquired after."

Thinking is thus lower than contemplation. Contemplation is the dream, the dream-world of speculation. Do not let sociologists, or psychologists, or psychiatrists destroy in us the power to dream. Even daydreaming; that is part of it.

It is actually difficult, in reading Emerson's "The Over-Soul," to put it all in a pat exegesis. He says, "The question and the answer are one." This is a deep saying, already poetical. Yeats ended "Among School Children" by saying

> O body swayed to music, O brightening glance,
> How can we know the dancer from the dance?

Emerson says, "Much of the wisdom of the world is not wisdom, and the most illuminated class of men are no doubt superior to literary fame, and are not writers." This is a canny, New England realization. We note that Wallace Stevens was a Hartford insurance businessman, dealing with the realities of men, not a man living in the ivory tower of a university. Emerson instinctively recognizes that reality is not limited to thinkers, professors and teachers. Perhaps the blacksmith in his day, the garage mechanic in ours, has a closer grip on reality. There is something down to earth in the prose of Emerson, while he is expounding the Over-Soul.

The New England individualism comes out. He says: "The great poet makes us feel our own wealth, and then we think less of his compositions." This phrase is worth pondering. The great poet serves the reader, ourselves, not himself or greatness. He makes us the more ourselves by opening up his doors in our consciousness.

The very sentence before this last one reads: "The soul is superior to its knowledge, wiser than any of its works." To put it most simply, there are the workings of the intellect, and higher than that there is the soul, a world-soul like that conceived by Plato, the Eternal Types, into which man reaches with his finer feelings.

But look how really radical Emerson is.

Shakespeare carries us to such a lofty strain of intelligent activity as to suggest a wealth which beggars his own; and we then feel that the splendid works which he has created, and which in other hours we extol as a sort of self-existent poetry, take no stronger hold of real nature than the shadow of a passing traveller on the rock. The inspiration which uttered itself in *Hamlet* and *Lear* could utter things as good from day to day forever. Why then should I make account of *Hamlet* and *Lear*, as if we had not the soul from which they fell as syllables from the tongue?

When you read *Hamlet* or *Lear*, do you feel this way? It is unusual, in fact radical. It shows a strong mind going to the roots of things. When I read *Hamlet* or *Lear* I keep to these works, bounded by the literary references I can find, by the knowledge I can get on them, and by the times I can see the plays, but neither I nor you, in 1963, probably would jump to the attitude expressed in this passage of Emerson.

Again, if you want to understand the essay, just take this one passage alone and analyze it. Emerson is not content to read *Hamlet* only as a play. He will not read it only as a psychological study of sensitive man in a bad situation. T. S. Eliot's essay on *Hamlet*—which makes perceptive statements about the Prince, incidentally enunciating his theory of the "objective correlative," while it is faulty in dealing only with Hamlet's Oedipal relation to his mother; a point corrected recently by Francis Fergusson, who stresses also Hamlet's relation to his father—sticks to literary criticism, stays on the plane of the play, and does not wander off into the soul endlessly far beyond the play.

But what does Emerson do? He goes beyond the whole play at once and summarily. He does not read *Hamlet* and *Lear* as *Hamlet* and *Lear*. He is concerned with the flow of soul out of which these works came; he sees them as mirrors of the soul. He here lauds the Over-Soul, the eternal flowing Over-Soul, the great reservoir of spiritual energy, the boundless heaven of reality above us, and puts Shakespeare with the two mentioned plays down as an example of soul-making, with the emphasis on the soul, and a de-emphasis on the complex, intricate plays which he does not have to consider more significant than a blade of grass, a mountain, or a mathematical proposition, since all of these phenomena only show and extrude the soul into sense. All sensory things are the glory of God's manifestation. Oddly enough, *Hamlet* and *Lear* are such things. Shakespeare might have tossed off a *Hamlet* and a *Lear* every week. It is instructive, however, that he did not.

The next sentence I wish to quote from Emerson's "The Over-Soul" is this: "The soul gives itself, alone, original, and pure, to the Lonely, Original, and Pure, who, on that condition, gladly inhabits, leads, and speaks through it."

The second set of words is written in capitals. By the mechanical device of capitalizing he sets them up in our minds in a new way as absolutes. They become like Platonic essences or eternal types. There are immortal realities of Lonely, Original, Pure. They are immortal concepts, perfect realities, timeless essences. He writes, in the same way, "I, the imperfect, adore my own Perfect" and, by capitalizing the second perfect, sets it up too as a Platonic original or archetype. His meaning is clear in the following two passages. "So I come to live in thoughts and act with energies which are immortal." "Man will come to see that the world is the perennial miracle which the soul worketh, and be less astonished at particular works." This explains his attitude toward *Hamlet* and *Lear*; they are particular works, they are not the whole show of the world. The whole show of the world is the soul. The soul is beyond the world but in the world; the world is the world but it is beyond itself and is the soul. The Over-Soul may be only "a little beyond," but you can see that it can also be as far beyond as you may possibly conceive in the most subtle reaches of your imagination.

How does Emerson end his essay? He was the practical Yankee, the man of worldly affairs and abilities. He partook of the religious feelings of his time so that he was a moralist, sometimes in spite of himself. He does not end his essay on metaphysical speculation, but on practical, sagacious precept.

The man who understands, accepts, believes in, and opens his heart to the Over-Soul is pictured as follows: "He will weave no longer a spotted life of shreds and patches, but he will live with a divine unity. He will cease from what is base and frivolous in life and be content with all places and with any service he can render." He wished to do good.

So Emerson ends on a moral tone, thus being a man of his time, a nineteenth-century moralist, and as R. W. B. Lewis remarks: "Transcendentalism was Puritanism turned upside down." I have quoted from Emerson's "The Over-Soul." Lewis also quotes Emerson's abrupt little sentence: "I hate quotations. Tell me what you know."

Let us look at Emerson's "Brahma."

This poem is about the nature of reality, but it is not realistic in the modern sense of the term. It does not say a thing is a thing. William Carlos Williams keeps saying in his poetry, "No reality but in things." Williams brings before our senses in his poems the things, aesthetically bright, stones, twigs, people, images, a red wheelbarrow. Williams says a thing is a thing. He shows you the things.

Emerson writes the poem and the words on the paper are, in a sense, a thing. It is a manmade poem, an object, an artifact, a literary creation. Emerson wrote it. Yet he makes Brahma speak it. It is thus transcendental, it is somebody speaking who is beyond Emerson, paradoxically. Think of it at first as Jehovah speaking, if you wish. It is Psyche poetry par excellence.

By making Brahma speak the words, Emerson at once intrigues us. He establishes at once aesthetic distance and spiritual involvement. The poem becomes a sort of condensed, concentrated sermon, saying the same thing over and over in slightly different ways, making a cumulative single point or impression, but so subtle that you can go on considering it for years, applying instances of life to it as a proposition:

If the red slayer think he slays,
    Or if the slain think he is slain,
They know not well the subtle ways
    I keep and pass, and turn again.

Far or forgot to me is near;
    Shadow and sunlight are the same:
The vanished gods to me appear;
    And one to me are shame and fame.

They reckon ill who leave me out;
    When me they fly, I am the wings;
I am the doubter and the doubt,
    And I the hymn the Brahmin sings.

The strong gods pine for my abode,
    And pine in vain the sacred Seven;
But thou, meek lover of the good!
    Find me, and turn thy back on heaven.

"If the red slayer think he slays." We think at once of our American red Indians, who slew whites a hundred years ago. It is a problematical statement, an "if" proposition. It does not say the red slayer has slain anybody. Then you think of Brahma as an Indian god of the country India, and may read "red" as the meaning of blood which the slayer sheds. This applies also to the American redskin. We may think of a red American Indian by perversity, and not at first.

The sentence is then turned around, as if a coin were seen on the other side. "Or if the slain think he is slain." It is at once a paradoxical metaphysical statement. A simple system of opposites is at once at work. If a man is slain he obviously cannot think; he cannot say, "I think I am slain." He might do so just before he passes out, but let that pass. It is Brahma, or Jehovah, talking, so it makes sense. It makes no moral judgment on killing, simply an overall statement. God, let us say, says if the red slayer thinks he slays, or if the slain thinks he is slain, they do not know well the subtle ways "I keep, and pass, and turn again."

The suggestion is that all this has happened before. There is nothing new under the sun, nothing new in the eye of Brahma, Jehovah, or God. It is seen in the perspective of continuous life. There is no statement of condemnation or forgiveness. It is a highly intellectual, impersonal concept.

The next stanza gives examples, more or less vague, more or less precise. "Far or forgot to me is near." Both "far" and "forgot" are rather abstract terms. They are both "near." We do not feel how near, merely near. "Shadow and sunlight are the same." This is unscientific, but the mind accepts it poetically. Obviously shadow and sunlight are not the same. No scientist would allow this. Poetry goes beyond science, envelops and contains it. God ultimately creates both shadow and sunlight. This is acceptable and true when so perceived. The mind has no trouble, poetically, in accepting it. Let the scientist stay with his measuring rods, not try for ultimate synthesis. "The vanished Gods to me appear." This is easy. Of course they do. The vanished are not vanished in the eye of God. They are there. The unvanished or present gods are also around, we should think. Time is not of the essence of God, but timelessness. "And one to me are shame and fame." The rhyme gives pleasure in these different terms, arbitrarily yoked together. They are arbitrary opposites in our usual, everyday world of so-called reality. In this world you would not ordinarily say that shame and fame are one, a unity. In the ordinary world they remain apart. Shame is really shameful, not famous, and fame is really famous, not shameful. Of course you can always in poetry extend your mind and play with words for pleasure, jumping the track in your locomotive intelligence. You could say that Hitler's fame was his shame, but Hitler himself would not have thought so. This may be stretching Emerson's skin too far. You may say that Hawthorne's Hester Prynne, whose sin made her shameful and caused the story, was famous because she was shameful, and that is closer. Her fame lasts to this day because of her shame and they can be thought of as one. Yet in the poem the two terms sit on the line, singly and unreferenced.

The next stanza begins on the same tone. The tone of the poem remains the same throughout. It is concentrated and even in tone, harmonious and whole. "They reckon ill who leave me out." You might suggest a slightly truculent attitude here on the part of God speaking, but there is actually none. This line takes care of all the unbelievers in the world, past, present, and to come. It sweeps them all into a bin, so to speak. It takes them all in. The proof is given in the next three lines. When anybody flies from God, God himself is the wings he is flying on. There is no escape. God is the doubting Thomas and the doubt itself. He is easily also the hymn of praise the Brahmin sings, God is God Himself.

The last four lines make up some more of the same, with their differences. "The strong gods" has gods in small letters, so these must be any minor gods throughout history. The word "pine" as a verb is characteristic of the nineteenth century, would not be used now. "Desire" would be a more modern term. The sacred Seven are the practical gods of classical antiquity, interested in Architecture, Music, Poetry, and so on. They, with the uncapitalized gods in the line above, are not the whole show and had better remember to keep their place. They are outcasts.

The last two lines make an abrupt turn from general rumination and law-dealing to direct address but ambiguous charge. "But thou, meek lover of the good!" with an exclamation point as if, ah you, there, you meek Christian one, you good one, you are my favorite, you know me, the Eternal God.

Then there is the last perplexing line, which is ambiguous. Ambiguity is one of the dense features of poetry. This poem would be less great if it were not ambiguous. It is grammatically ambiguous in the last line. "But thou, meek lover of the good! / Find me, and turn thy back on heaven." You would think at once that if the meek lover of the good had found God he would be in heaven, or at least integrated with heaven. Note that heaven is not capitalized, as if Emerson, the down-to-earth New England Protestant, was protesting against giving its final due to this word. Yet just two lines before he had not hesitated to give a capital to the classical Seven. Maybe they are more worldly, so maybe pumped up, whereas one stands in awe of Eternal Reality, and heaven had better be kept down on the street somewhere where it can be handled, taken care of in a homely way. Neither the strong gods nor the sacred Seven pined for His abode but in vain, but the meek lover of the good finds Him, and may turn his back even on heaven to turn his face directly to God Himself. There is also a teasing sense in the last two lines of a kind of game of hide and seek. God has hidden Himself and says, "Find me." Turn your back on heaven, come and find me. This reading makes the verb sense into an adjuration. The last four lines have a teasing particularity. The whole poem, however, is wonderful for its general unity.

Let us turn now to Wallace Stevens.

I first called on him some years ago in his polished office at the Hartford Accident and Indemnity Insurance Company. He took me out to lunch at the canoe club. But first I asked him some business advice which he gave precisely and practically; it was about how to go about selling wax to cover the thousands of square feet of floors in his vast building. After I had seen the proper person I returned to his rather austere office, sat at one end of it while he finished some work at the other behind his big desk. I noted that he was executing some papers. After reading a large file for a while, he put his signature to it, tossed it into a big wastebasket beside his desk, pressed a buzzer or used the phone, and one of his business colleagues came in. We were introduced with the statement, "I hope you do not mind if Mr. B. comes along so we won't have to talk shop." After this jollification, I drove them to the canoe club a few miles away on the river. Stevens pointed out that there were no canoes; nobody had canoed past the club as far as he knew for thirty years. But there were martinis. After two or more of these and during lunch, shop was talked. It was poetry we always came around to, which was enjoyed by Mr. B. also.

This was the beginning of a series of meetings at the canoe club, down the pike to Naher's, a charming old German restaurant which had just the right cuisine, or at our house in Cambridge, where Stevens used to leave his car when he went to the Harvard-Yale game, or let me drive him around Cambridge before a Harvard reading. I remember the last time, when he allowed as how he was getting too old to get easily in and out of these small modern cars; I recall the buildings he pointed out from the Harvard of his day, and especially his surprising inability to see any virtue in the new Graduate School buildings of Gropius, which he passed by with a wave of the hand and pointed to some stolid old nineteenth-century ones nearby, wondering why they couldn't make something as good as those anymore? I thought the new architecture was analogous to the newness of his poetry, was at a loss to understand his love of the old buildings so unlike his modern imagination, but said nothing. He had pointed out an old house on Garden Street where the last member of the regency had lived. And on the Square he pointed to what was a loft above what is now the Harvard Trust Company and said Robert Frost lived there when he was in college but was five years his senior and he did not know him.

But what about those huge files tossed into the wastebasket? When quizzed, he laughed and said the receptacle was fitted to a conveyor system which whisked the executed claims periodically away to various far parts of the building for final action after his allowing or denying signature.

Stevens is nine-tenths poet, one-tenth prose writer. Maybe less than ten percent. He wrote only one prose book, *The Necessary Angel*, in 1951, at over seventy. His *Collected Poems* appeared just in time for him to relish this large volume of a lifetime.

Where one can secure the kernel of significance in Emerson in studying one poem, one cannot get the meaning of Stevens without reading many, absorbing his wide air breath by breath, poem by poem for a long time.

Emerson is relatively easy, straightforward, and simple. Stevens is nothing if not complex, subtle, difficult, strange, and profound.

You may read Emerson on your own level. You read Stevens to exceed yourself. You can go on exceeding yourself a long time before you have begun to exhaust this master of imagination. Each poem in him is like chipping a bit off a block of marble. The form he is trying to make will take a lifetime; you cannot see what the statue will look like; it will take a lifetime for him to compose his statue of man, of man's mind, of the human imagination.

A third distinction is that Stevens is witty where Emerson is usually not. Stevens is full of jest, of blague, of gothic ornament, of newly minted, freshly invented phraseology. Emerson had no jest, no make-believe, no pantomine. Emerson was too earnest. Stevens is earnest, but covers it up in elaborate shows of whimsy, verbal encrustations, grammatical flourishes.

Emerson spoke at the center of the consciousness of a New England which recognized him as in the center when the center was known. Stevens is always paradoxical. He is in one sense peripheral to our times, which being in the center of our consciousness. He is an aristocrat of the imagination in a welter of democracy. He is not central to Americanism as one might think of Carl Sandburg. Sandburg was explicit. He sang of the Midwest as it was or is. He offered less charm to the imagination. He was realistic. A thing was a thing—he named them. They were not always on the verge of becoming something else. Now many read Stevens. He is the darling of the universities. He may not be read by the so-called common reader, whoever he is, but he is read by the thoughtful, the alert, the intelligent. He is at once poet's poet and poet of the highest taste in the intelligent reader. Stevens has been a long time building. His edifice is now complete and indestructible. The ornate palace will live for centuries. While he seems peripheral, is not realistic in an ordinary sense, actually Stevens is central to our times. From the grand chaos, if chaos can be called grand, that is, from the muck and ruck of wars and depression, societal upheavals, he has thought about the meaning of imagination. He has exalted this word. He has made imagination itself his hero and written in manifold ways of this hero, who is ambiguous and scintillant.

We should consider many poems of Wallace Stevens to approach his core. Stevens is at once the supreme dilettante, the supreme man of fictions and the juggler of meanings, the possessor of life's significance. He is the artful one, full of linguistic cunning. He gives an elaborate and subtle pleasure. Of poetry he says, "It must be abstract. It must change. It must give pleasure." Stevens's titles are flamboyant, excessive, colorful, impish, aesthetically delicate or startling.

To try to reduce Stevens to some simple formula is difficult. He is huge and amorphous, many-tongued, mountainous. I wish, however, to make two points about his poetry in relation to Emerson. The first makes him out to be quite unlike Emerson, a contrasting element. Emerson believed in another world, was not in one way very worldly, and believed in intellectual dominance, in reason. Stevens is unlike Emerson in his long celebration of the senses, of sensuous, of sensual things. He believes in the flesh, in this world. The flesh is the temple we certainly inherit and inhabit. Without it we are either in nothingness or in heaven, both of which can only be contemplated while we inhabit the flesh. Stevens has a lot to say about nothingness and much to say about probable or possible heavens. Or about reality. He is actually talking always about reality and about the imagination. The imagination is the true reality; the imagination is Psyche. He throws out thousands of lines, forms, tropes, images, about the imagination as the reality of the world. He is at once airy and gauzy, plastic and malleable.

First, the contrast with Emerson. You would not expect Emerson to speak like this, which is Stevens in the last section of "Esthetique du Mal":

> The greatest poverty is not to live
> In a physical world.

This poem exalts and celebrates the physical world, enjoyed most in sensuous realizations. Stevens, while using a grand mind, often derides the mind, which pleases us. He thinks of thought as giving false happiness. Here is his "Crude Foyer":

> Thought is false happiness: the idea
> That merely by thinking one can,
> Or may, penetrate, not may,
> But can, that one is sure to be able—
>
> That there lies at the end of thought
> A foyer of the spirit in a landscape
> Of the mind, in which we sit
> And wear humanity's bleak crown;
>
> In which we read the critique of paradise

> And say it is the work
> Of a comedian, this critique;
> In which we sit and breathe
>
> An innocence of an absolute,
> False happiness, since we know that we use
> Only the eye as faculty, that the mind
> Is the eye, and that this landscape of the mind
>
> Is a landscape only of the eye; and that
> We are ignorant men incapable
> Of the least, minor, vital metaphor, content
> At least, there, when it turns out to be here.

A third poem might be his famous "Sunday Morning." A woman, in the beauty of her flesh, thinks of the meaning of religion. Late coffee and oranges in a sunny chair, the green freedom of a cockatoo, all lovely things of the senses are brought up against ancient questions of the meaning of some other world than this, the meaning of religion, the meaning of death. The poem celebrates aesthetic beauty, the tangible beauty of this world, against the claims of another world. Emerson, in his strict Puritanical times, could not have written it and he wouldn't have written it if he could, so straitlaced was he, and prim.

The first reductive point, then, is that Emerson believes in the soul but Stevens believes in the flesh, in this world.

The second point in comparing these two poets is that in spite of himself Wallace Stevens is a transcendentalist, or maybe it is because of himself, in his deepest way. One has to read many poems by Stevens to get his measure. It is a big measure. It always remains grandiose and amorphous. He is known as a poet of the élite, a poet of the most subtle nuances, a poet's poet, a man who spins and weaves, always saying things in endless new elaborations, each seemingly more ornate and elaborate than the last. The fact is that one can select many lines, in the vast contradictory array of so rich and trenchantly stored a mind, in which his spirit transcends the flesh, this world, mortality, to invent purely artistic architectures for the soul. In "Certain Phenomena of Sound" he writes:

> Someone has left for a ride in a balloon
> Or in a bubble examines the bubble of air

The balloon is real, but it is a bubble. The air it rides in is also a bubble. It suggests the transiency of this life, suggests some other life. In "The Motive for Metaphor" he writes:

> The obscure moon lighting an obscure world

> Of things that would never be quite expressed,
> Where you yourself were never quite yourself
> And did not want nor have to be.

You were never quite yourself, nor had to be. This is a sort of under-mind submarine statement, or understatement, of an oversoul. The over-soul is not there, explicitly stated, but it is suggested.

Now I realize that criticism is sometimes special pleading. I am trying to make out a case where another critic would deny the allegation, where another reader would make out an opposite or another case. Let that be. In "The Creations of Sound" he says:

> We do not say ourselves like that in poems.
> We say ourselves in syllables that rise
> From the floor, rising in speech we do not speak.

Is this not a statement of the struggle to get "a little beyond" oneself? The last two lines of "Holiday in Reality" read:

> Intangible arrows quiver and stick in the skin
> And I taste at the root of the tongue the unreal of
>   what is real.

The tongue is the organ of speech as well as of taste. The poet is the speaker of truth, who has tasted the world. At the last Stevens says he tastes the "unreal" of what is real. You may yourselves determine what is real, or what is unreal for you, but his belief in the unreal embedded in the real is, again, Stevens's partial assent to the over-soul. He admits something beyond, although he is always heavily pulled back into the senses, making gaudy grammatical shows and propositions of the world. He never explicitly states what his over-soul is, which gives us the pleasure of trying to find out. So he is actually not like Emerson, yet he partakes, in some parts of his make-up, of the Emersonian transcendentalist view.

Pretty close on the above point is No. IX of "It Must Change" from *Notes toward a Supreme Fiction*. It reads:

> The poem goes from the poet's gibberish to
> The gibberish of the vulgate and back again.
> Does it move to and fro or is it of both
>
> At once? Is it a luminous flittering
> Or the concentration of a cloudy day?
> Is there a poem that never reaches words
>
> And one that chaffers the time away?
> Is the poem both peculiar and general?
> There's a meditation there, in which there seems

> To be evasion, a thing not apprehended or
> Not apprehended well. Does the poet
> Evade us, as in a senseless element?
>
> Evade, this hot, dependent orator,
> The spokesman of our bluntest barriers,
> Exponent by a form of speech, the speaker
>
> Of a speech only a little of the tongue?
> It is the gibberish of the vulgate that he seeks.
> He tries by a peculiar speech to speak
>
> The peculiar potency of the general,
> To compound the imagination's Latin with
> The lingua franca et jocundissima.

See how he is the self-wrestler! He admits the vulgate, he does not deny a Bible, symbol of absolute religious meanings, yet he calls it gibberish. This is the reaction of a spiritual yet doubting man of the twentieth century, as compared with the more nearly absolute spirituality of a nineteenth-century mind like Emerson's.

And, to choose a stanza to destroy my argument, there are many passages in Stevens celebrating this world only, limited to the loved human. The nineteenth stanza of "Chocorua to Its Neighbors" reads:

> To say more than human things with human voice,
> That cannot be; to say human things with more
> Than human voice, that, also, cannot be;
> To speak humanly from the height or from the depth
> Of human things, that is acutest speech.

That is an explicit passage, needing no commentary. This attitude is large in Stevens, yet he is usually ambivalent, tentative, suggestive of new imaginings.

Emerson was a Yankee, born and bred. Wallace Stevens is significant in that he was of Dutch descent and came from Pennsylvania. Yet he adopted Hartford as his home, where he lived for decades, and made that rather jewel-like city on the Connecticut a mecca for poetry. He made it, singlehandedly, the literary Boston of the 1950's. He speaks for a strange, more complicated, more aesthetic, wider-ranging congeries of attitudes than has been spoken for before. The Harvard Dutchman has spoken, as one new voice, for a New England no longer unified with the dozens of voices of the time of her flowering.

Robert Frost is in the direct descent from the old New Englanders. Frost is less spiritual, knottier, earthier, less complicated than Stevens. Frost is in an old, direct tradition of simple, trenchant speech. He does not have the enticement, the feminine grace, or the aesthetic oddities, or the brimful imaginative violence of Stevens. He has his own great qualities. Frost's mind is nothing like, or very little like, Emerson's. Stevens's mind is not seemingly like Emerson's, yet the case can be made out for its Emersonian quality, and you are invited to adumbrate my examples.

There are many more contradictions in Stevens than there are in Emerson. Emerson exemplifies a unified body of thought. The fact that there are so many contradictions in Stevens reflects the lack of a unified body of thought in our time, while it exemplifies his will toward a unity that is not there. Therefore he flies off in a thousand ways, by analogy, tautology, ambiguity and sophistry, every kind of intellectual and grammatical legerdemain, writing hundreds of poems trying to integrate life into a system of aesthetics. Hence the paradox of Stevens that the more diverse and spread out his poems become, the less he loses his center. The more he throws himself away, the more he finds his aesthetic meanings. But when the whole poetry is read and all the meanings are in, he has inhabited a gauzy world, a playful world, a world of abstractions and elaborations, a very real world of the imagination, and he has, in spite of himself and by paradox, produced a poetic world of the over-soul. He thus joins in our time in a strange way with the Emerson of a century ago. He once wrote a poem called "The Comedian as the Letter C." Emerson never got up into the comic. Stevens goes from the comic out into elaborate imaginative terrain. They both hanker after the over-soul, however, the one explicitly, the other by implication. Wallace Stevens is lately dead, yet he is all the more alive in the wonderful superiority of his poetry, in magics of ideational invention and in diction. To these high properties of human excellence he was not superior, but the noble bondsman. He possessed a metaphysical, psychical mind, but he could not get to heaven. He was always pulled back to the real essence of the sensuous in this world, which he celebrated. But for him imagination itself becomes the hero. His imagination is not without clearest soul, the soul of a bright light being broken up by the prisms of poems. He is a pleasure to have to put in a special place in our spectrum, no ordinary man of Will, a poet of fictions who had a powerful grip on poetic reality.

If the poetry of Wallace Stevens is remote from the concerns of the common man, it is nonetheless human, dignified, resplendent, and charged with multiple meanings for the pleasure of our understanding. If the man in the street cannot comprehend it, he has his world and shares the universal and sensuous air stated for him by a poet whom he does not know and cannot share. Both live in the live American air, the world of sight, scent, and touch. Both feel the earth and embrace the stars. Stevens is the aristocrat of emotional and intellectual fascinations, the giver of beauty back to beauty itself, if not technically to God, the beholder of infinite, intimate analogies and correspondences, a man enabled to do wonder work in the common work of the world.

We have seen Stevens as a transcendentalist in his own fashion in spite of his earthly quality, one who does not embrace the orthodox Christian answer as such, a man of many fine Psyche balances and proliferations.

From the scintillation of his work it is difficult to choose one poem to defend his middle but spiritual ground. In Stevens we get multiple aesthetic meanings, we secure a new location of our sensibility; we encounter difficulties of meaning which please us and tease our reacting powers. We possess an aesthetic piece of art for long contemplation, for reimagining and for sensitive enjoyment. A Stevens poem is a modern poem, by indirections finding directions out; it is a parcel of magic, a web of imaginings, a fresh structure of English syllables, a glance of craft.

Let us try, as an example of the typical, No. VII of "It Must Be Abstract" from *Notes toward a Supreme Fiction*:

> It feels good as it is without the giant,
> A thinker of the first idea. Perhaps
> The truth depends on a walk around a lake,
>
> A composing as the body tires, a stop
> To see hepatica, a stop to watch
> A definition growing certain and
>
> A halt within that certainty, a rest
> In the swags of pine-trees bordering the lake.
> Perhaps there are times of inherent excellence,
>
> As when the cock crows on the left and all
> Is well, incalculable balances,
> At which a kind of Swiss perfection comes
>
> And a familiar music of the machine
> Sets up its Schwarmerie, not balances
> That we achieve but balances that happen,
>
> As a man and woman meet and love forthwith.
> Perhaps there are moments of awakening,
> Extreme, fortuitous, personal, in which
>
> We more than awaken, sit on the edge of sleep,

> As on an elevation, and behold
> The academies like structures in a mist.

May I give a musing commentary on this poem? Things that pop into and cross the mind while reading. It has a neat look on the page, as if it were a well-trimmed tree. This has a leafiness. One is used to the Stevens three-line stanza without rhyme, a satisfying device allowing extensive rhythmic and linguistic variations.

We are at once in the realm of the aesthetic and the ambiguous. We have a momentous feeling that something is about to happen, that there is a charge within the poem which meets our submerged charges. It feels good as it is without the giant—what giant?—we feel good because "It feels good." Is the giant the thinker of the first idea, or is the poet or am I a thinker of the first idea? Was there ever a first idea? What is it? Pleasing speculations are to hand in a line and a half. "Perhaps" is good at the end of the line, then a plain line which we accept, "The truth depends on a walk around a lake." Why so it does, or why should it not? This is a lake, no specific lake. "A composing as the body tires," how human, so he tires too, I am with the poem, he knows about being tired without being destroyed, this is natural. Then "a stop/ To see hepatica," I suppose I ought to know what hepatica is without looking in the dictionary, nice-sounding word, a suggestion of an ought, it ought to be a goddess; rather, this is description of a flower. Reiterate "a stop to watch," this stop set in a little from the end of the line against the extreme right for the stop "to watch/ A definition growing—like the hepatica?—certain and." Why this is very pleasant, he is saying something and that "and" at the end is expert, it has been used before by others but is not a worn counter. I count this good usage, "and/ A halt within that certainty," this is philosophic and good, no one simple notion but a complexity adjoined to a central idea, then "a rest" equated with the first "a stop" above "a rest/ In the swags of pine-trees bordering the lake." Here we have original Stevens, for nobody before has said "swags of pine-trees," isn't that good, swags has its very special flavor and savor and weight, swing or plunder or bushman's luggage, a swag, why swag itself, the pine trees are swaggering maybe, or are as a man bent with swag, they are going and they have their purpose but can be rested in. "Bordering the lake" so plain and straight English a phrase. Then "Perhaps there are times of inherent excellence" which we accept at once as truth, as truth-telling, neither overt nor undone, harking back in kind to "The truth depends on a walk around a lake." We are in the poem and loving it, here is a comma, run on to "As when the cock crows on the left and all," that is the end of the line, quickly on to "all/ Is well." Is this idiosyncratic, why should a cock crow on the left, is there some biblical reference here, do I need to know, is it not enjoyable as is? Then the explosive great phrase "incalculable balances," this wonderful terminology, securely set in the short line after "Is well," and we feel that there are incalculable balances, the poem has them and we have them and incalculable is incalculable and one had better not try to calculate them, we are soaring off into the beauties of the incalculable. Then the even-feeling line "At which a kind of Swiss perfection comes," easier than "swags of pine-trees," which is so new and original; a Swiss perfection is acceptable, we think of Swiss watches, it is all right, not hard, but not bad either. Then "And a familiar music of the machine" with here an ambiguity, what machine, is it the human body, is it Stevens's body, is it mine? We take the intellectuality of the familiar music of the machine, properly nonsense, it quickly "Sets up its Schwarmerei," a soft-fleshed word full of suggestion, German to the Swiss, then "not balances/ That we achieve but balances that happen," and this is a heavy knock of reality and truth, he is deep here, it is the philosophy again. All sorts of ramifying thoughts now, we do not cause the times of inherent excellence he is saying, there is no use to human will, it is the harmony that happens, the "balances that happen," that come, the poem is in its stride now. Then, after a comma, "As a man and woman meet and love forthwith." How good and crisp that "forthwith"; the line is natural and human, true and free.

Then a generalization, "Perhaps there are moments of awakening," is he dealing with dream or reality, the subconscious or the objective world, or in between somewhere, then the perky line with three eventful words, "Extreme, fortuitous, personal," each so weighed and telling, and the good grammarian will not let us down with too many of these, he eases off the line with "in which" and then we are at the last stanza "in which/ We more than awaken, sit on the edge of sleep," this is good as actualizing metaphor, we have all done it, "As on an elevation," here a vague but compelling generalization, then "and behold" at the end of the next-to-last line "The academies like structures in a mist." It ends magnificently in ambiguity, is he denigrating somehow the academies, what academies, like structures in a mist, as feeling his own personal reality so much more true than objective things of the world, or is it that we sometimes awaken, or may awaken, to a historic vision of culture rampant in some roseate world, a vision of an imaginative world totally desirable?

And what, after all, became of the giant, and who was or is he?

Such is a musing run-through of a reading of this poem by Wallace Stevens, not a conceptual study, not thorough, not exhaustive, reactions at once to the wonderful pleasure of the variously drawn-out lines and the sumptuousness of the manifold meanings.

On Theodore Roethke's Poetry

It is a sad thing to have to talk about a colleague a year after his death at fifty-five when he should have had ten or twenty more years to give us more of his marvelous poems. It is necessary now to talk about his work as an accomplished fact rather than, as one felt when he was living, an organic and a growing thing. We must now see his poems as out of time, in a way, as timeless, which they are, to be enjoyed for their fixed and static purity, rather than as each a new thrust and effort of the imagination confronting life, making of it what he could.

Roethke made a large world of the imagination in lyric poetry, which was at once his limitation and his strength. He insisted on the autonomy of his imagination and became, as it were, an oracle giving forth high warnings against the crass, inventing measures of the fine. He established personality as a gain, rather than a loss to poetry. He delved within the depths of his own personality until he knew the inner world as well as the outer, and finally wondered if he could distinguish between the two.

He was a true creator who finally came to a mystical point where the world was a mirror to his insight. His psyche was subjective and drew into its re-creating and verbal-making power creatures of the earth, birds of the air, voices of the sea, persons and things, and from the whirling vortex of his egocentric sensibility he made poems that are unique, and sometimes sublime. He had an instinctive sense of the

Delivered as a lecture at San Francisco State College on October 27, 1964. Omitted from the published version above are five poems by Roethke which Mr. Eberhart read with commentaries: "Root Cellar," "Night Crow," "The Waking," "I Knew a Woman," and "The Shy Man." At the end of the lecture Mr. Eberhart read his poem, "The Birth of the Spirit" (For Theodore Roethke, 1908–1963), which appears in the *Harvard Advocate*, April, 1965. This lecture was first published in *The Southern Review* 1, no. 3 (Summer, 1965): 612–20.

justice of words, their economy in use, their connotative values, their combining strengths to give delight and to increase in us, the receivers, the large increase and heady flow of his intellectual, sensuous, and spiritual knowledge. He was like a spring that gave down sparkles of water over a high cliff year to year. He was like a mountain, brooding in fogs and long soft nights, murmurous with strange enchantments. Or he was like the sea, a natural force, welling or shrinking, or ebbing, always restless, changing, showing new subtleties to the beholder. He praised life with his powers of discrimination and adoration, a respecter of excellence complexly motivated, but simple in his undeviating devotion to craft, style, freshness, newness, and depth of meaning. My criticism shall be that of praise. We no longer have the living, the suffering and the joyful man, but we have his works, and these earn my privilege of praise.

But before speaking further of Theodore Roethke's work, I would like to speak of the relationships of life to poetry in certain other poets I have known, also among the dead, their spirits in a poetic or historic domain, to wonder at the nature of poetic achievement in our country. It is not only that poets appear who have sensibilities, but there is the incontestable fact of the nature or quality of a time in which the poet finds himself enmeshed, against his will, for he could not determine the time of his birth and must confront his time-spirit, the quality and nature of the times in which he finds himself.

Perhaps an ultimate critic can speak a final truth about a poet, knowing everything of his life and of the nature of his times. I am not that ultimate critic and I do not presume or wish to make final judgments. I suppose Ben Jonson gave an ultimate criticism of Shakespeare. I would like, rather, to make some comments on some poets I have known, before returning to Roethke.

The first poet I would like to speak about is James Agee. He came from Tennessee and went North to school. He had a marked early poetic sensibility. The time was the Thirties, certainly a difficult time. I remember Jim Agee well. He was thin, rather handsome, nervously alive. It seemed as if he were going to be a leading poet of his time. His first, and as it turned out his only book of poems, *Permit Me Voyage* (a phrase from Crane), carried an introduction by Archibald MacLeish. I did not see Jim Agee often, but I observed him through the years. Perhaps if there had been such offices in those days as poet in residence, Jim could have carried his pronounced poetic gift farther than he did. He was a poet who saw that there was no way of making a living from poetry. It is for the biographer to consider the facts and meanings of his three marriages.

He was adept at prose, and he early went over into the other rhythm of prose, if you will recall the critical phrase. I remember there were years when I, as I felt other poets did, felt that he was letting the art of poetry down. He had to face his time-spirit with what fortitude he could. Now we have the letters he wrote to an Episcopal priest and recently the whole corpus of his movie criticism, much of it written for *The Nation,* considered by some to be the best movie criticism written by an American, the most intelligent, judicial, and essentially interesting and lively.

James Agee died early, in his forties, but his poetry, in my estimation, has yet to be assessed. What makes a poet primarily a poet? What forces in Agee's case kept him from being totally and only a poet? I do not know enough to know, but I was pleased to see that in a fairly recent book Elizabeth Drew compared his Knoxville, Tennessee, poem with a sonnet of Shakespeare, detailing the reaction of each poet to the matter in hand, comparing and contrasting Agee's confrontation of his subject with that of Shakespeare of his. This collocation and perceptive conjunction was a criticism of high praise.

The fact remains, however, that Agee's prose outweighs his poetry. One feels that something in his psyche and in his American times kept him from giving the world further poems that I intuit were potentially in him. My intuition may be wrong. We have a small body of excellent work to enjoy.

The next poet I would like to mention, whom I knew, is John Brooks Wheelwright. His work also has not been sufficiently assessed. His father was the architect of the so-called pepper-pot bridge between Boston and Cambridge. Jack Wheelwright was a well-born Bostonian but, confronted with the Thirties, he suffered the conflict of the people versus established society, and while he was known as being to the left, he never was sufficiently anarchistic to leave the Beacon Street home of his parents. He never married. He had a highly developed eccentric personality, and his poems were highly intellectual and ornate, while he supposed them to be revolutionary in intention. He was the first to get poets to read their work over the radio, I believe, in the middle or late Thirties. I first read for him in Boston, much enjoying his management of the affair, and later repaired to his family house for tea, amazed at the obvious dichotomy between the great Paul Revere silver tea service, and the like, the elegance of the appointments of his family house, in contrast to the radical ideas he liked to express. I was confounded by the rigid nature of this dichotomy and felt that he should either belong to the Paul Revere silver or get out of the house, go to New York or elsewhere and work for the people. I could not mention this, and he never took such action but maintained a two-faced life characteristic of that of other intellectuals of the time.

Jack was tall, thin, handsome in a non-robust Bostonian sort of way and always wore a great coonskin coat when he came to poetry readings at Harvard. These were then held in Sever Hall, and Jack invariably came in late in his straggly raccoon coat about five minutes after the speaker and the audience were settled for their give and take of poetry. He invariably disrupted the order of the occasions as he strode from the back of the room always around to the left (symbolically) and invariably found a seat toward the left front into which he settled with a good deal of fuss. Once seated, he demeaned himself as others did. It was supposed to be amusing. Everybody had to put up with Jack's eccentricity. Probably the poets were tipped off so they were not too much annoyed. One had to suffer the eccentricities of the old Bostonian, and actually people were supposed to be pleased. They were. He was a delightful and a witty man.

While I am at it, perhaps I ought to recall a memorable jape of Jack's. It was before the war, when Allen Tate read at Harvard. Afterward a group repaired to the rooms of Theodore Spencer in Eliot House. The talk, in small groups, was heavily intellectual over the cocktails. Then Jack Wheelwright performed an act the likes of which I had never seen before and shall no doubt never see again. It was a strange attention-getting device, yet without a word said about it before or after the event. Jack must have been about six feet tall but he got down on his knees on one side of the room, pulled up the rug, and wormed under the rug on the floor, slowly across the room, taking a long time to make this strange passage, or eccentric poetic voyage. The society was such, of a certain sophistication, that while as I recall all could not help notice this unique behavior, the conversation went on unbroken and when Jack finally emerged at the other side of the room, having gone more or less on a straight line through his psychic ordeal, he stood up and began talking to somebody as if nothing had happened and all the guests kept to their conversations and drinks without apparently noting, as they did not mention the occurrence of this extraordinary incident.

His poetry was not all that eccentric and should be assessed, or reassessed, today. There was a strange fate in his death. At the Boston side of the bridge coming over from M.I.T., he was killed early in the morning when coming home in a taxi, at Beacon Street, by another car, a few blocks from his ancestral home.

Theodore Spencer also died much too early. He was not eccentric and was a fine Shakespearean scholar, a popular professor at Harvard, a perceptive literary critic, and a poet. Perhaps he held his own poetry as the matter closest to his heart, but, as with Agee and Wheelwright, he was not toally a poet. Again, someone far more learned than I would have to delve into the intricate reasons why this was so. Does a poet not become totally a poet because of some defect of the psyche, or is it because of the exigencies of society, or because of complex causes unable to be raveled out?

Theodore Spencer was perhaps the first poet in America to adapt the refrains of Yeats to his own uses. His was a schooled and learned verse, deep student as he was of the entire history of English poetry, and he had a terseness or concision of expression that was characteristically his own. He was able to roll up a whole look of experience into one ball and make short poems that said much in little space.

Handsome, elegant, refined, polite, Ted Spencer was as unforgettable as his running-mate and co-popular professor, the critic F. O. Matthiessen, who also died, but by suicide, much too young. Their Harvard was lively and had an ambience and color and tone of the world of T. S. Eliot. Indeed, Mr. Eliot gave the first Theodore Spencer memorial lecture, which this last year was given by Mr. Spencer's friend, Professor I. A. Richards.

One feels in Spencer that poetry was a lesser accomplishment when compared with that of his scholarly and critical work. It is clearer to see in his case that America dictated that he should not be primarily a poet because of the nature of his admired and high professional life, but again this may be wrong, and a case could be sought in some obscure depths of his psyche and personality.

Theodore Spencer was the only American who had the distinction of being taken back at Harvard after being one of several professors ousted by President Conant when he became president of Harvard. He was made a professor at Cambridge University, but the war was on and Harvard took him back and he stayed in the same rooms and office in Cambridge, Massachusetts, as a professor from Cambridge, England.

Only last year somebody told me the curious story that after these events Mr. Conant and Mr. Spencer approached each other near the Square, walking inevitably toward each other. Mr. Spencer, no doubt relishing his own wit, said, "Pardon me, Sir, I am a professor from Cambridge. Could you direct me to the Widener Library?" Mr. Conant pointed the way, but nothing else was said.

With these glimpses of other poets known to me, who were partial poets, with poetry as only one part of their lifework, it is now my pleasure to speak of the work of Theodore Roethke, who was totally a poet. We feel in Roethke that poetry was the mainspring of his life. Although he earned his living by teaching, and finally came to be made poet in residence at the University of Washington, he gave all to poetry, lived his intensest times for it, gave it total devotion, and discovered his true nature and scope in relation to it.

The thesis of my remarks is that there is a mystery about poetry, why it becomes partial in some poets and totally engrossing in others. I have suggested that there is the initial brunt of talent and ability, but that no man is an island unto himself, as Donne said, and all partake of our common humanity. When the bell tolls for others, it tolls for us. No man can live to himself alone. The nature of life is social. There are endless relations and interrelations between the poet and others, the poet and life, the poet and the life of his times. The question remains of the relation of a poet to himself and to his times, to his contemporary situation, to the time-spirit.

I do not expect to unravel the mystery in the case of Roethke. I do not wish to entertain his biography, which others could probe better than I. The fact remains that he was fundamentally a poet, and I rejoice as his contemporary to be able to praise his effort, which resulted in some of the best poems of our time.

I would like to make a few modest points.

But first, let me say that we were at Yaddo for a month or more at the beginning of the Fifties and had lively times and discussions. When he brought his bride to New York, my wife and I saw them, and Ted came to our hotel with his manuscript, wondering what poems to put in his book. I remember the last time I saw him, at the National Institute of Arts and Letters, in 1960. I remember at Yaddo that he began playfully calling me the Commander (a reference to Navy days—he was not in the war) and I always called him the Maestro. If I could get a point on him in tennis I was lucky.

I should think that Roethke's life should scotch the notion of Eliot that in poetry there is no competition. Roethke realized that he was competing with everybody, and he was out to win. Not only was he competing with his contemporaries but he perceived that he was competing with the poets of the past, those who embodied the deepest truths in poetry. This is a most subtle consideration. We all know we are mortal, and when we die we have no knowledge of how our works will fare. We do not know of the fate of man and we do not know of the fate of the English language. We do not know our own fate. Thus the problem of the staying power of poetry is profound and complex. One can do his best. Roethke managed his own career for the best making and showing of his poetry, and he won the major prizes of his time. He brought about his results in a characteristically individualistic way. He was Teutonic in his positive approach to life and his own work.

I make the point of his far-seeingness in that Roethke, who began with rather simple, perhaps classical rhymed poems, perceived that time passes quickly and that one or two decades is not enough to try to mate in the writing of poetry. He perceived, I should think, that what is called fashionable or current today will be outmoded tomorrow. Therefore, he wanted to get at the heart of lyric utterance in English, to make poems that, if they were at the heart of experience, would transcend the current time and have lasting power. We should use the word "timeless" with the realization that every feeling of timelessness is related to time; time is the root of the term.

As an obvious instance, while the Beatnik poets were being most timeful, most timely, seizing on the instant, Roethke, who could not have been like them had he wished, still must be supposed to have perceived that poems should be universal in significance rather than of the moment. He rejected the moment, as it were, having, of course, many momentary things to convey, too, in favor of large utterances and deep feelings which could be good at any time.

Another point. He was aware of the brevity of time, our brief stay on the earth, and so he tried to penetrate the ideal essence behind the mask of time; he tried, at first through writing of newts and worms, and later and last through mysticism, to penetrate the heart of life and to give, through sensuous, sometimes sensual images, the feel of nature as most sensitively apprehended by him.

It was a deep, intuitive relationship to nature that he had as a lyric poet. He was enveloped in self, in the ego, so deeply that, as I said at the beginning, at times he could not distinguish between the inner and the outer world of reality. It was one reality to him.

Thus his poetry is intimate, oracular, prophetic, entertaining joy and despair both as essential to knowledge, but his is a poetry of praise more than it is a poetry of despair. It is highly subjective, rather than objective in the large sense of depicting the conflicts of people. Once he threw up his hands, in a gesture not quite of despair, and said, "I could never write verse drama." His limitation would not let him sympathize with characters as such, to the point of communicable projection. He knew what he knew thoroughly and deeply; from his wellhead or fountainhead of perception he has given us highly individualistic poems which sometimes rise to splendid heights.

Robert Frost: His Personality

Now that Robert Frost is dead at the age of eighty-nine, time forces us to see him irrespective of his personality. This is not to say that personality does not inhere in his works, but it inheres now in a different way. The works are in cold print for any assessment. What I refer to is the lively personality of the man, a personality which pleased and charmed many on platforms, indeed, throughout the whole literary estate of America for decades. He also pleased and charmed those who knew him fairly well or intimately, in small gatherings, at dinner parties, or after readings. And while some writings refer to his testy nature, his sometime truculence, or his downright rudeness, even an unmerciful laying about of adversaries, by and large the general impression of Frost is that of a genial man, so ambivalent in his attitudes as to seem always supple, interested in what was directly going on, and able to cope with life at all times, if seemingly mostly in talk. He was a great talker, could stand for an hour, even hours talking with somebody. Perhaps it was his native keen interest in life which made him seem much younger than he was. He followed the goings on of the world with a natural avidity for experience. He belonged to the world and brought his mind and his sensibility always to bear upon it.

He was in no way a reclusive poet. He did not retreat to the woods to get away from life. If he did not participate in certain decades, if he disapproved, for instance, of Roosevelt, he spent considerable time writing satirical verses on the state of the American world at that time. He was having his say as a contemplative artist.

Delivered as the first annual Robert Frost Memorial Lecture, San Francisco Public Library, October 28, 1964. First published in *The Southern Review* 2, no. 4 (Autumn, 1966): 762–88.

It is unfortunate that many persons who knew Frost well are either dead or getting old. This brings me back to the point of his personality. I myself knew him and think of him only as an old man. It was mostly from 1946 on, after the end of World War II, that I began to see something of Frost, first at Cambridge when we were living there and he would give reading-talks at Harvard, or at his place on Brewster Street, where, incidentally, once I went to see him and stood inside the door where he expanded a greeting to a talk of well over an hour. Another time he came over to see us, probably in 1946 or 1947, when we were living in a third-floor apartment at 117 Lake View Avenue. I felt that I should go down to the ground floor and help him up the flights of stairs. But nothing of the sort. He brushed aside any indication of help and practically bounded up the flights of stairs. He did not even seem to be out of breath. I was amazed. He was eager to talk all evening.

During his lifetime his personality was inseparable from his poems; the personality was ubiquitous, tangy, memorable. It was as if every lover of his poetry, from schoolboys to emeritus professors, had seen the twinkle in his gimletlike, deep-set, small gray-blue eyes; had heard him talk offhand about almost anything; or had heard some anecdote about him or his poetry, the legends of his youth, his going to England, his fame there and here, his academic and farming career, the last popular years of his wide fame ending in Kennedy's invitation to his inauguration and Frost's final trip to Russia to encounter Khrushchev.

As it is a living hand which writes a poem, it is reasonable to assume that most readers of the poems they like best relate, however they are able to do so, the written word with the living poet. They do not see a poem by Frost as an impersonal object on a paper, as an abstraction from life, or as a work of art somehow unrelated to the man who made it, but feel the man in the poem, in ways perhaps far too subtle to unravel or explicate.

Some followed his career and connected his new poems with what he was doing. Some followed his old poems and thought of what he had already done. Some studied his progressions and regressions of thought, and his new forward leaps, relating these to what went on in America vis-à-vis the world, as the decades passed. Some wondered upon his inability to change. Some compared him with others, his peers and colleagues, or to poets of the past.

This is to indicate my point that in all of this activity, of many persons in very different ways, the personality of Robert Frost, the impact of his living presence, was known as inextricably bound up with his poetry. His mastery was also in what he would not do, in his recognition of what he could not do.

Some studied this facet of the man, the negations which he felt as positive artistic necessities. For example, he disallowed himself to write reviews, or to write commentaries or blurbs for other poets' books. Some put this down to an insatiable vanity; others saw in it good sense and artistic integrity. He drew a stern line somewhere as to what a poet's role should be in relation to the literary world; he was always refining this line to a hard reality. In this way he was a sort of absolutist. If some English reviewer, in late years, slighted his work in a way he felt was unjust, simply not true, he would write this person off from consideration, set him in some personal limbo from which the critic could never climb again to grace in the eyes of Frost, who considered himself the master of the poetic value of his own work. He kept his own masterful evaluations in his own mind. If some critic could not intuit these, this critic was understood as false and value-less. He was seldom publicly harsh, but he made harsh individual evaluations, sometimes expressed to friends. And nothing was more characteristic of his cunning than to feign modesty and to say that it was, after all, for the critic or the reader to say whether he was a poet, and how good a one.

If Poe showed a disintegrated personality, and if Emily Dickinson possessed one partly so, Robert Frost exhibited an integrated person-ality. He was integrated with the life of his times and his nation. He was integrated with nature because he began when man could feel a less urban sense of where man exists on the face of the earth and in relation to the universe. More Americans then lived on farms. It was the time before the electric light, the car, the radio, or television, and the clusters of our populous cities with their vast interrelating traffic patterns. Frost's poetry goes back to early American farm life, partak-ing of a pastoral feeling which, in turn, goes back to the Latin authors who formed his style.

He understood the music of the scythe sweeping along the ground. Now there are millions who do not know what a scythe is, or was. There are millions of city boys who never saw a cow. In my time the horse has practically disappeared. But Frost understood the drumlin woodchuck, as well as the tramps in mud time, and the farm wives. Tragedy was as available to the common man as it could be to any exalted personage. He wrote of the subtle tragedies of poor people, giving them a universal dignity and relevance to the whole of life.

While Frost was integrated with what might be termed the rural life of his times, and wrote a sort of elegant pastoral, there is a question

whether in future his relevance to the whole of life will increase or
diminish. It does not look as if we could go back to pastoral life in
America; but it looks as if we will become more and more urbanized,
with greater numbers of citizens living in cities, less life being lived on
farms, more life being represented by automation and further compli-
cations of automatic devices.

If this proves to be the case, perhaps in the future Frost's vision will
be pushed farther back in the past, in a sense, than would be expected,
and he will be considered as dated and fixed to his times by the year
2000 as Longfellow is now for the most part only considered in relation
to his times. This is a guess. A further guess is that a poet of comparable size in the near future, or in the far future, must be one who speaks
not of country things, but holds a mirror up to the central doings, the
goings and comings, the preoccupations and hazards of an almost
totally urbanized population.

One reason why Frost is almost universally admired is that he
believed in this world. He is skeptical of any other. He celebrates the
possibilities of life as it is, its large and rich resources. In "Away!"
(1958) he tells us, with a deeply reserved humor, that he'd like to come
back to earth "from having died," if he doesn't like it over there.
Earth's the best place for love.

This poem also shows his basic sense of will, the assumption that
man should be able to control his own destiny. He has to admit that
ultimately he cannot, but he can make a sort of joke out of it and as
poet have it his own way, as in this meaningful poem. This poem
endears him to readers, as do many of his; it assumes that they may
feel as he does, that communication may become communion. Titian,
if I remember my college art course accurately, painted one of his best
nudes when he was eighty-five. Frost wrote one of his best poems as
an octogenarian. Without being sentimental, readers are prone to
applaud when artists at great age produce admittedly great works of
art. Frost never courted the sensual in poetry, and the sensuous in
him is masked by a sternness and rigor, an intellectual discipline
everywhere in his work. His new poem is not like Titian's painting,
but the earth or life itself is his to adore in his restrained fashion. Here
is "Away!":

> Now I out walking
> The world desert,
> And my shoe and my stocking
> Do me no hurt.
>
> I leave behind
> Good friends in town.

> Let them get well-wined
> And go lie down.
>
> Don't think I leave
> For the outer dark
> Like Adam and Eve
> Put out of the Park.
>
> Forget the myth.
> There is no one I
> Am put out with
> Or put out by.
>
> Unless I'm wrong
> I but obey
> The urge of a song:
> "I'm—bound—away!"
>
> And I may return
> If dissatisfied
> With what I learn
> From having died.

An artist has a right to his own ideas as a free spirit. Frost here rejects the Adam and Eve, Garden of Eden story, protesting that he stands outside it. "Forget the myth." The strong last four lines show again what I have indicated elsewhere as predominant in him, his will. He wants to hold that he shall have the power to decide whether he "may return" to earth if dissatisfied after death. This is a most characteristic stance and notion of Frost. It is not without its humor, and the reader may contemplate it as he sees fit.

While we are on this notion of death, it might be pointed out that in "A Soldier," written about the time of World War I, he goes as far toward spirituality as he ever does. He does not go as far as to embrace Christianity or any other religion, but his sensitivity for the dead soldier ends the poem as follows:

> But this we know, the obstacle that checked
> And tripped the body, shot the spirit on
> Further than target ever showed or shone.

It should be said that, although Frost's style and basic attitudes have not changed in a world of remarkable change, he was not paid attention to in the Thirties and part of the Forties as he was earlier and later. Having spoken of World War I in poetry, he left it to other poets to address and assess World War II. Having spoken for individualism, even optimism, and not being for any form of socialism, he was somewhat eclipsed for about two decades. It should also be said that the importance and religious convictions of T. S. Eliot cut down during this period on the interest in Frost's different kind of mind. Students of modern literature learn with amazement and joy of the great last period in the poetry of Yeats, wherein he perfected a new, austere style to express his mature convictions. In the late life of Frost there is no new style, rather, a consolidation of the old; there is a flowering of influence in the continuance of his old, excellent style which is almost without parallel. In his eighties Frost achieved and enjoyed the peak of his fame, having gained and maintained the deep applause of thousands of listeners to his poetry on many stages across the nation. Where Yeats at the last came to an "artifice of eternity," believing in mind alone, Frost offers a full humanity of head and heart. He also offers simplicity and understandability as essentials of poetry. And, as I said before, he believes in the world as it is, the visible and experiential world, showing it forth in rich terms. He comes to and stays in reality as men know it. His sometime sarcasm, even savagery are saved by a grace of wit which he knows well how to employ. It is not a withdrawn or a too fastidiously complex poet who maintained throughout his life a keen interest in the game of baseball. Poetry, the analogy is, must be a game too. While it is a matter of life and death to the poet, it must not be taken too seriously, in one sense. One must know how to manipulate it as a game or device. But, again, poetry is taking life by the throat, Frost told one unexpecting audience. It is also simply being oneself, speaking naturally. Consider "The Silken Tent":

> She is as in a field a silken tent
> At midday when a sunny summer breeze
> Has dried the dew and all its ropes relent,
> So that in guys it gently sways at ease,
> And its supporting central cedar pole,
> That is its pinnacle to heavenward
> And signifies the sureness of the soul,
> Seems to owe naught to any single cord,
> But strictly held by none, is loosely bound
> By countless silken ties of love and thought
> To everything on earth the compass round,
> And only by one's going slightly taut
> In the capriciousness of summer air
> Is of the slightest bondage made aware.

"The Silken Tent" has a more delicate feeling than we get in many of Frost's poems, an aesthetic feeling, wonderfully tender. It is one of the subtlest of his poems. It is a poetic triumph, a Shakespearean sonnet in one sustained sentence. The poem accords with Milton's specification for poetry that it should effect linked sweetness long drawn out. The subtlety of the poem is visual, as fine as the activations of the slightest breeze, yet the poem tantalizes beyond visual pleasure to induce, by "countless silken ties" of ideation, empathy with a natural world of harmony. Many of Frost's poems have a more prosaic feeling, and some have a dark fatalism about them. "Design" is also a sonnet. It is one of Frost's compelling poems, based on visual aesthetics, but, not suffusing the tranquil quality of "The Silken Tent," it disturbs the sense with a dark message although the colors shown are white. Yet the pleasure in reading the poem is so keen that the darkness of the message is masked as if by a withdrawal into undynamic aesthetics. Let us look at this poem and compare it with "The Convergence of the Twain," by Thomas Hardy, with whom Frost can claim some kinship of spirit. First "Design":

> I found a dimpled spider, fat and white,
> On a white heal-all, holding up a moth
> Like a white piece of rigid satin cloth—
> Assorted characters of death and blight
> Mixed ready to begin the morning right,
> Like the ingredients of a witches' broth—
> A snow-drop spider, a flower like a froth,
> And dead wings carried like a paper kite.
>
> What had that flower to do with being white,
> The wayside blue and innocent heal-all?
> What brought the kindred spider to that height,
> Then steered the white moth thither in the night?
> What but design of darkness to appall?—
> If design govern in a thing so small.

This poem perfects a little drama of nature. Frost was always interested in botany. The heal-all is a common plant which is said to have healing properties, yet is usually blue: this variety is white. The white spider holds a white moth. Here is a strange juxtaposition in nature. The octet of the sonnet describes the scene. The sestet asks fundamental questions about what brought these three things together as they are. Spider, flower, and moth are the subhuman characters in this little drama. The dark question is in the next-to-last line. There is a sinister undertone as Frost leaves ambiguity in the line, "What but design of darkness to appall?—"

Hardy's poem is also from observance of nature, but from contemplation of a happening that shocked the world when it occurred, the sinking of a ship which man had boasted unsinkable. Here is "The Convergence of the Twain (Lines on the loss of the *Titanic*)":

> In a solitude of the sea
> Deep from human vanity,
> And the Pride of Life that planned her, stilly couches she.
>
> Steel chambers, late the pyres
> Of her salamandrine fires,
> Cold currents thrid, and turn to rhythmic tidal lyres.
>
> Over the mirrors meant
> To glass the opulent
> The sea-worm crawls—grotesque, slimed, dumb, indifferent.
>
> Jewels in joy designed
> To ravish the sensuous mind
> Lie lightless, all their sparkles bleared and black and blind.
>
> Dim moon-eyed fishes near
> Gaze at the gilded gear
> And query: "What does this vaingloriousness down here?" . . .
>
> Well: while was fashioning
> This creature of cleaving wing,
> The Immanent Will that stirs and urges everything
>
> Prepared a sinister mate
> For her—so gaily great—
> A Shape of Ice, for the time far and dissociate.
>
> And as the smart ship grew
> In stature, grace, and hue,
> In shadowy silent distance grew the Iceberg too.
>
> Alien they seemed to be:
> No mortal eye could see
> The intimate welding of their later history.
>
> Or sign that they were bent
> By paths coincident
> On being anon twin halves of one august event,
>
> Till the Spinner of the Years
> Said "Now!" And each one hears,
> And consummation comes, and jars two hemispheres.

Hardy posits the Immanent Will as implacable. The Spinner of the Years is implacable, too. The processes of nature are relentless and bring about the fatal collision beyond man's power of imagination to hinder or change. There is no escape in Hardy. Note that Frost's poem, in being a sonnet, is conventionally contrived. It is easier to read and has no odd grammatical turns or old-fashioned, outworn words like "thrid." Hardy has invented a new stanza form for the poem; he has also conceived the philosophical terms we have noted. Both poems could be called subdued dramas. Each has a presentation and a climax. Hardy's, being longer, has more chance to build up to its climax. Frost's poem shifts and holds off to a disinterested view the implacable workings of nature; then with a deft last stroke, as if not wishing to oppress the reader with dogma, it gives him an out or a leeway that maybe the vast design of the universe, however fixed, final, or fatal, may not be mirrored in a situation "so small" as that of the juxtaposition of spider, heal-all, and moth. This is a turn of Frost's nicest wit, a leaning back into the human as against the absolute confrontation of inhuman or superhuman forces in Hardy's poem.

Two other poems by Frost and Hardy invite comparison, Hardy's "Under the Waterfall" and Frost's "Directive." Let us read them both, giving our initial attention to "Under the Waterfall":

"Whenever I plunge my arm, like this,
In a basin of water, I never miss
The sweet sharp sense of a fugitive day
Fetched back from its thickening shroud of gray.
　　　　Hence the only prime
　　　　And real love-rhyme
　　　　That I know by heart,
　　　　And that leaves no smart,
Is the purl of a little valley fall
About three spans wide and two spans tall
Over a table of solid rock,
And into a scoop of the self-same block;
The purl of a runlet that never ceases
In stir of kingdoms, in wars, in peaces;
With a hollow boiling voice it speaks
And has spoken since hills were turfless peaks."

"And why gives this the only prime
Idea to you of a real love-rhyme?
And why does plunging your arms in a bowl
Full of spring water, bring throbs to your soul?"

"Well, under the fall, in a crease of the stone,
Though where precisely none ever has known,
Jammed darkly, nothing to show how prized,
And by now with its smoothness opalized,
　　　　Is a drinking-glass:
　　　　For, down that pass

> My lover and I
> Walked under a sky
> Of blue with a leaf-wove awning of green,
> In the burn of August, to paint the scene,
> And we placed our basket of fruit and wine
> By the runlet's rim, where we sat to dine;
> And when we had drunk from the glass together,
> Arched by the oak-copse from the weather,
> I held the vessel to rinse in the fall,
> Where it slipped, and sank, and was past recall,
> Though we stooped and plumbed the little abyss
> With long bared arms. There the glass still is.
> And, as I said, if I thrust my arm below
> Cold water in basin or bowl, a throe
> From the past awakens a sense of that time,
> And the glass we used, and the cascade's rhyme.
> The basin seems the pool, and its edge
> The hard smooth face of the brook-side ledge,
> And the leafy pattern of china-ware
> The hanging plants that were bathing there.
> By night, by day, when it shines or lours,
> There lies intact that chalice of ours,
> And its presence adds to the rhyme of love
> Persistently sung by the fall above.
> No lip has touched it since his and mine
> In turns therefrom sipped lovers' wine."

Now let us read "Directive":

> Back out of all this now too much for us,
> Back in a time made simple by the loss
> Of detail, burned, dissolved, and broken off
> Like graveyard marble sculpture in the weather,
> There is a house that is no more a house
> Upon a farm that is no more a farm
> And in a town that is no more a town.
> The road there, if you'll let a guide direct you
> Who only has at heart your getting lost,
> May seem as if it should have been a quarry—
> Great monolithic knees the former town
> Long since gave up pretence of keeping covered.
> And there's a story in a book about it:
> Besides the wear of iron wagon wheels
> The ledges show lines ruled southeast northwest,
> The chisel work of an enormous Glacier
> That braced his feet against the Arctic Pole.
> You must not mind a certain coolness from him

Still said to haunt this side of Panther Mountain.
Nor need you mind the serial ordeal
Of being watched from forty cellar holes
As if by eye pairs out of forty firkins.
As for the woods' excitement over you
That sends light rustle rushes to their leaves,
Charge that to upstart inexperience.
Where were they all not twenty years ago?
They think too much of having shaded out
A few old pecker-fretted apple trees.
Make yourself up a cheering song of how
Someone's road home from work this once was,
Who may be just ahead of you on foot
Or creaking with a buggy load of grain.
The height of the adventure is the height
Of country where two village cultures faded
Into each other. Both of them are lost.
And if you're lost enough to find yourself
By now, pull in your ladder road behind you
And put a sign up CLOSED to all but me,
Then make yourself at home. The only field
Now left's no bigger than a harness gall.
First there's the children's house of make believe,
Some shattered dishes underneath a pine,
The playthings in the playhouse of the children.
Weep for what little things could make them glad.
Then for the house that is no more a house,
But only a belilaced cellar hole,
Now slowly closing like a dent in dough.
This was no playhouse but a house in earnest.
Your destination and your destiny's
A brook that was the water of the house,
Cold as a spring as yet so near its source,
Too lofty and original to rage.
(We know the valley streams that when aroused
Will leave their tatters hung on barb and thorn.)
I have kept hidden in the instep arch
Of an old cedar at the waterside
A broken drinking goblet like the Grail
Under a spell so the wrong ones can't find it,
So can't get saved, as Saint Mark says they mustn't.
(I stole the goblet from the children's playhouse.)
Here are your waters and your watering place.
Drink and be whole again beyond confusion.

"Under the Waterfall" has a lighter tone than Frost's poem has, and perhaps we notice at first that it is in quotation. Somebody is saying it. It is odd about this poem that you cannot tell on first reading who is speaking, man or woman. It is not until the next-to-the-last line that we know the poem is spoken by Hardy's woman protagonist. The poem is charming in its long recall. Love is recalled when, plunging an arm into a basin of water years later, the speaker of the poem recalls how the lovers "plumbed the little abyss/ With long bare arms" to retrieve a drinking glass below the waterfall. They could not retrieve it. Now the water basin recalls the early event. The drinking glass is now spoken of as a "chalice." Times have changed but "No lip has touched it since his and mine/ In turns therefrom sipped lovers' wine." It is a subtle poem with a certain lightsome touch, although Hardy's language is rather dense, requiring slow and careful reading. Note the experimental quality of the two short inworked quatrains. It is a poem about lost love and its recapture in memory. Frost's poem is heavier, although its lines are easier to read and are not broken up toward experimental form. Frost is speaking as poet directly to the reader. Hardy's poem is about lost personal love. Frost's poem is about the loss of a whole way of life. There is the sense of a lost world, a wide world when compared with Hardy's lost narrow, personal world. Hardy's protagonist thrusts arm "below/ Cold water in basin or bowl" to receive the sensation leading to the retrieving of a past experience. In Frost's poem there is also the idea of coldness, that of "an enormous Glacier/ That braced his feet against the Arctic Pole" and that of a brook "Cold as a spring as yet so near its source,/ Too lofty and original to rage." This last phrase is highly imaginative. Its comment on the meaning of rage is fortified with the parenthetical afterimage of "tatters hung on barb and thorn," this only.

Both are poems of deep acceptance. Where Hardy uses the word "chalice," Frost describes "A broken drinking goblet like the Grail" which he has "kept hidden" "Under a spell so the wrong ones can't find it." He ends by saying: "Here are your waters and your watering place./ Drink and be whole again beyond confusion." He says parenthetically, just before this, "(I stole the goblet from the children's playhouse)." We are meant to sense meaning as spiritually as Frost will let us sense it in this poem. It should be noted that it is a will poem; Frost's will is the driving force behind it. It is Frost the poet who is casting the spell. He is not going to let anything in nature be spell-originating. He goes back to "the children's house of make believe" in the old, desolate place of the poem for the essence of the lost meaning of life, the beginning of the long pilgrimage of man's experience through time, and he gives us the vision of his Grail as the means to "be whole again beyond confusion." If the last two words may seem to some to be redundant, they make of the sentence a reasonable, prosaic statement; without them the sentence would be nearer to an explicit Christian analogy with Holy Communion and would thus be beyond the Classical restraint we find at the peak of the most spiritual parts of Frost's poetic consciousness and poetic evocation.

Let us now consider some other poems by Robert Frost.

"Neither Out Far Nor In Deep" represents the humanistic nature of his thinking. He wishes never to go too far in any direction, but to keep his perceptions in the middle of his heart. He is thus able, in many poems as in this one, to speak for feelings that are universally valid. The situation is simple. People on land tend to look at the sea when they stand at the edge of the land. "They look at the sea all day." It is as if the sea might be or become a natural symbol of something beyond themselves. They note a passing ship, a gull. In the third stanza, shifting back from the possibility of the sea as some illimitable symbol, he declares, "The land may vary more." We are given this to take as it is, that for him the earth may provide a symbol, the earth being posited as more various, yet immediately we read the conditional "But whatever the truth may be"; and we are suspended in a fine, delicate balance of possibilities. There is then a flat recapitulation of the beginning of the poem: "The water comes ashore,/ And the people look at the sea." The last stanza makes two broad generalizations out of the depths of Frost's feelings. These are based on strong restraint. "They cannot look out far./ They cannot look in deep." Behind these two sentences lies Frost's realization of the limitations of man. They suggest that there is something far and something deep to which man cannot get, but instead of erecting some new symbol for this farness, this depth, which a Romantic poet might do, Frost characteristically brings the matter home to a usable, natural consideration. When was the fact of our inability to perceive life as it may be a hindrance to our keeping watch on life as it is? Keeping watch on life as it is is what we have to do every day. It is this basic necessity which Frost celebrates in this poem.

The restraint of Frost's strongly balanced and Classical nature is shown again in "The Onset." With the beginning of winter, man may feel that he can do something about life or nature, but he knows that he cannot hold back winter. Frost says:

> I almost stumble looking up and round,
> As one who overtaken by the end
> Gives up his errand, and lets death descend
> Upon him where he is, with nothing done

> To evil, no important triumph won,
> More than if life had never been begun.

It is said as if in an aside, this hope of man to do something to evil. It is as if wit were the final motive for this, for any natural man knows that evil is ineradicable. The phrase is a kind of shadowboxing, a wish fulfillment, as if it were slipped in or allowed by the unconscious, not the conscious mind. It is a telling phrase; it tells us a great deal about Frost, driven by a demon of the will. Then the poem goes on in an arbitrary way to state that spring will overcome winter. He says: "Winter death has never tried/ The earth but it has failed." We accept the end of the poem for what it is talking about; we warm to the poet's emphasis upon spring rather than winter, but with an equal logic he could write, if he wanted to, that an "April rill" has never run but that spring and summer have been defeated again by winter. The point of the poem is that it expresses man's universal wish for the death of winter.

Criticism of many of the poems is so easily available that it is not my purpose to adumbrate and elucidate many of his well-known poems. I would prefer to point up his powers of concentration in the shortest type of poem, the couplet or distich.

Frost has a group of couplets in which he can be arch and succinct. These are concentrated essences of meaning and suggestion.

"The Secret Sits" reads as follows:

> We dance around in a ring and suppose,
> But the Secret sits in the middle and knows.

This is an admirable closed statement. It admits the limits of man's knowledge. It is a truth-telling. Despite the frenzied actions of man, there is a still center. My question is whether by capitalizing "Secret" he improves the connotations. The capitalized abstraction would be less abstract in lower case. The rhythm of the two lines compels a kind of verbal ritual. The rhythm is slightly interrupted by the capital S. These two lines succinctly posit the human situation. The first line represents devotion, the second line final austerity, judgment.

In "An Answer" he writes:

> But Islands of the Blessèd, bless you, son,
> I never came upon a blessèd one.

This couplet presents two clever turns. It is light, mocking, and bantering in tone, yet with a rapier thrust that pierces. He jeers at Romantic conceptions. The bare sense of the sentence is that there is nothing behind or beyond appearance. Realism and the present scene are all. Frost is not one to "bless," so that "bless you, son" is said in imitation of colloquial jargon; but yet half in belief, as of one who has lived long and looks back to bespeak the way to an oncomer. The repetition of "blessed" in the second line is what gives pleasure here, alerting the reader to an ambiguity held instantaneously in mind, that "blessed" is the same as "Blessed" in the first line but equally the main part of a colloquial phrase. It is characteristic of Frost that he masks the darkest part of his pessimism by veils of wit which make the intake of his words a pleasure, whether the meaning is approved or not.

In "The Span of Life" Frost writes:

> The old dog barks backward without getting up.
> I can remember when he was a pup.

This distich depends more upon what is not said than do the other two. At first sight and sound the poem is so banal as not to be arresting. It may seem at first to be entirely unpoetical, two barefaced prosaic statements. One may read a great deal between these two lines. A whole philosophy of life may be found there; if not philosophy, a depiction of the actuality of life. The old dog has lost his fight. This is inevitable. If one lives long enough, one is bound to be old. If you live to be old you lack fight. The old dog does not get up, and he turns his head to "bark backward." The poet's phrase "I can remember when he was a pup," when contemplated long enough, provides the delayed reaction of a full charge of meaning, although the line does not seem made with this possibility when first taken in as flat prose. Actually it is richly connotative and conjures up the whole of life. In this line we contemplate our own youth, the immediacy of life, the vigor, the hopes, the aspiration, the fresh upthrust. Into this line you can read your own advent in time, and, in addition, apply it to all of mankind's if you wish. These two lines connote much more than they actually say. They effect a life-inclusive poem in the shortest possible space. However, it may be said that "barked backward" is problematical. I had never heard of a dog barking backward and had to ask what it meant. Probably somebody in the hills of New Hampshire would have known the phrase for fifty years. While I have not had opportunity to ask a country person, others have told me that they assume the tired dog only turned his head backward to bark. The more you read these two lines, the deeper seems Frost's commentary.

Frost unmasks himself in relation to God in "Not All There." It goes:

> I turned to speak to God

About the world's despair,
But to make bad matters worse
I found God wasn't there.

God turned to speak to me
(Don't anybody laugh)
God found I wasn't there—
At least not over half.

The last line redeems the poem by some pity beyond derision. I assess it that Frost thinks God would want man to be whole. To make God find man only half there gives us a wry comment on life. This poem shows the artistic balance of Frost. The first four uncompromising lines are compromised in the second four. He allows the reader to have it both ways, an atheistical negation balanced by a dualistic system which can be read in terms of either God or man.

To speak not only of this poem but in general of Frost's attitude to God, the trouble is that Frost does not give God credit for making him what he is. Instead, he takes something away from God for withholding something from him. He is a maker, a maker of poems. In what religious portions of his mind there are he does not see why he cannot or should not make God. Man does not assume the primacy of God. But if you put it with a small "g" it is all right. Primitive man is a natural maker of gods in his own image, totems, idols, icons, artifacts. Frost is a maker of poems, primitive in some ways, sophisticated in others. A poet should be permitted the freedom of his own ideas. As a skeptic, Frost has every right to put his first reliance in self-trust. The reader has every right to evaluate what the poet's convictions are in relation to God.

When you read and make part of your consciousness and knowledge of life many of his poems, you may agree to a generalization that Frost stands firmly in this world and that his poems deal with an astute knowledge of others as well as of himself. He wants each of his poems to be in some way dramatic. He often told his audiences to note how different they are one from another. While he has deep personal lyrics, such as "Stopping by Woods on a Snowy Evening," Frost never lets himself go in a piercing, self-revelatory, Romantic way as Gerard Manley Hopkins did. Listen to the octet of Hopkins's "The Starlight Night":

Look at the stars! look, look up at the skies!
O look at all the fire-folk sitting in the air!
The bright boroughs, the circle-citadels there!
Down in dim woods the diamond delves! the elves'-eyes!
The grey lawns cold where gold, where quickgold lies!

> Wind-beat whitebeam! airy abeles set on a flare!
> Flake-doves sent floating forth at a farmyard scare!—
> Ah, well! it is all a purchase, all is a prize.

The sestet of this poem is concerned with the Christian mystery which enclosed and enfolded Hopkins's struggling spirit. In the first part we have quoted there is a breathless quality, an immediacy quite unlike Frost. Who else but Hopkins would write seven lines ending in exclamation marks? Hopkins writes in "I Wake and Feel the Fell of Dark":

> I am gall, I am heartburn. God's most deep decree
> Bitter would have me taste: my taste was me;
> Bones built in me, flesh filled, blood brimmed the curse.
>   Selfyeast of spirit a dull dough sours. I see
> The lost are like this, and their scourge to be
> As I am mine, their sweating selves; but worse.

Frost is a different kind of poet. His self-revelations are temporal and are embedded in poems showing human situations. He is not a confessional poet in the sense that Hopkins is a totally confessional one. Hopkins is committed to the Christian view. Frost is a secular poet, functioning and thriving in a Christian society. He never writes so personally or so passionately as in the above quotations from Hopkins.

Perhaps another example, quite the opposite of Hopkins, will make us better able to appreciate the even temper of Frost's poetry, its large humanity and its central stance. Following is another example of a kind of poetry Frost could not write, but its spirit is nearer to him than the religious spirit of the poems of Hopkins. The poem is by Robinson Jeffers, born in 1887. He moved to California and built with his own hands a stone house overlooking the Pacific. While Frost's mind was skeptical, we find in Jeffers a belief that things are stronger than man, that man is only one datum of nature no more valuable than other phenomena, that we must learn to love the inhuman. It is a stark and bleak doctrine. We face it in his "Signpost":

> Civilized, crying how to be human again: this will tell you how.
> Turn outward, love things, not men, turn right away from humanity.
> Let that doll lie. Consider if you like how the lilies grow,
> Lean on the silent rock until you feel its divinity
> Make your veins cold, look at the silent stars, let your eyes
> Climb the great ladder out of the pit of yourself and man.
> Things are so beautiful, your love will follow your eyes;
> Things are the God, you will love God, and not in vain,
> For what we love, we grow to it, we share its nature. At length

You will look back along the stars' rays and see that even
The poor doll humanity has a place under heaven.
Its qualities repair their mosaic around you, the chips of strength
And sickness; but now you are free, even to become human,
But born of the rock and the air, not of a woman.

Incidentally, in another poem, "Return," Jeffers has an image similar to one in Hardy's waterfall poem: "I will go down to the lovely Sur Rivers/ And dip my arms in them up to the shoulders!"

Frost loved man as well as things. He does not turn away from mankind but speaks for it in some way in every poem. His great popularity is due in part to the love of life and of man, imperfect as, they are. All readers can share in varying ways with this sympathy and this human understanding.

Those who were privileged to hear Frost "say his poems" in his last years, if they got to hear him several times, were delighted that he always had something new to say. He often began a performance by talking offhand on some philosophical topic that had been engaging him, before saying his poems, often from memory, but with his *Complete Poems* in hand.

I recall him saying that poetry places the greatest meaning on the world as it does on the word. I recall a preachment that the word began back in the land of the Scriptures, traveled in a northwesterly direction for centuries through Greece, Rome, and civilized Europe to land, rather happily and rather wittily, on Frost's own New England. He didn't specify what would happen in his view if it kept on across the Pacific. He also talked in his final years about poetry as risking spirituality to materiality. This idea goes back decades in his thought. He announces the primacy of spirit. The challenge of the West is with spirituality put into materiality. He observed, in one lecture, that we all now have bathroom scales. We want to know how much we weigh. He sees this as a risk of the spirit, a risk the spirit has to take, such interest in materiality, a word he consciously used in distinction to materialism.

Let me recall a certain incident. In 1960 at the fiftieth anniversary dinner of the Poetry Society of America in New York to honor Marianne Moore, Robert Graves, and Robert Frost, I had the honor, as consultant in poetry to the Library of Congress, to welcome to our shores Robert Graves, who had come here for the occasion from Majorca. Miss Moore received a medal, in a box, which had a Pegasus on it. Mr. Graves had a gold medal pinned on his lapel. He made some witty remarks about the gold standard and took a touchstone out of his pocket to test the metal and treat the audience to a little talk on alchemy, incidentally saying that poetry was an impossibility, it was so high a thing, and saying that of all the poets there only Frost was assured of poetic immortality. Mr. Graves said he would rather have had Miss Moore's medal because it had a Pegasus on it, the symbol of the poet's ride in the heavens of the imagination. Frost arose and in his inimitable and much-loved way took up the notion of Pegasus. This was an example of his quick, opportunistic wit, which never failed him in something trenchant to say. He said of Pegasus that it was all in who had the whip handle and that "you've got to drive Pegasus along." He made the point with an energetic gesture.

This was a true, impromptu expression of the genius of Frost. It was a simple statement or two, most effective and most human. It meant that for him, the humanist, the materialist if you will, the man of this world and the skeptic of any other, the marvelous poet who was also a common man, the universalist in his way, it is man who is the master of all things, it is man who makes art, man who must master his art and that he does, can, and must whip Pegasus along through the skies of imagination. It is not as if art were a Platonic abstraction, a Platonic idea, or could fit into a world crucible into which the imagination of man must delve to realize a purity imposed from without, or some purity implicit in the skies of imagination, but it is actually as if man must begin with his own flesh and blood, his own condition, his own possibility and his own limitation, and there is a touch of masterful ruthlessness in the forceful charge that the poet must command art, from first knowing and commanding his own nature, that the poet must whip and drive Pegasus along through the skies.

These impromptu and chance remarks by Frost were wonderfully characteristic of his whole attitude toward life. It is a Classical attitude rather than a Romantic one, and he was an Aristotelian rather than a Platonist. The Aristotelian attitude begins with the things of this world and believes that they can be measured, arranged, codified, and argued from empirically. Aristotle as scientist was our first methodical codifier, arranger, and measurer. The reality of the objective world, to a man like Frost, is approached and known through his senses, then through the sorting and balancing mechanism of his mind.

Platonism is "the belief in a world of Forms or Ideas—an *idea* being, as the dictionary has it 'a supposed eternally existing pattern or archetype of any class of things, of which the individual things in that class are imperfect copies, and from which they derive their existence.'" I. A. Richards in his essay on Shelley goes on to say, "Logically, it was a theory of Sameness: how can there be any stability

197

or constancy in anything, in our own selves, for example? Many things are white, say (or beautiful), at many different times and in many different places. But how? Plato suggested that it is Whiteness (or Beauty)— a being not in time or space—which makes them white (or beautiful) . . . . For Plato there is something more, even beyond the world of Forms; there is the Idea of the Good, from which the Forms receive their Being—as beautiful things in their turn receive their beauty from Beauty."

Frost was not a Platonist. He refused consciously throughout a lifetime to use the word "beauty" in his poetry. He was rooted in the here and now, the actual and the real, and it is easy to see that Frost belongs in the Aristotelian camp. He was not, of course, like Aristotle. Aristotle, while being almost everything else as a thinker, was not a poet. But Frost was also not at all like Shelley. It might be interesting for a momont to compare them. Shelley plucked poetry out of the air, as it were. He was protean, fertile, variable, quick, malleable. Frost is nothing like this. His poetry is rocklike, not ebullient; quiet, not wild; factual, not hallucinated; solid, not evanescent; relevant to things, not creating a dream world; rational, not irrational; well tempered, incapable of what the Greeks called divine frenzy; plausible, not an extremist; well grounded, not aerial; given to quatrains, couplets, and other set forms, not inventing new measures; recording man deep and sure, not strange and high.

But to get back to the poetical dinner party. The remarks of Frost mentioned above were said with his usual twinkle and verve, pleasing everybody. Frost had a natural way of saying his severest things with a chuckle of good will as if to mitigate the stings. He would be less popular if this were not so. Underneath the winning manner sometimes lurked radical remarks uncompromising in their bleakness. On this occasion, before he sat down, he repeated what audiences had often heard from platforms in the last few years: "Forgive, O Lord, my little jokes on Thee/ And I'll forgive Thy great big one on me." Everybody laughed. This statement when heard from Frost's lips in public was arresting and calculated to shock, which it did initially to some extent. Said with his characteristic eye twinkle and mirth, it titillated and pleased an audience. It is an "if" proposition, an equation. If you'll do something for me I'll do something for you, an eye for an eye, a tooth for a tooth.

The reasoning is actually queer. He equates a small thing with a great thing. He asks to be forgiven for his little jokes on God which he makes in a playful way, but not outright, only as a proposition. If the Lord will do this, he will in turn forgive the Lord's great big joke on

Frost, as man, and thus on mankind, the joke being, I assume, that the Lord is greater than mankind and in His nature keeps man from knowing everything. God is mysterious about the purposes of mankind, of good and evil, of life and death. Frost is piqued because this is so and puts it up to God to give him parity. I can't see that the little and the great joke are on the same plane. There is a deep, brutal recognition in the second line. If one is not a Christian, if one views this pith of Frostian wisdom from an agnostic or an atheistic point of view, then it may reside in our memories as a good humanistic proposition. As a humanistic proposition, divorced from religious considerations, it is cogent. The reader has to decide where he stands in reading it. The saying seems to ask not to be taken too seriously but to exist as a sort of daring revel of healthful audacity in a man who wants to be loved, not rebuked for saying it.

I should try, perhaps, to make up a picture of a composite evening with Frost. He has read at Webster Hall, or in Dartmouth Hall, let us say, to a crowd of students; he has spoken his marvelous poems, although he would not use that word about them, and then it is time for the quiet aftermath. He wants to walk, but is got probably into a car and is brought to a professor's house, usually a different one each visit in offhand, friendly rotation. Robert Frost requests to see a small group of his men friends; it is a fact to note that these are all-male occasions. No wives are allowed. This is a fact of some importance, let the psychiatrists make of it what they will. Frost has eaten nothing before his reading. After the reading, his host or hostess, in the house of choice for that night, gives him a snack in the kitchen, whatever he likes, something simple, and then he comes into the main room. He sits in the main chair, a king surrounded by ministers, as it were. This is his court. His essential goodness and humanity radiate throughout the room. He is an old man, but he is younger in some ways than his auditors, it seems, and he demands to do all the talking. There are opening questions, but sooner or later all settle for the fact that this experience is primarily a monologue. Everyone is well pleased to hear Frost, as he always has something lively to say. At length, having wearied several listeners, Frost at over eighty is still going strong into the night, hates to leave, and demands to walk home! His protestations may be countered, and all remember a splendid evening!

The remarkable thing is that throughout his long, fruitful life Frost was able to write so many masterful poems, so consistently, and with so little deviation from the central excellence of his early work. He modestly said that he only wanted a few poems that men will not wish to get rid of; the few are, in fact, many. And no doubt men will be saying them "ages and ages hence." It may be that some of his attraction lies in the fact that urban man longs to remember a closer association he had with nature, going back only as far as his grandfather's time, or even his own early life, and derives this natural insight into nature from Frost, who knows it well from his farming days and living among country folk. Our urban civilization is relatively recent. Frost goes back to the soil from which it sprang. Certainly some of his attraction lies in the rare ability he has of appealing both to unsophisticated and to sophisticated readers of poetry. He cuts across all classes, is a classless poet. Children and young students can understand him; at the same time he appeals to the most learned men in many professions due to the subtlety of his thought. He is at once simple and profound. He has great range of interest and great breadth of technical resource. I have indicated repeatedly that his natural bias is in favor of this world; he engages us totally in what is commonly known and felt to be reality, and this may be his greatest gift. He is more of a realist than he is an idealist, as he is more a localist than an internationalist. But let me philosophize.

The brutal fact is that no man knows whether there is anything beyond death. This is a prime baffling fact of existence. Let us suppose that there is nothing to life but appearance, nothing to death but the appearance of death and therefore obviously no life after death. If this is the true state of things, then Robert Frost's poetry becomes more valuable than if this were not true. The fact that we do not know adds to the fascination of his ideas and to the potency of the poetical charge of his poems. For then we will have to admire him for his robust, stronghearted resistance to any idea of life after death. We will have to salute him for persistent doubt. We will incline to give him credit for his doubt. We will call him a hero of unredeemed man and applaud him for adding mirth as a palliative. We will probably by natural sympathy admire him the more for thinking of man as less than immortal and being able to communicate an orderly, realistic, fearless poetry out of his wry convictions and for approaching a defiant attitude, the attitude of a human in his strongest self-realization, in the will to wrest from nature the most superb, harmonious words he can select to make permanent nature's manifestation to him. Also, if we are like-minded, we will incline to think that his poetry is more nearly right than wrong. He has to stand and have his being on reason, on rational grounds, with a nature-penetrating imagination, not a mystery-piercing or a God-piercing one.

However, a deep idea in the world is that there is something beyond it; a deep look at appearance will see right through it that there is something behind or beyond the realm of appearance; an idea as ancient and persistent as man is that there are ultimate mysteries beyond our mortality, that God exists, that there may be life after death. One generation of men rules that there can be no life on any other planet, another generation holds that the mathematical probabilities are that there must be life beyond what we can see. There are notions of eternal recurrence in Oriental religions, the notion of Redemption in Christianity. If these ideas are true, if reality is not in appearances, but must include what does not appear, and if reason is not the highest faculty of man, but intuition is, then we are at liberty to adjust the value we set on Frost's poetry according to our own most intimate values.

Societies have a natural way of preserving their own images in literature. Frost is one of the vital poetic spokesmen of our time. Our society and our culture are sufficiently like his presentation of the meaning of life so that many Americans can read him with conviction.

Robert Frost is large in scope. He teaches us courage in the face of the enigmas of existence. We feel that he wears no mask and speaks the truth directly, and that his truth, if not the whole truth, is worthy of our serious, steadfast, and continuing love.

Remarks on Auden

The death of Auden shocked me because only recently at the London Poetry International '73, from June 25 to 30, I thought he looked better than he had when I last saw him in this country some time ago. I am now glad that I saw him and spoke with him on several occasions during the literary week. He was urbane, kindly, and intelligent as ever, a civilized man.

In the Thirties he became a prime spokesman for a new feeling of those times. He was linked with a group, his name being followed by Spender, Day-Lewis, and MacNeice. As decades passed, Auden stood out as amazingly productive in poetry, essays, reviews, and as librettist. He became a monumental figure, leaving England to live in America from 1939 and becoming an American citizen. Yet his voice was always English, and he was no more American than Eliot was British, who left our shores to become a prime literary figure in England.

As time passed it appeared that Auden best represented the Thirties in poetry, and although he kept on writing remarkably until the end, he did not uniquely capture the spirit of his later decades.

He mated with his times, though, as I think of his whole life, rather than being prophetic. Few poets are prophetic. Hopkins was one of these, who wrote in the nineteenth century but speaks directly to us in the twentieth, as Blake had been prophetic earlier.

I do not think of Auden as speaking to the future, but he will mainly be studied in the future, I suggest, as a master of form and feeling of an earlier part of this century. He had a generalized and even-tempered sensibility. He could not have been as howling as "Howl," nor could he have been as solemn as Eliot sometimes was. He stood grandly in

First published in *Harvard Advocate* 108, nos. 2–3 (1974).

the middle of things, yet would not have liked the word "grand," which has a Miltonic ring, being plainer and more like Dryden than Milton.

When he last read at Dartmouth in Spaulding a few years ago, we had a bottle of wine for dinner. Wystan always liked wine. He asked me if we could have another bottle. Fortunately there was another bottle in the house. There was a flannel effect. When he stood up to read he was flannel mouthed. His words were thick, slow, and low. My wife had the daring to stand up in the packed hall and ask him, after a painful few minutes, to speak directly into the microphone. This shook off his drowse, he did so, and the rest of the reading was sprightly, memorable, well communicated.

I cannot remember when I first met Auden, but it was in New York and he was with another Englishman, maybe Isherwood. He seemed amazing to me. He looked like a clown but talked like a sage.

It was my pleasure to ask Francis Parkman, the headmaster of St. Mark's School, where I was teaching, if he would invite him up to teach for a while. Auden came and stayed about five weeks. He was open throated and always wore slippers. He enchanted the boys by his teaching. It was Spring, 1939. He drank a lot of tea and had books sprawled over the floor. He was always picking books up off the floor to read or refer to, which seemed strange and un-American. He was writing his early poems and would change a line on the instant if you suggested it and what you suggested seemed better. I think I watched him write "Voltaire at Ferney." He was lively and high spirited, very much alive, well mannered in a friendly British way.

He always sat on my right when I sat at the head of a table in the dining hall. After a time I tried to get him to sit with other masters, but he did not. He was rather shy. One time toward the end, I recall it was on a Sunday morning, he placed a small round white pill at the top of my plate. I rejected it, saying I had no need of drugs. He said they gave him a lift of several hours every morning. It was benzedrine. How innocent we were in those days! I thought it was some terrible drug.

Decades passed. I recall Auden coming to Washington for the Kennedy inauguration. Hundreds of artists of all kinds were there. I remember sitting almost directly across from the Kennedy stand in front of the White House on the chilly, windy day. Beside us were Auden and a cousin of my wife's family, Fritz Gynrod, an opera singer from Germany who had escaped Hitler and who was somewhat the same size and shape as Auden. They were both Europeans. When our marchers came around into Pennsylvania Avenue, both men remarked on how badly the American military turned corners.

Each said his country was much better at marching. (Also, as many hundreds filed by, for some strange reason many lost their rubbers. When the parade ended, the street was strewn with rubbers which had come off.)

I remember how cold the thighs of the young girls looked in their scanty costumes, girls from the South braving the chilly day. Most remarkable of all was a Western cowboy type, a man maybe fifty, who approached astride a buffalo. When he got within a hundred or two hundred feet of the Kennedys he spurred the bison, which charged. At the full pitch of the bison's tremendous effort the big cowboy doffed his big Texas hat to the President and Mrs. Kennedy, who responded with cheers and waves, immensely pleased, as were we all. Pure American!

That evening at our Georgetown house Auden, the only unmarried man, outdid himself in good will, bustling in the kitchen to help bring in things for the dinner. Everybody was happy; we thought it the dawn of a new bright time for America. I cannot recall who all was there, but I recall Tate and Lowell, and Katherine Anne Porter, who came with Madame Perkins, the founder of social security, and a lady friend who had been the first woman to go with Shaw to Russia long ago. Katherine Anne said she had on only her little pink slippers and worried about the slush and ice of the streets in getting into the armory, where we all repaired for one of the large dances honoring the new President and his family. We luckily found a large booth in the packed hall, replete with champagne, and claimed it as our own. It was a gala night, and after midnight old Robert Frost stalked in and crossed the floor to sit with political dignitaries on a raised platform. But "Whizz," as I always called Auden from first knowing him, declined to come to the inaugural ball, requesting to remain in our house to read and rest. Katherine Anne dared more with her little pink slippers than Auden would with his sloppy big ones.

Robert Frost in the Clearing

At the London Poetry International '73 last summer I felt a rich sense of our mother tongue in poetry in Britain, the deep and long love the English have for poetry, their sensitivity to it, its naturalism to them. I thought of Frost starting there, and of my own beginning at Cambridge. Last fall, invited to say something about Robert Frost, I fell into a long mood of doubt and criticism of Frost. What did he have to say to us in 1973, ten years after his death?

What I objected to was little overt joy, little despair or anguish, no feverish exaltations or airy graces, little heightening of the senses, no profound humility, no religious ecstasy or tantalizing ambiguities, and in the form of verse itself no experiment.

I felt that he was much too controlled, much too staid, afraid to let himself go, much too classical. And in 1973 I felt that he had not spoken on the problems of our age but was already a classic poet of the past, best enjoyed beyond contemporary confrontations, best known in timeless configurations, a kind of absolutist of the natural soul. He did not like the Roosevelt administration but would not use poetry as politics to take sides against the New Deal. He would not write a poem against Roosevelt. Last year he probably would not have written a poem against Nixon and Watergate. You couldn't come to him to learn how to behave in the present situation of our nation.

What was the matter with me was that I wanted Frost to be a Romantic, to be as wild and as original, say, as Hopkins, whereas he was a Classicist based on Latin and the rule of reason. I wanted more irrationality, more excitement, dangerous descent into the depths of the ego, more despair and humility, but Frost was too reasonable and wrote a middle-of-the-road poetry, not too far right or left. His poetry

First published in *The Southern Review* 11, no. 2 (Spring, 1975): 260–68.

has no high quiring or nervous lacerations of the spirit. It has no record of intolerable anguish. It has no dependence on mercy. He does not search the struggle of the lost soul for grace.

I kept on reading and I kept on doubting and finally seemed to conclude that Frost was too sane, too rational and rationally cunning, too proud, too ignorant of forgiveness, a managerial mind without excesses. Again, a man of classical balance and order, of strong natural harmonies in unelevated language, a man who is universal standing in the middle of the road viewing good and evil, not taking sides, a man with an Olympian view keeping his cool, never being outrageous or outraged, too strong to give in to weakness, never able to shout or loudly protest, keeping control of everything by control of niceties, a man so calm and worldly as never to be defeated by anything in the world, equal to the world and able to manage it as it is by acts of will.

It is interesting to me that I felt this way about Frost in 1973, because I never felt that way about him before.

It must have been due to the extraordinary governmental break-downs of honesty which induced an irrationality to think that our great poets can save us. While I said above that he was not irrational enough, I now counter my irrational claim that his poetry could save us, believing this a false claim although maintained by Arnold of poetry, as you will recall.

What I have said above I should take back in face of the monumental reality of Frost's poetry and truth. What is the use of criticism? My criticism of Frost does not change his words on paper nor a consensus of his excellence held throughout the Western world. I can say that Hardy's "Under the Waterfall" is better than his "Directive" because the language of the former is crisper, there is originality of style in the insets, there is artistry in the fact that only at the end do you know the poem is spoken by the woman, and because of the tenderness of the emotion, and say that Frost's poem lacks something in the com- parison, but this is only an opinion and a point of taste. And if I ad- mire the originality of style, of stanzas in Hardy's "Convergence of the Twain," also the bleak doctrine he enounces, comparisons are odious and you can find plenty to admire in Frost. I may carp at a lack of tenderness in Frost, and a lack of gaiety, but he is such a large figure that you can find a whole world, his whole world, in him.

He was so much older than I was that, although I saw a good deal of him from after World War II, the generation gap precluded real friendship. Yet this must not be the answer, because I enjoyed real friendship with Stevens, only five years his junior, and with Williams, also an elder when I knew him. At any rate, I held a conventional view widely held of Frost's charm, amiability, kindliness, and keenness of mind and personality. I never saw any other side of him except in a few instances and was shocked at the dire view of him taken by Lawrance Thompson in his second book of biography.

I recall, though, at a Dartmouth reading late in life that he spied a student sleeping about halfway back in the audience while he was reading. He pointed his finger at him and called out harshly for him to wake up. This startled the audience as well as the student. It was a cruel gesture for an admired elder to make. After the reading the student came up to him and said that he was not asleep but that, as some like to enjoy music with eyes closed, he liked to enjoy poetry with his eyes closed. Instead of showing humility in the face of this truth, the arrogant Mr. Frost brushed the matter aside as if to protect his vanity.

I also recall an error in his thinking at one of those last meetings when he posited that Western culture began in Greece and went ever northwestward. He announced that civilization and culture went northwest to Europe and the British Isles, then crossed the water and came happily to rest on his own native New England. He did not think to project his missile farther, and if he had it would have landed on Communist China and Communist Russia. He was not prepared for such an eventuality but I never could guess why he had not thought of it. Some have talked of his chauvinism, his narrow New Englandism or Americanism, and indeed it may be that these limitations, his inability to take a world view, were parts of what denied him the Nobel Prize.

He was taken by the high tide of the Kennedy inauguration and ended his preliminary history in rhyme on these last two lines: "A golden age of poetry and power/ Of which this noonday's the beginning hour." These assertions, including the cliche the "golden age," do not read well today. Indeed, they do not seem worthy of the best thought of Robert Frost.

The day after the inauguration we met Frost at the Coxes for cocktails near our house in Georgetown. He had been to see the President alone that morning. I asked him immediately and rather excitedly what President Kennedy said. He came back immediately, saying, "I did all the talking." This was a stroke of his best and characteristic wit, but he did not go on to say what he had said to the President, and there would have been no point in asking him.

In dealing with a poet as massive and "rich with gifts, alone" as Frost, I want to narrow speculation down to *In the Clearing*, his last book, published in 1962, a year before his death, and to speak only of certain poems and ideas in this book, as if by noting what a man said latest in life one could come close to some ultimate nature of his thought. It may be a false premise, but is worth a try.

What I want to wrestle with is whether he was a Christian, what he felt about life after death, what he felt about God. There is more in Frost about God than about Christ, to whom or about whom he had little to say. But he did say something, guardedly, in a letter to Mrs. G. Roy Alliott dictated from the hospital shortly before his death on January 29, 1963. Here is a part of the letter:

> Why will the quidnuncs always be hoping for a salvation man will never have from anyone but God? I was just saying today how Christ posed Himself the whole problem and died for it. How can we be just in a world that needs mercy and merciful in a world that needs justice. We study and study the four biographies of Him and are left still somewhat puzzled in our daily lives. Marking students in a kind of mockery and laughing it off. It seems as if I never wrote these plunges into the depths to anyone but you.

Note how typically Classical and guarded he is. He says Christ posed the whole problem and died for it, but he does not say that His is the final word, and he does not say that he goes over to Christ as a believer. Instead, note the Classical balance of the sentence, "How can we be just in a world that needs mercy and merciful in a world that needs justice." To write this sentence takes control and balance of mind, qualities at the heart of Frost's thought. Frost is a pugnacious man, often dreaming of something beyond the show of appearances but never willing to systematize his dreamings by joining them with any established religious system. He is always individualistic, embedded in the limitations of the human condition. But how far will he go?

There are two poems in *In the Clearing* which show how far he went. The first is only two lines long. It says

> Forgive, O Lord, my little jokes on Thee
> And I'll forgive Thy great big one on me.

When I first read this I was startled and thought it a kind of blasphemy, but later on I had to take it as perhaps he would wish, as itself a kind of joke, to be enjoyed but not taken too heavily, to be enjoyed lightly. Again, it has a Classical balance of ideation. It is an "if" proposition. If you will do something for me, I will do something for you. It does not admit that God is supreme and greater than man. It talks to God man to man. These two lines show Frost reasoning, not writing out of abject humility. The great big joke God plays on man is to hold a veil against total knowledge. Behind the lines is the admission that God has a final secret or secrets man does not or cannot know, yet Frost will not defer to God but invites him into a partnership. If you will forgive my little jokes on you, I will forgive your great big one on me. He wants a dialogue in which man is on a par with God. The suggestion of the "if" proposition is that only if this is so can there be any forgiveness on either side.

As I said, when I first read this I was startled. I now consider it a possible poetic device for speculation and one of truth for Robert Frost.

The other poem is longer, twenty-four lines, entitled "Away!" It has a beautiful look on the page, Classically controlled short lines rhymed regularly ab/ab.

When I first read this, I thought it was blasphemous. He makes a playful turn about Adam and Eve "Put out of the Park." Then he says to forget the myth. This is explicit. He has got over one of the great myths of mankind. But then what? There is serenity in the next four lines, wherein he expresses a harmonious sense of being human, not being put out with or by anybody. There follow four poetic lines. Unless he is wrong, which suggests that he is not, he only obeys the urge of a song, "I'm—bound—away!" with helpful dashes between the three words to slow them down and reach us into some kind of momentary dreamy association.

The shocker comes in the last four lines. In these lines he arrogates to himself power usually accorded to God. He thinks he is God and gives himself the audacity to determine life or death. Frost will announce and determine his own fate, he will not let God do it. He says that, if he is dissatisfied with what he learns from having died, he may return from beyond death to this life, something no man has done. (I leave out Christ here, as Frost is not talking about Christ but about God.) Readers will recall an early poem stating that earth is the best place for love, he doesn't know where it would go better.

Again, let me say that when I first encountered this poem I thought it was blasphemous. Now, aside from the aesthetic merits of the make of the poem, I accede to the notion that any poet can talk about God this way if he wants to, and as Frost was urged to do so at the end of his life, we are invited to accept his ideas if we wish to.

I did not think I would stand here arguing for Frost in this connection, yet I am compelled by reason to do so. Since man does not know the ultimate secrets or meaning of God, that is, by reason, and if reason is the strongest thing in Frost, stronger than any devotional feeling for any established religious system, why is it not quite human, even humane, for him to praise the living, life itself, and deny death by saying that he may come back from it to the living if he wishes to? I do not think it is the greatest idea in the world (Christ's is much more mysterious, challenging, and unresolvable) yet it is Frost's own idea, a unique perception after living long, and perhaps it even took courage to come by and to write into a poem.

Let me be clear. I do not believe that man is greater than God. I believe that God is greater than man. I do not believe that man can come back from the dead whether he wishes to or not. Nobody has done so thus far, as far as I know. Yet I come to the conclusion that we ought to prize a poet for stating this, rather than condemning him for blasphemy, since he honestly felt it, and probably meant us to take the whole poem in some sort of playful way as well.

Probably the poem should be taken as a fantasy, a myth itself. In this same book Frost says, "It takes all sorts of in- and outdoor schooling/ To get adapted to my kind of fooling." So, he was just fooling around with ideas, this one outrageous, untrue to the nature of things, but why not employ imagination and imagine anything? And why not give him a palm for trying to do the impossible, which poets often try to do, in this case for man himself to try to overcome death?

Wallace R. Alstom of Agnes Scott College writes, on October 6, 1963, "So far as the Church is concerned, obviously Frost had little place for it in his life. He often poked a bit of fun at churches and preachers, but it was harmless enough. He said last January [January, 1962]: 'Eliot is more churchy than I am, but I am more religious than Eliot.' "

Alstom goes on to say something that has a bearing on the poem we have been talking about. He writes, "When I shook hands with Robert Frost on his eighty-eighth birthday, he said to me that he had been so ill in Miami after leaving Agnes Scott that he had peeped in to see what it looked like in the 'great Beyond.' Then he added in characteristic fashion, 'I like it better here; I turned around and decided to come back.' "

Before leaving *In the Clearing* here are a few observations I would like to make.

In "One More Brevity," about a stray dog "Gustie, old boy, Dalma-

tian Gus" who comes in, leaves the next morning, the imagination of
the poet thinks of him as "Sirius/ The star itself—Heaven's greatest
star,/ Not a meteorite, but an avatar" come to call. He ends,

> A symbol was all he could hope to convey,
> An intimation, a shot of ray,
> A meaning I was supposed to seek,
> And finding, wasn't disposed to speak.

This shows Frost's ability to believe something unlikely, his doubt,
and his sly, characteristic ending that he won't tell everything.

In "Accidentally on Purpose" he thinks about Darwin, saying, "We
were just purpose coming to a head."

> Whose purpose was it. His or Hers or Its?
> Let's leave that to the scientific wits.
> Grant me intention, purpose, and design—
> That's near enough for me to the Divine.
>
> And yet for all this help of head and brain
> How happily instinctive we remain,
> Our best guide upward further to the light,
> Passionate preference such as love at sight.

And here is an admonition, in "A Concept Self-Conceived":

> The latest creed that has to be believed
> And entered in our childish catechism
> Is that the All's a concept self-conceived,
> Which is no more than good old Pantheism.
>
> Great is the reassurance of recall.
> Why go on further with confusing voice
> To say God's either All or over all?
> The rule is, never give a child a choice.

In "Kitty Hawk" we receive a notion he talked about in his late
lectures and readings, the idea of spirit descending into matter:

> But God's own descent
> Into flesh was meant
> As a demonstration
> That the supreme merit
> Lay in risking spirit
> In substantiation.

And where I said above that if culture went northwest from Greece
through Rome, France, and England to our country, but that he did
not carry the line on to China and Russia, he actually has a chauvinis-

tic turn in "The Leap—the Leap!": "It belonged to US, / Not our friends the Russ."

Perhaps I could end on notes of his strong self-identity. In "Auspex" he ends:

> I have remained resentful to this day
> When any but myself presumed to say
> That there was anything I couldn't be.

And the last poem in the book, "In the Winter Woods," reads as follows:

> In winter in the woods alone
> Against the trees I go.
> I mark a maple for my own
> And lay the maple low.
>
> At four o'clock I shoulder ax,
> And in the afterglow
> I link a line of shadow tracks
> Across the tinted snow.
>
> I see for Nature no defeat
> In one tree's overthrow
> Or for myself in my retreat
> For yet another blow.

Perhaps I may end on a poem of my own entitled "Worldly Failure."

> I looked into the eyes of Robert Frost
> Once, and they were unnaturally deep,
> Set far back in the skull, as far back in the earth.
> An oblique glance made them look even deeper.
>
> He stood inside the door on Brewster Street,
> Looking out. I proffered him an invitation.
> We went on talking for an hour and a half,
> To accept or not to accept was his question,
>
> Whether he wanted to meet another poet;
> He erred in sensing some intangible slight.
> Hard for him to make a democratic leap.
> To be a natural poet you have to be unnaturally deep.
>
> While he was talking he was looking out,
> But stayed in, sagacity better indoors.
> He became a metaphor for inner devastation,
> Too scared to accept my invitation.

I have entitled this paper "Robert Frost in the Clearing." Now that we have seen how definite his ideas were on certain topics, principally on coming back from the dead, I perhaps should have named it "Robert Frost in the Clear." As to his thinking: Frost is the only poet who could think to say that *homo sapiens* is the only animal who could think to think.

Reflections on Wallace Stevens in 1976

It is rather dangerous for me to read Wallace Stevens in 1976; it would have been better in 1956. I felt him to be the large general mentor of the times, whom I looked up to as commanding the scene. I took comfort in this. I knew my man and believed in the excellence and durability of his stance. To me it was a high artistic position comporting with an acceptance of an America it represented. Having suffered T. S. Eliot and living in the surround of Eliot for decades, as had those of my generation, it was a distinct refreshment of taste to transfer to Stevens one's beliefs and wishes. He was above the battle, while happily engrossed daily in the business of business. There was this secure moment, a moment of a few years, when Stevens satisfied the capacity to live with belief within a sophisticated poetry. It seemed to have everything: the serious, the grand, the concise, temperamental extravaganzas, periods made memorable by fantastic grammar, a love of this world seen through a repetitious philosophy, a sinister darkness still with the power to charm, a colorful grotesquerie with the skill not to abate interest. His poetry succumbed to endless resources to overcome itself. He overwhelms sensory predicaments by tactile arrangements of style without overwhelming the substratum of sheer and embroidered intelligence. He could write problem poems like "The Emperor of Ice Cream" and the "Anecdote of the Jar," but he was not limited to anthology exercises and could walk and ramble through miles of Stevens territory in his long poems which never dragged foot. He was my specialist of the exquisite, the refined, and he was my expert in the grand, the noble, the generous, a poet of large statements and design. He was as readable as his handwriting was unreadable. One wanted to go on reading and reading, making the

First published in *The Southern Review* 12, no. 3 (1976): 417–18.

Stevens voyage into infinities of metaphors and tropes, a great health of the spirit. I thought he represented America at its best.

Now we have to look at Stevens in another way. Unlike Frost, he did not woo college presidents, college audiences, or a President of the United States. He would not have been asked to go to Russia to meet Krushchev. He did not get to Europe, although he spied out French paintings and had them sent here. He engaged in long letters, writing to persons in South America and India, and he and I exchanged thirty-five letters during our friendship in the last eight years of his life. Wallace Stevens stuck close to the office and went his accustomed ways. He was embedded in materialistic America and lived well, while not trying to become a millionaire. I do not see his nature as schizoid and feel that his dictum about a worst thing being not to live in a physical world comported with going to work every day. Poetry was another kind of work. He made up poems while walking to work and had his secretary put them in order when he got to the office. For all the florid nature of his poems, they were natural, not Poe-tortured, and he seemed so normal, even tempered, and robust that you would not imagine him jumping off a boat like Hart Crane.

The times changed, and now is a different time. Stevens is ensconced in the Huntington Library. He was part of America, while I lived in his work and relished his poetry as the main poetic statement. It is good that our country produced William Carlos Williams at the same time, more closely allied to city life, to objectivity, to an infinite variety of people in his works. It is a matter of taste which of these two one prefers. To me it is splendid that we have both, that a democracy produced both poets, and that there are other major claimants on our attention as well.

What we need now is a poetry of the people, a poetry to represent the wilderness of new feelings we have in this turbulent time, perhaps a prophetic poetry to tell us where we will go or may be going as a nation. Poetry appears in subtle ways and for various reasons. In 1976 Stevens represents a part of the American poetry scene of the past quarter-century or more, but maybe what we yearn for is less nobility, less imaginative detachment from society; maybe we want a man as big as the continent we live on, a Walt Whitman or his like, a poet of universal, not particular, consciousness. But Stevens was universal in his way, too.

PART THREE

An Interview *(Shenandoah)*

The scene was Undercliff, Cape Rosier, Maine, where the Eberharts spend vivid, extrovert summers. It was my first meeting with Richard Eberhart, with whom I had corresponded for several years: I was spending a torrid summer (torrid by Dublin standards, anyway) teaching poetry and drama at Harvard. I arrived at Bar Harbor, dressed as if I were looking for a job in an advertising agency; Eberhart met me, dressed exactly right for such a marine occasion, all windswept and open chested. Despite such incongruities, we had a fine time.

But the incongruities persisted in the interview. I wanted to push things; he insisted (rightly) on the mysteriousness of the whole poetic business. I wanted to bring other poets into our discussion; he said (rightly) that the poetry he knew most intimately was his own. I sometimes tempted myself to drag in Big Questions; he preferred (rightly) Little Facts. I'm not sure what the interview proves. I gave him his head and he ran on merrily.

Interviewer: It is particularly appropriate that we should discuss poetry in general and your poems in particular here at Undercliff, the title of one of your books of poems, because you are very much a poet devoted to time and place and specific occasion.

Eberhart: Well, that may be so, but I think poetry is a mysterious business. As you know, I have been writing poetry for a long time now, ever since the late Twenties. I wouldn't have held so much twenty years ago that I was a poet of place in your sense, but since World War II we have been coming up here to Maine and going to the same place, and I have derived several poems from this specific re-

First published in *Shenandoah* 15, no. 4 (Summer, 1964): 6–29. The interviewer is Denis Donoghue.

gion that would not have been written but for the place in which they were engendered.

Interviewer: Yes; and I wonder if this is perhaps the result of a larger commitment to the whole human condition of which place and time are manifestations.

Eberhart: I would like to think so, but I must say I'm open-minded about poetry, and I think a poet can do anything that he can do, to state it that way. It is a highly imaginative, subjective operation as far as I am concerned, and always has been. My first book, *A Bravery of Earth,* which came out in 1930, was in a sense a large place poem because it took a voyage around the world as its total emplacement. Yet, I was trying to make the distinction between the spiritual subjectivity of poetry, in me at least, and the fact that it comes from some complexities that are not totally understood and it resolves these complexities in some way. The whole process has always seemed to me mysterious, and through the years I have come to have definite notions about what I think poetry is and what my poetry in particular is. For instance, I believe in what some people, I am sure, would think an old-fashioned notion, the idea of poetry as a matter of inspiration. This is an unpopular view, yet it seems to me that it has been true of me almost from the start, that in a sense a poem is a gift of the gods, a laying on of hands, and that when you write sometimes the poem is dictated to you. Not quite in the Yeatsian way, I don't believe—I haven't played around with Madame Blavatsky in the way that he did; I don't mean it quite in that sense—but it is something beyond rationality. The fire of it is a potent force which is given to you and in which the personality is held in abeyance, and the personality is a vehicle for the utterance of the poem. Some of my best poems—some that have lasted now for decades—have been given in this way and they have been emitted in a high state of consciousness and control and one has not had to change a word, or maybe only a word or two. This seems to me strange from a prosaic point of view, so that the writing of poetry is entirely different from the writing of prose. Now, to get back to the matter of place. I was opposing these ideas to that, because if you believe in inspiration, I don't think the idea of place would be so important. On the other hand, poetry is a house of many mansions. There are all sorts of poems, one writes different kinds of poems, one changes with the years, and I notice in my work that since World War II I've become more objective in some ways. I think that is tied in to the commitment of place, to a central place.

Interviewer: More objective; but you don't mean this to repudiate what some readers would call your early romanticism?

Eberhart: No, not at all. It's just the difference of approach, I think.

Interviewer: Well, what does it mean, objective? Do you mean that the commitment is more to the human events themselves than to significances which you are prepared to "declare"?

Eberhart: Yes, perhaps. For instance, in my new book I have two poems which are character sketches. I got excited when these poems were "given to me," when I had them, when they were presented to me and I wrote them. One is called "A New England Bachelor," which is a character study, and the other one is called "A Maine Roust-about," which is about an old Maine character. I was pleased that I was enabled to write poems about specific persons.

Interviewer: These were stories; specific people.

Eberhart: They were not literally transcripts of true lives, but they were based on real lives, you see, and I thought at once, oh how marvelous, if I could only write twenty of these, I would have a new dimension to my poetry and I would have a book of what I would call Objective Verse, and it wouldn't be as subjective and personal and individualistic as my lyrics have tended to be throughout the years.

Interviewer: Is this a desire to write dramatic monologs?

Eberhart: Ah, now you are touching on something very real. Yes, there was a period in my life—I can pinpoint it at 1950—when I had a tremendous urge to break away from everything I had done before, that is the lyric principally, any kind of poems that might come under the lyric utterance, and to embrace mankind and see if I could make studies of character in poetry, and, of course, that meant the attempt to write verse plays. You have been good to me in devoting a chapter to my plays in your book *The Third Voice*. As you know, we had a theater in Cambridge, the Poets' Theater, which was very lively and a viable thing for a few years. There was this attempt to enlarge the domain of poetry, that is within my limits, I'm talking just about myself now, not about American poetry in general, or poetry in general.

Interviewer: Yes. Of course, you have always been a poet of the large theme. Do you feel that poetry should commit itself to the large theme, the worldwide preoccupation; war, for example?

Eberhart: I love to talk with you, but I am not a dogmatist and I have no dogmas. Maybe that is my dogma. So I think perhaps this is true, but on the other hand I believe a poet—again, to go back to an old cliché—can do anything he can do. But certainly in maturity, after you have had your first years and your first flings at it, if you have something to say you must entertain the whole of mankind. You must entertain the great problems, and it's only in the last few years that I have become aware that poetry must in a sense engage political ideas. I wouldn't have held this twenty-five years ago. I was very much in one sense the Cambridge University or the Harvard Ivory Tower poet. But as one lives, one wants to cope with larger ideas. You mentioned war; well, yes, when I was in World War II, as you know, two or three poems came out of it that are read to this day, principally "The Fury of Aerial Bombardment." That was an attempt to say something about the totality of war. And then, certainly, poetry must engage the reality of its time. As a matter of fact, it can do no other, unless it wants to put its head in the sand.

Interviewer: Yes. And am I right in recalling a time when you rebuked Wallace Stevens for not tackling the big themes, the great preoccupations?

Eberhart: I can't remember I ever did that. Maybe I did. I can't remember everything I have said. I would think it rather unlikely because I have always adored Wallace Stevens and been very much devoted to him, and I would say paradoxically that from your point of view he has engaged the great themes. He has engaged the greatest theme of all, from his point of view, the theme of imagination. He has made imagination itself his hero, and he has written magnificent poems to glorify the scintillating state of the imagination. So, I'd think that was the great theme, but I know you mean it on a more worldly level. There are many people who couldn't read Wallace Stevens, because they wouldn't think he related to their lives in any way. That is true, he was a high poet, and he was a university-type poet, I suppose.

Interviewer: Many people would ask: Does this man vote for the world or not? After all, a great Stevens poem like "Notes toward a Supreme Fiction" moves engagingly and beautifully, but as soon as you turn away from it you find all kinds of things are happening; famines, wars, fears; and many readers are disengaged from the poem because it has nothing to say directly about these things.

Eberhart: This is all fascinating to me. It depends upon what you think poetry is, and what it should do, and also it depends upon who you are, what is your state of education and sophistication. Certainly it is as bad to be overly sophisticated, I presume, about poetry as it is to be ignorant of it.

Interviewer: Yes, but think of the current situation in American poetry; clearly, many young poets who were influenced by Wallace Stevens are now turning much more, I think, toward a poet like William Carlos Williams to find a much more strenuous engagement with actual people, an actual world situation, what I have already called, in your case, a commitment to people in place and time. This change seems to me very important. I think to many poets Stevens's values are thin, and the more committed poet, like Williams, is becoming more important. Or, to put it bluntly, more "useful."

Eberhart: What you say is true, and yet in England and Ireland, too, I gather, William Carlos Williams has never received his due, is hardly considered at all, whereas more people read Wallace Stevens. How do you account for this?

Interviewer: I'm not at all sure that I know. You see, the kind of thing I have in mind is that passage in "Paterson Five" where suddenly Williams turns away from his theme and describes an entirely anonymous woman walking down a street in Rutherford, New Jersey. He describes her vividly, but with no claim at all to intimacy or recognition, and he says that it is for her that he has written all his poems. Now, it is that sudden humane acknowledgment which is terribly important in Williams, and the importance of it, I think, will be more and more recognized, but there is nothing like it in Stevens.

Eberhart: I agree to that, yes. When Stevens, for instance, attempted to write plays, you know how poorly he did; he had practically nothing, his efforts were inconsequential. But as a rejoinder, I would like to say how splendid I think it is that America has both of these poets, and I cannot get over the ideas of dichotomy, ambivalence, and irony, and all these ambiguities, and all these absolutes that have been with me all my life. I think it is marvelous that America has produced these poets. We have both of these poets, we have both points of view, I happen to have been friends with both of them and admired them both very much.

Interviewer: Of course, it is not a matter of giving alphas to Williams and betas to Stevens. But, I think there is a point where you have to vote on a very large issue; namely, are you *for* the human world?

Eberhart: Ah, yes.

Interviewer: In some sense you have to vote, and I think your own later poetry will drag you over to my side. After all, think how warmly you have committed yourself in your poems to certain large terms. A term like love, for example. I'm thinking now of a very recent poem of yours, "A Commitment," where you say, "Love is long and art is good to stitch the time." It is this pouring of the feeling into a large term such as love; this kind of commitment seems to be terribly important.

Eberhart: I believe that these great topics of which you speak are still available and that they are the central ones for poets. I find it difficult to talk about poetry because I know a lot about myself, I think, in my own psyche, and what I want to do and can't do. But I find it difficult to be a critic, that is to try to speak for poetry in general or for the state of American poetry. I would say, for instance, that some of these great topics are birth, hope, love, and there are ideas of evil and hatred, and death. You will notice that in the history of English poetry there have been more great poems about death than there have been about birth. You think of Milton's poem "Nativity"—but how many? A little poem by Blake—but how many? Isn't it interesting that, for instance, birth is positive, life-giving, death is negative and life-taking-away, and yet death transports the imagination of a poet much more than birth. I believe that only good poems last, and man only retains through the centuries, or through the decades, poems that are moral. This is a point that you can argue about, but we do not save poems that do not speak deeply to man and that he does not want to keep, what I would call immoral poems, which I call bad poems. He wants to keep the good poems and the good poems are more often about love, it seems to me, which is a positive thing, however complex and subtle, than poems about hate, for instance, or evil.

Although I must say that as much as anyone I admire deeply someone like Baudelaire, who had a great deal to say about evil and hatred and decadence.

Interviewer: Is it that the reader wants the poems to comfort him in his affliction, and love is an infinitely more comforting commitment than hate?

Eberhart: Well, yes. I think hate opens your eyes violently in poetry to things you already know, but it isn't as good for you.

Interviewer: But hatred will sharpen the blade of the mind, and that is about all it will do.

Eberhart: Yes. On the other hand, the worst thing about poetry I suppose is sentimentality. You have to be careful when you talk about love poetry. There is not so much pure love poetry after all. Maybe "The Phoenix and the Turtle" is one of the best love poems in the language and yet it is a hard, intellectual, metaphysical poem. Incidentally, William Carlos Williams in his last years, you know, wrote some of the best love poetry we have in American poetry, I think.

Interviewer: In *Pictures from Brueghel*?

Eberhart: Well, in the one before that, too.

Interviewer: The Desert Music.

Eberhart: Yes. And *Journey to Love,* marvelous love poems written by a man in his seventies. This gives one a great deal of comfort about the possibilities of mankind. Whenever I get too cynical or too pessimistic,

I think of things like that. For instance, that a man could write his greatest love poems in the mid-seventies. Just as Titian painted one of his great nudes when he was eighty-five, I believe.

Interviewer: Yes, but why should this be surprising? In one's eighties, I take it, the world has narrowed down and we retain only what we need.

Eberhart: But usually it's fallen apart if you haven't been long in the ground before that.

Interviewer: I'm thinking now of several poems; indeed, from Undercliff, where we are this morning, especially I think of poems like "The Human Being Is a Lonely Creature." I think this is a very characteristic poem of yours; or a poem perhaps not quite so characteristic in its title anyway, "On the Fragility of Mind."

Eberhart: I rather like that other one.

Interviewer: It's a good one, but would you be prepared to enlarge on it, do you feel that the mind is utterly fragile?

Eberhart: Well, I don't; I remember writing that poem and feeling that way, and that was written quite a few years ago. Yes, I think this has become a rather persistent theme of mine, now, a deep feeling in me that the mind is not enough. Most poets are so intellectual, yet poetry isn't an entirely intellectual operation, it depends upon perception and intelligence and adjudication, delicate perceptions of weights and balances, depends upon vision in a physical way. Wallace Stevens once told me, when we were driving from Hartford to the canoe club where he took me to lunch—he said, in our profession you have to have the eyes. I thought that was very nice.

Interviewer: And he meant what? I take it he meant what Blake meant by vision?

Eberhart: Yes, he didn't say not through, you know, through the eyes. He didn't make it as specific as that; I think he meant it in a physical sense. You see, he belonged very much to the physical world, he believed in the sensuous world, and I think he really meant that you couldn't afford to be blind to be a poet, you can't be a blind poet, and yet there is the theory of blind Homer, and I'm against Stevens in this to some extent, because in a metaphorical way I have a poem just recently to say in "The World Situation" which came out in *Encounter* in April, I think it is, that there is the paradoxical idea that it is only when you are blind that you see best. I don't mean this in a literal, I mean it in a metaphorical way. But the idea has become strong in me as I've grown older, say after the age of fifty, that the mind is not enough, and whether the critics like it or not, poetry has to be an engagement of the whole personality, the whole being you know, the heart is quite as important as the head. But I wouldn't say either is more important. I think it's the whole suffering, living, breathing organism that must work on the world and make a poem if it can.

Interviewer: Well, then, is this an answer to one of the leading assumptions of our own time, that the mind is good enough, that it will do everything that has to be done?

Eberhart: Yes, I should say so. Of course, I wasn't really answering any philosopher in that, but yes, I certainly believe that.

Interviewer: How would a poem like "On the Fragility of Mind" be related to one of your earlier and, indeed, one of your most celebrated poems, "If I Could Only Live at the Pitch That Is Near Madness"? Isn't there a comment going both ways from these poems?

Eberhart: Well, yes, I think that "If I Could Only Live at the Pitch That Is Near Madness" is the better. It seems to me in retrospect (and now one is getting way up in the fifties, and one has retrospect, and it is a very fine thing to have; I never thought I would have it in the way that I do now) I can see that this poem epitomizes for me the 1930's. It was written in the heart of the depression years, which were fierce and hard. At that time I was a struggling poet and had hardly any, I had just started, you know, had no status. I didn't know where I was going or how good my poems were, whether they were good. I was in that state of almost total love, psychic violence, which most poets have for a long, long time. And this poem represents to me something that is deep in me, and I call it a Platonic poem. It has a Platonic idea. It's the idea that the child is the father of the man. It goes back to Wordsworth's "Ode on Intimations of Immortality from Recollections of Early Childhood." It has that idea, that when we were young at some point, I wouldn't know at what age to describe, we see the world in its pristine glory, and after that there is a falling off. I envisaged the Platonic idea as a great world soul, a cloud in the heavens, as it were, and when we are born, part of the world's soul is put upon our bodies, and the body and the soul go together. This is rather like the Christian concept. Then at death the soul goes back to the world soul, the body goes back to the earth. So, this is dealing in a lyrical, quick-tempoed way with these ideas, and then one had to resolve the poem, so you will see that the resolution is in the last four lines.

> I gave the moral answer and I died
> And into a realm of complexity came
> Where nothing is possible but necessity
> And the truth wailing there like a red babe.

Interviewer: Of course, you were later to think that a good deal more was possible than necessity, weren't you?

226

Eberhart: Yes, yes.

Interviewer: Indeed, as in "The Goal of Intellectual Man," where you speak of human love. You remember those stanzas—

> But it is human love, love
> Concrete, specific, in a natural move
> Gathering goodness, it is free
> In the blood as in the mind's harmony.
>
> It is love discoverable here
> Difficult, dangerous, pure, clear,
> The truth of the positive hour
> Composing all of human power.

How would these poems, then, be related to perhaps your most famous poem, "The Fury of Aerial Bombardment"? If, in keeping with our earlier theme, the mind is fragile, then what was the feeling behind "The Fury of Aerial Bombardment"?

Eberhart: I think the feeling behind it was a total engagement of the personality which was infuriated at the calamity of war. As you know, I was an aerial machine gunnery instructor in World War II and taught thousands of our young men to shoot out of aircraft at the enemy. I volunteered to serve because I believed in my country, but I always had a sense that the conscientious objectors who didn't wear the uniform had a deeper moral understanding of man than I did in condoning killing by belonging to the war, you see. But I taught many of these boys, and then all of a sudden, much too quickly, maybe in three weeks' time after they went off to the Pacific, their names would be posted as dead. One time this made me so gloomy, I remember sitting on the steps of a barracks in Dam Neck, Virginia—I have another poem called "Dam Neck, Virginia." In writing this poem, I should tell you that the poem is in the form, as I thought, of a prayer. It is three stanzas of asking questions, as it were, a prayer to God, and wondering how God could allow this to go on. Then I put the poem aside, and about two weeks later I read it over and thought it needed something added to it. This is one of the poems unlike the inspired ones that I told you about. So, in an entirely different frame of mind or state of being, not a passionate one at all, but in a cool, reflective mood, by reason and intellection, I composed the last four lines. It has always been interesting to me that the critics have said that it is the last four lines, especially the last line, that make this particularly a contemporary poem, and I also believe that if I hadn't added the last four lines that it probably wouldn't have gotten into anthologies at all. So, you see what fate is always hanging over poetry, and it's a fascinating sort of thing. One critic, my friend John Ciardi, wrote a long criticism of this poem in which he invented the idea that every poem has a fulcrum point, indeed, it may have fulcrum points, but each poem has a major point of balance, maybe, say, a hundred words on one side of the scale and only ten on the other, but it is balanced in some way, and he found the fulcrum point at the end of the third stanza, before the last four lines, and he made a very reasonable thing out of this, the weight as it were in this poem, the weight of the last four lines is equal, in a sense, to the first three stanzas, and he put it in a graphic way. In the book in which he printed this, *How Does a Poem Mean?*, he had a large diagram across the page in heavy ink, showing the fulcrum point, and then he went on in the most ingenious way to study this form. That was quite a fascinating idea.

Interviewer: In "The Fury of Aerial Bombardment" you are talking about two furies, aren't you? Fury is a word you use very frequently, I think, in that book. And there is, of course, the Platonic fury which you have praised in "If I Could Only Live at the Pitch That Is Near Madness." Do you see any relation between the two furies?

Eberhart: Well, you have posed a new question to me. No, I should have thought that the "If I . . ." was a good fury and the Moloch fury was the bad fury.

Interviewer: The pitch that is near madness?

Eberhart: Yes, that's a good fury. It's good to be at the pitch that is near madness. That's when you are nearest to the divine insight. The war experience had fury, but this is the absolute objective fury of destructiveness.

Interviewer: You wrote quite a number of poems arising from this situation, didn't you, poems like "At the End of the War," but again you are speaking to a God deemed indifferent. Did that question persist right into your later poems, or was it resolved through the great God-term, love?

Eberhart: Yes, I think that is more nearly correct. Obviously after the war I didn't write further war poems, and it is interesting in retrospect that "The Fury of Aerial Bombardment" has been anthologized and read by many people, whereas "At the End of the War" has not. If a student wishes to study these two poems, he could probably learn a lot about what we think in these days is poetry, in this connection. In other words, there is more artistry, probably, in "The Fury of Aerial Bombardment," there is more economy. The passion is more controlled, which I think should be a good thing, whereas the other is much more a direct outpouring; and then it is longer, too.

Interviewer: It's interesting also that the question you ask in "The Fury of Aerial Bombardment" is at least provisionally answered in "At the End of the War," especially in the last stanza where you pray.

Eberhart: Yes, it is about a man who has been doing massive killing, and now hopes somehow that it wouldn't have to be so in the future, but we know from the beginning, from the Garden of Eden and the Cain and Abel story, that there is no end to it short of the redemption of man. Man is always being redeemed but he never is redeemed. It is always a process of coming to that or trying to, getting away from the evils, and yet they are inherent in the human condition. The end of this poem says:

> May we learn humility
> May humility be insinuated
> More subtly than evil
> Which brought ruin rocking him
>
> May he turn the other cheek
> Not bitten yet by worm of hate
> May joy be his abandonment
> In Thy forgiveness early and late
>
> And may he learn not to fight
> And never to kill, but love,
> Never, never to kill, but love,
> May he see Thy holy light.

Interviewer: Are these basic terms—forgiveness and love—meant to have Christian meanings and overtones?

Eberhart: Well, yes, I think they are indeed. Yes.

Interviewer: And does this also apply to a term like "human"; is this word within any particular tradition?

Eberhart: No, I think that is a universal term, a Greek term. Not limited to what we call humanistic philosophy, or the humanistic studies. I meant it in an overall, general, large way that any English-speaking person could understand.

Interviewer: Isn't it strange that you are using Christian terms, and yet so differently from the way in which, shall we say, T. S. Eliot used the terms in "Four Quartets"? I think Mr. Eliot would regard many of your commitments as self-indulgent. You remember the passage where he talked about the humanist abstractions, the gifts reserved for age, and so on. Clearly, his vision of life is much bleaker than the one which is celebrated in your poems. This is partly what I meant by talking about the relations between poets like Williams and Stevens; I don't want to go back to this, but isn't there a sense in which even if poets do not compete, as Mr. Eliot has said, isn't there a sense in which there is a complicated dialog going on?

Eberhart: I think there is a large dialog going on, surely , but I believe that every poet is limited, nobody has a universal mind. There is no world poet; I wish there were. We had Dante, but I would say that Dante, in my idea, was limited to Catholicism. Now, you, I believe, are a Catholic, you probably wouldn't agree to this idea, but even Dante is limited to a certain set of ideas, a certain whole commitment of form and architecture of ideas. And Shakespeare for his so-called universality left something out of life. And Goethe, too. These three are often mentioned. So that poetry is possible because of its limitation. I admire the "Four Quartets," but I must say I am more moved by "Ash Wednesday" than I ever was by the "Four Quartets," and I think the reason is that "Ash Wednesday" is, in my opinion, a pure form, one of the great religious poems of the century; it moved me very deeply because of its lyrical quality, Now, you speak of his commitments. I think in the "Four Quartets" I dislike two things. One is their prosaic nature in comparison with "Ash Wednesday." They were more nearly like prose, the lines were flattened down. And second, I suppose, though I have not read them now for some time, but if I remember correctly, as with Eliot's work in general, it is so interlocked with technical Christian theology and dogma that I found this a blemish rather than a release.

Interviewer: You mean it has attenuated the poem rather than—

Eberhart: Yes, I would say that, for me. Other people probably don't find this. In comparison with my work you were just bringing up, I haven't thought of this, this is offhand, in other words just talking back and forth. But it seems to me that the twelve lines I have just read you here, when you talk about love and forgiveness, are more individualistic and they come right out of me as an individual. I find it difficult to give up the idea of individualism and to accept completely a system. Therefore, although this is not an occasion for theological discussion, I find it difficult to try to be a Christian as a poet, although I think I am, and not many of my colleagues are, you know, they are so intellectual most of them, and so there are few Christian poets; many of them are very much against it. They don't think Christianity is a subject for poetry, so I find that I am ambivalent, I wouldn't say that I am a totally Christian poet in some way. But I am with Blake in that way. I admire Blake very much for his individual stance. Everyone thinks of Blake as a Christian poet. He wanted to have Christianity his way. He wanted to make Jesus over into his own image of Jesus Christ as a man in society, and he wanted to bring it right down to the political level. That appeals to me. But he did not accept the church as such.

Interviewer: But also you are probably working on an assumption which I believe to be valid; namely, that if you are a Christian your words will have a Christian resonance or intonation no matter what you do about it. But if you use a term like "human" or "forgiveness," these terms will pick up a kind of Christian inflection, the Christian feeling will come over in the words anyway. "The Horse Chestnut Tree" is a humane poem, and it has no specific Christian references, but it moves very comfortably within a Christian setting, wouldn't you agree?

Eberhart: Well, I'm not so sure about that. It depends upon how you read it. It says in one line toward the end that we are "outlaws on God's property." Now this is more nearly an Old Testament poem than a New Testament one. It's more a Hebraic idea behind this poem than a Christian one.

Interviewer: Do you mean it to be like "The Fury of Aerial Bombardment," asking questions of a God indifferent to our purposes?

Eberhart: Yes. Incidentally, there is a story connected with this. This poem was written after the war when we were living in Cambridge, I think it was written in 1948, and was based on a real happening when troops of wild Irish boys, adolescent boys, would rush down Lake View Avenue in the fall, every fall it happened, and they would come into my father-in-law's garden and break down his great horse chestnut tree and throw sticks and stones and they were really very destructive. My father-in-law was getting rather old and I was feeling very strong, and I said one day I woulld take over from him and I would handle the situation. The boys were ruining the tree. So, I rushed out and grabbed one of these fellows by the shoulder. I had every feeling that I knew what I was doing and that what I was doing was right, and I grabbed this strong lusty sixteen-year-old and he immediately shouted in a loud voice "Police, Police." So, I confess, I went back into the house, I gave it all up. I thought the Irish were now in cahoots with the police, they had it all under control. And these boys didn't care anything for capitalism or for private property. But I got my revenge on that boy. About six months later this poem came to me, in a way that many of these poems have, it welled up into consciousness in a moment of meditation, say, six months later, or sometime in the winter, in my study. This is one of the poems that I can adduce as having been given to me, because I wrote it all, and I don't think I changed a line—certainly not a line, maybe a word or two, but not more than a word or two. I like this idea, that a poem when it is ready to be born may be born whole. It comes and there it is.

Interviewer: I remember when reading this poem, and often in the meantime, the phrase "outlaws on God's property." I see what you mean by saying this has an Old Testament ring. But it seems to me that you were invoking a certain feeling, that we do not hope to take possession of God.

Eberhart: Well, yes, I'll go along with that. It is a poem of adoration, isn't it? I mean, "the great flowering world unbroken yet," it adores this idea, and the world will still be there no matter what man does to it.

Interviewer: It reminds me of John Crowe Ransom's "God without Thunder."

Eberhart: The early book.

Interviewer: Yes, the early book, toward the end of which he says in resonant terms, "restore to God His thunder." I think he felt that the twentieth century was hoping to turn God into a pet, and to have Him on a lead, and he was rejecting this notion. Could we discuss some of the poems that have arisen very specifically from the situation around us here in Maine, at Undercliff?

Eberhart: Yes. As a matter of fact, we are looking now right out to the open ocean through about ten miles of beautiful islands. And right around the corner there as far as you can see is an island called Pond Island, and right to the westward of that, you cannot see it over this headland, is an island called Western Isle. And a few years ago I was in a rowboat—it had an outboard on it—but I was lolling on the oars off Western Isle, between Western Isle and Green Ledges Light, which is a marine marker, in a little pool of water, probably five hundred feet around or long, and I was just lolling there and up came to view a half-dozen seals. We have many seals here. They are curious animals, they are charming and they have great big eyes, superhuman eyes. Whenever I see the eye of a seal I think of Hart Crane's marvelous line "the seal's wide spindrift gaze toward Paradise." I liked to stay very calm in the boat and see how close they would come. They never come more than twenty feet or so, fifteen or twenty, and then if you move they will scoot away. Well, I wasn't thinking poetry at all, I was having a pleasant day on the water. At the same time, two or three hundred fork-tailed terns came in close-packed formation across the sky, so swiftly it was as if a scarf or a silken handkerchief had been drawn quickly across the sky. I noticed that the sun was beautiful on their underbodies, they were some two hundred feet up. Here were the birds above and there were the animals below, and yet no poem was in my mind then, and by this same curious amalgam, or whatever you might call it, months later I thought about it, at least the ideas got put together into a poem, "Seals, Terns, Time," which shows man, who thinks he is so solid and present, so real, actually a fragile creature sitting on a filament, the boat in the water, between two gigantic symbols. The birds are the symbols of our spiritual nature, and the animals, sea animals, are the symbols of our animal nature and of evolution coming up from the slime.

The other one I had in mind was caused by an actual happening on this coast, over on that headland. We had a boat which we sailed around in—it was a motorcraft, only about twenty feet long—some years ago, before we got to the Reve which we have now and in which you have had a cruise from Mt. Desert Island and Northeast Harbor all the way down here, forty miles of exciting sea voyage that we had the other day. But this little boat was put up on shore, and actually the man who put it on shore put his fist right through the sides, so he congratulated us all on being alive, and said we should have drowned months before in riding around in this rickety old boat. We put it up on shore at grandmother's house and filled it with flowers and had the children play in it. My mother-in-law, whom we call "grandmother," has a brother who is also in his early seventies who was at the Naval Academy when he was a young man. He is very fond of ships and vessels and he kept arguing all winter that we should not leave this vessel on land because a corpse should be buried, you should burn it up or sink it. We argued this back and forth all winter, and he finally won and we decided that we had to burn the vessel. So a man who owns an island down the Bay, Timothy Rhodes, came up in the middle of August, he knew when the tide would be farthest out, and about half a dozen of us pulled the boat off the shingle down to the very edge of the water at the lowest tide. And then a marvelous thing happened. Somebody brought little red glasses, and somebody brought spirits (I call it spirits, it was actually whiskey), and about sixty people came from all around the country, around the countryside here, to see the ship burning. This appealed to my imagination, it was so exciting. I felt alive to the ancient Greeks, or to the Norsemen for that matter, in the burning of a ship on the shore. We poured kerosene on the prow and stern, and I stood in the middle, I remember, and we lit the fires and I stood there with a red glass in hand and everyone had one, and I made up a toast to the immortal transubstantiation. And then when it had all burned down, we sat on the harsh rocks of the coast of Maine, which you know now, and we watched the tide come in and take the last debris, and the end of this poem is literally true. That evening there was the most magnificent comet that I had seen since I was a young boy and saw Halley's Comet. It was a long comet with an enormous tail, and in the middle of the tail was a star, right in the center of the farthest out part. It was like a jewel in the sky and it was like a benediction.

I tried to put down what I thought poetry was about this last year, and I came up with the following. First, the inner life is stronger than the outer life. Poetry defends the inner capacities of man. Second, life is ultimately mysterious. Poetry orders our extremest imaginings. Third, poetry makes the spiritual real. It erects value and substantive meaning. Fourth, poetry defends individualism, and is actually written to master time, sub specie aeternitatis. *By the actual, I mean historical permanence, for the best poetry of the time exceeds its time.*

—Denis Donoghue

An Interview *(William and Mary Review)*

Interviewer: Mr. Eberhart, I would like to welcome you to our campus on behalf of the College of William and Mary.

Eberhart: Well, let me say that I am happy to be here and delighted to come back to Williamsburg, where I believe I first came in about 1943 in the midst of World War II and spent a weekend. Also, I've been at your college and seen its environs, but this is the first I've been invited to your college, although I read for the Poetry Society of Virginia here in Williamsburg in May, 1961. The second thing I'd like to say, if you don't mind, in a pessimistic sort of humor, is that I have some distrust of the machinery into which I am now speaking, because I want to tell you of a very distressing experience I had last July. An Irish literary critic and professor at University College, Dublin, named Denis Donoghue, who conducted the Yeats Festival one summer in Ireland, and who lectured at Harvard last summer, and with whom I had corresponded for years, wanted to meet me. We made arrangements for him to come up to Maine. He flew to Bar Harbor, and we voyaged in our cruiser about fifty miles to Northeast Harbor to meet him in order to cruise him down the coast to our place. The formal purpose of his visit was to have a conversation with me by way of one of these machines. He had an invitation from the London BBC to tape a conversation on literary topics. We both looked forward to this very much. So he came and we enjoyed him ever so much, and one morning we went upstairs in our seaside home and talked about poetry. He asked me questions as you are going to do now. We talked back and forth and I was really delighted, because we put so much enthusiasm into it and one tried really to say what one meant, only to

First published in the *William and Mary Review* 2 (Winter, 1964): 1–12. The interviewer is Mr. Marshall.

learn just a few weeks ago the sad news from the BBC that he didn't have our machinery turned on correctly and the entire tape was unusable. When I think of all the energy and the preparation and the truth we tried to say, it is hard to say it over again just the same way. I hope your machinery is working.

Interviewer: By way of introduction, I am interested in a remark you made in *Twentieth Century Authors* that "I am not a dogmatist. I am a relativist." In your verse play *Preamble I* the Author bids the Poet "to be a poet of the relative," "to find the absolute in the relative." Would you mind commenting on these statements?

Eberhart: To answer the question about relativism and absolutism in poetry, I think the passages you've read are self-evident. I think the words explain themselves and that I don't need to adumbrate very much. I suppose many of our attitudes are crystallized from *a priori* points of view. I suppose that there must be something dogmatic in me that makes me not want to want to be a dogmatist. I did not want to have a system of poetical ideas that is absolute. I do not want to be dogmatic, but maybe it is some sort of excessive earnestness that makes me want to possess this more relativistic attitude. Maybe we have to say precisely what we mean in a sort of dogmatic way sooner or later. But my intellectual and aesthetic position is, and always has been for a long time, that you can have more of a handle on the truth, you can see life and poetry in a better light, if you think in relative terms rather than in absolute ones. That is, no poem, for instance, is absolute. Every poem can be interpreted differently, or slightly differently according to the age. A poem must have some universal core of meaning and a good or a lasting poem must have about 90 percent of cognitive value that is transferable from one age to another. But depending upon the taste of the time or depending upon your difference from me as a person, poems will be interpreted differently. For instance, we know that Shakespeare, when he wrote and lived, was one of fifteen or so very active playwrights. And we know now, but they didn't know in 1623, when the first folio came out, that Shakespeare was incontestably greater than his contemporaries. It took the world a hundred years to place Shakespeare where he is now, and this next spring we're celebrating his 400th anniversary. This always strikes me as a very strange thing. I mean, Ben Jonson was very much in the swim, you know, and Marlowe, all kinds of people, all sorts of people were functioning in the Elizabethan state, and yet the words we read in poetry now were the same then. They're right there in the books. How could it be that the world could not see that Shakespeare was head and shoulders above his contemporaries until a hundred to a hundred and fifty years later; but this is true, this is a historical fact.

We change all the time, as we grow. I dare say that you don't react to a poem the way you did five years ago, because you are more mature than you were five years ago, and I dare say that the poetry that you like now, you will like either less or more, probably less, later on. I'm suggesting maybe you outgrow the poets that you like now, and when you're thirty you'll have a different approach to them. I like to recall one change in myself that I've found. Up to about the age of forty, I was so earnest a man that I thought Marvell's "To His Coy Mistress" was a serious poem. I took it with deadly earnestness. However, it wasn't until I was well over forty years old that, in reading further criticisms of it and coming to this poem and seeing it with different eyes, I saw it as a comic poem. If you read it as a comic poem, it seems to me that is a more mature reaction than to read it with the devastating seriousness with which I took it. Now I still am not enough of a scholar to know precisely what Marvell's attitude was when he wrote it. I don't know whether anyone actually knows. This would be the pleasure of scholarship to see if you could tell. I don't think people really know. All you can do is work from the tripartite build of this poem and see how he moves from one point to another. I'm sure now that to read this poem with an ironic sense of humor, or to take it with a certain lightness, is a better reading than to take it with heaviness.

Interviewer: Have there been any poets of this century that have influenced you in approaching poetry in such a manner?

Eberhart: Well, that's a hard question to answer. I don't know how I could trace this back offhand. You mean how I got the idea of relativism? I think it came from my own temperament, my own philosophical disposition and the wish to be able to explore continuously a matter further. It seems to me that if you are a dogmatist you have to take dogmas on faith, and you have to believe that they are absolute. Well, I have a contentious mentality, and I like to contend against such propositions, and I think that there is always another way to look at something. Now as to who has influenced me, that's very hard to say. I think that I would have to go back to the beginning, and I might as well tell you that I began writing when I was about fifteen as a high school boy in southern Minnesota, where I was raised in Austin, Minnesota. The poet whom I first admired and imitated as a boy was Tennyson. Well, that is almost laughable to go back so far that you begin imitating Tennyson. But Tennyson was the poet who was read most in our household. We had a beautiful edition of Tennyson on our library table, and I got to know Tennyson the same way your generation got to know Dylan Thomas and the way the one before you got to know Eliot and the way my college generation got to know Housman. But if I go back far enough, I go way back to Tennyson. I tried to imitate the musical quality of his verse and the regularity of it. Now all my early work (before I went to Cambridge University) was, I suppose—obviously was—derivative, and yet I found in a chapbook that I wrote when I was about sixteen years old, a few years ago, a poem that was so perfect in its form and in its expression that I drew it out, had it typed up, submitted it to my publishers, and in my collected poems, if you want to read a short poem called "Indian Pipe," you will see a poem written when I was sixteen or seventeen. I took the greatest pleasure in embedding that poem in a text where it cannot be distinguished. In a way this is the marvel of poetry. Poetry is a mystery. How it's written or how it is perfected is very hard to tell. This form stood out as against the others, which were derivative, but there is where I had my own voice in a kind of impeccable style, and it was picked up, let's see, about forty years later.

I suppose there are only two or three poets who have seriously influenced me, but none of them for long. You go through a poet and then finally you get your own voice, you know. I know that I was much influenced by Wordsworth. Wordsworth was a deep influence on me. My first book, written when I was at Cambridge University, was written maybe partly because I was at St. John's College—which had been Wordsworth's college. Listening every night in my gown to the Latin prayers before meals, I would sit under the Pickersgill portrait of William Wordsworth. I adored Wordsworth, and I loved "The Prelude" and I wrote a long poem as my first book, *A Bravery of Earth*, and if you will take the trouble to read it you will find some Wordsworth in it. I was reliving, in my own way, his spiritual growth as a young man. Then, as you know in those times, John Donne was very much in the air, and I had a passion for Donne, but it wasn't as deep as that for Wordsworth, and I think, if you look in some of my early work, you'll find Donnean emphases. We were all indebted to T. S. Eliot for bringing Donne to the fore, but that Donne feeling was passing, and there was a depth in my psyche that mated with a depth in Wordsworth's. I think the greatest, the most mysterious, and the deepest influence on me was Blake, whom I've always adored, and, who is—well, it's hard to talk about Blake, he's complex and yet so simple. You can never exhaust him, which is remarkable. Many critics for twenty years or so were always likening my early works to Blake. I notice that they don't do this so much any more. But there was a real kind of Blakean thing in me, and I think it had to do with a tension between opposites. I was always interested in good and evil, life and death, age and youth—these opposites, so strongly opposed one to the other. Yet, there was a kind of a truth suspended between them. I think those are the main literary influences—or have I left out somebody? Oh yes, I must say that in my Cambridge years I was tremendously taken with Hopkins, and this was fairly early, because Hopkins, as you know, had only been published in 1918 and I was on the scene ten years later and when I came to the scene, as it were, the English scene over there, the great spate of books about Hopkins had yet to be written. People were still baffled by him, by his style, and amazed by his intensity and troubled by his career. But I had a very strong attachment, a completely excited realization of Hopkins, and I remember critics pointing out lines of mine in the early books that seemed to stem from Hopkins. I think that's about it.

When I was an undergraduate at Dartmouth, we all loved A. E. Housman, but he never influenced my style. I loved the temper of Housman. I still admire him very much, but I wasn't influenced by him. So I'm not answering your question as to this century, because I don't think there is anyone. I don't think I have been influenced by any of my contemporaries. I certainly have never been influenced by any of my elders who are still living that I can think of. For instance, there is nothing Eliotic in me, and I am not at all like Pound. I'm not like Jeffers or anybody else. I had two wonderful friendships with older poets in their later years: Wallace Stevens and William Carlos Williams. As a matter of fact, a couple of critics have noticed a few things like Stevens in some of my lines, but I don't think that's very deep. But I admired Wallace Stevens very much and still do, and I admired William Carlos Williams very much. But I believe that poetry is individualistic and that it cannot be otherwise. I think it's a contradiction in terms to think of a school of poetry, yet I know that schools of poetry exist. I know, for instance, that when Empson and Kathleen Raine and J. Bronowski and T. H. White and I were starting to write at Cambridge and publishing together in the same magazines, we had no idea that we were in a school or founding a school, but now, thirty years later, they're beginning to see that this was a kind of school. They can write of it as a school, just as a couple of years later Auden, Spender, Day-Lewis, were all the Oxford group, and Mac-Neice, too, was associated with them, and for many years that was a firm so-called literary school, and yet it's taken all these years for Mr.

Spender to come out in print about it within the past year. I think it was a couple of years ago, or was it Auden? I forget. One of the two of them said that they never were all of them in the same room together, never met each other when they were young men in their twenties—well, Auden and Spender met, but not all of them, and it's really absurd to have thought of this Auden, Spender, Day-Lewis school. This was something made up by the readers of poetry or the critics to help themselves to identify certain attitudes. I find this is all fascinating. I think I have been lucky in not having been endangered in belonging to a school in America. There is something or was something called the beatnik school. You know, it's still going on or waning now, but three, four, or five years ago the beatnik movement came up to a high pitch of fury in this country, and in a sense there was a school. You can name at least half a dozen people who are all writing in the same way or saying their poems to jazz, and they belonged, more or less, to the same set of ideas. But now if you think of these people, this movement, as historical, it still comes down to individualism and you still have to name the one or two poets and you have to think of them as highly individualistic. You may like Ginsberg or Corso or Ferlinghetti—after all, they're all very different aren't they?

Interviewer: Do you feel that the modern poet in his verse has become too introspective, too selfish and egocentrical, too vague and pedantic in his images and allusions, so that he can no longer communicate with his fellow men and comment on society and the dilemmas of his times?

Eberhart: Well, that's a very good question. I'd like to put it over into a slightly different form and talk about it from that point of view. It will come to the same conclusion, perhaps, but I'd like to formulate your question a little differently and oppose the poetry of the academy to the poetry of the street—let's make that dichotomy. The reason I do this is because I attended a meeting at Princeton last June, and this problem came up in the discussion from the floor: that is whether poetry was becoming too much ivory tower, too far away from the people, and therefore far away from life. I have lived with ambiguity, and ambivalence, and irony all my life. I belong to the generation which was controlled by these concepts or had them to deal with all the time. So again I do not have an absolute view. I would like to make some remarks on this. In the first place, I think it is just as possible to get at the truth if you write in the academy as it is if you write from the point of view of the street. You have only to look at the facts to see that by all odds the greatest percentage of the best American poets have belonged at some time in their lives to the academy. I use the word "academy" to stand for any college or university or educational institution. I do not mean a technical academy such as the National Academy. I mean the term in a generic sense. The academy in this century has been the mother of poetry and has reared up a whole school of excellent poets. If it weren't for the academy, I don't believe that American poetry would be at its high level of achievement. It is at a very high level of achievement and has been for thirty years. Criticism, perhaps, has outweighed creation. You could easily argue on that side. But even so, it is the academy that has made the high level possible and the discriminations of critics which have made it possible for poets to write a high kind of poetry. Now I suppose if we were going to do this thoroughly, we should parade a lot of names. I don't know that it's necessary to do that here. There have been a few poets who are anti-academy and who have been great, and obviously I believe in them as much as in the academy poets. But if I were to give an argument I would be on the side of the good to the art the academy has done. But to mention only one that you think of immediately —Hart Crane, one of our great poets, who was not a member of the academy. He eschewed going to college; he couldn't make a go of it. He wanted to work away from his father's candy business in Chagrin Falls, Ohio, and come to New York and read Tourneur, Webster, and Shakespeare and be a great poet. I'm glad that his life took the turn that it did—perhaps he would have been ruined by an academic job, or by being an academy poet. If you think only of one from the other side, Dylan Thomas was a fine example of a man of poetic fire and genius whose academy was the pub. I would have been sad to have Oxford or Cambridge as a substitute. I believe again on relativity that poetic genius can spring up anywhere, and I believe the next great poet, if you can use that term, might come from some remote part of our country and far afield from an academic situation. On the other hand, that's just a guess. It's more likely that if we are going to have a great poet he will probably come out of one of our great universities. Again you think of many of the modern poets. Let's just name a few—Wallace Stevens, a magnificent poet—very much a Harvard man. Frost, although he was running away from universities all the time, can hardly be thought of apart from the academy. Wallace Stevens, William Carlos Williams, to come down to our own time. Just take Lowell alone, an academy man. But they could come from some other situation. When I think of the opposite of Wallace Stevens, for instance, I think of Carl Sandburg. Now, I would like to argue in favor of Carl Sandburg, who is very unpopular, who is not read in the universities, where Wallace Stevens is adored. Carl Sandburg is either forgotten or tolerated, because he dealt so closely with reality back in the Teens, Twenties. He was so limited to sectionalism, to speaking about midwestern reality, Chicago, the prairies, that his poetry is simple rather than complex. His poems are so simple that you can get everything out of them in one or two readings. So that's why he's only read now historically, but you do not enter now into the mind of Sandburg as you do into that of Wallace Stevens. Stevens is oppo-·site by being subtle, complex, mysterious, ambiguous, redundant, tautological, and all sorts of other things intriguing to us. You can hardly exhaust him. You can read, you can study a Stevens poem twenty times and never exhaust the meaning, or you can get new reactions to it. In other words, his mind was so much more subtle. It wasn't dogmatic again, it wasn't just one to one. There was always a question mark somewhere in his thinking.

I would say that there is a sense in which you are right concerning poetry becoming hidebound, straitened, or held in by the academy. Thus it will suffer and dry up and become uninteresting and unskillful—bad. There is that possibility that you get too many poets who write only for poets, too many poets who can be understood only by one another, and too many poets who write only with critical estimation in mind. I indicate those who write to the taste of the critics. I would agree that, if this were a universal manifestation of what I call the academy, it would be bad. On the other hand, I don't think it's universal at all and I think that poetry is a matter of skilled use of intelligence and the subtle use of words and the deepest feelings that you have. How can you say that it would be better to write these from a university situation or from a cold-water flat in Greenwich Village? Hart Crane ended up by jumping into the ocean. I think poetry ideally must be universal and that it should appeal to the deepest feelings in man. I would be the first one to welcome a new William Shakespeare, if it's not comic to entertain such an idea. Supposing a great writer like Shakespeare should appear in our midst, if he could be a street poet as against an academic poet and if he could synthesize the whole of the second half of the twentieth century, if he could speak to the very soul of America and in political terms, too, as well as in intellectual ones, I would be the first to welcome him. I'm not at all against the idea of the anti-academy approach. I think, to repeat, that where you could name four or five poets offhand who belong to what I call the street poet you could name twenty with the greatest of ease, all of them marvelous poets like Ransom or anyone you want to mention who is an academic poet and an excellent poet.

Interviewer: Do you feel that students today fear poetry, tend to shy away from it, or mistrust it, and turn to various critics and explicators rather than confronting the poetry or poem itself?

Eberhart: That's a very good question. I don't think they do. One has to limit one's answer. I would have to answer principally from teaching young men students at Dartmouth. I can't think of speaking for the whole country really upon this topic. It seems to me really not only do they not fear poetry as they used to, but they aspire to it and admire it and learn to love it. I think the whole country is much farther advanced than when I was a young man. There used to be, when I was a young man like you, the idea that all poets were queer in some way, that they were odd or that a poet was a fool, or a madman, or crazy or anti-social, or somebody you wouldn't associate with—that the poet was really a strange being, and it seems to me that that idea was much more widespread than it is now. And I think that part of it's due to the fact that there are so many poets who are sane and healthy and who have made their mark in the world of our civilization so that people have seen these poets from Eliot and Frost right down to the youngest ones. Furthermore, we've got to the point of education now where educated people realize that the hardest thing in the world to do is to write a great poem or even a good poem that will last for a hundred years, and people respect the genius of poets now—the way they didn't when I was your age. Now as to leaning on criticism, let me say that I think by the nature of things young people at this college and every other one lean on criticism much more than they did when I was your age, because there wasn't so much criticism in those days. There were fewer critics, many fewer critics, and there were older critics, the critic of the past, but some about 1925 or 1930 knew the whole vast movement of the new criticism was being perfected. Thousands of students have been influenced by all these critics: I. A. Richards, Empson, Leavis, and on this side Tate and Ransom and Blackmur and all the rest; and they should have been, and it's a fine thing that they have got the enlightenment that these critics have been able to show. I don't think that there's anything to worry about on that score. I think if they come to criticism along with the poetry they're better off. They have a better understanding really than if they just delve into poetry alone. I think we're all maybe more sophisticated than we were earlier. Maybe earlier we read a poem more for sheer pleasure. More than we do now. You read a poem, and if it said something to you, you thought that was wonderful. You didn't have to feel any social weight of criticism, whether it was a good poem or a bad one, or whether your attitude was a good or bad one in reacting to it. Maybe we've lost something there. That would be really individualistic. But we know now, for instance, what some of the bad poems really are. There are schoolroom exercises about why Joyce Kilmer's "Trees" is bad. Okay, maybe the man I am talking about was a man who simply thought "Trees" was wonderful in 1920. Now we are more sophisticated. You read the criticism, and you know what's wrong with that poem, so you cannot any longer think it's good. But I hope that doesn't mean that everyone cannot react to a poem in his own way nowadays. You have to react to it in your own way, and you have to have the stamina and character to stand up for your own likes and dislikes. Again, if I get anywhere near dogmatism, it would be the dogma of saying that the worst thing that could happen to a young lover of poetry would be to have his taste dogmatically formed by critics. In other words, to like a poem only because it was approved by one of these major critics. I think that would be a very bad state of things.

Interviewer: What has led you specifically to write verse plays?

Eberhart: That would take a long answer. I know pretty much why. It was simply the excitement in the air around Cambridge, Massachusetts, a few years after World War II. This is a profoundly interesting thing to me. After World War II, it happened (and it came to a head in 1950) that there were about ten people, ten poets, who were living close to each other, or in the same town, or within a near radius, and they read their poems to each other and discussed them. Then there were other people vitally interested in acting and in the theatre. All of this coalesced to a powerful affirmation of the belief that it would be marvelous if in this country we could have a new and vital verse theatre, if we could all graduate to writing verse plays. This feeling was explosive. Now I'm sure that, if there hadn't been all this lively proliferation of ideas about it around me, I wouldn't have written a verse play of my own. I don't think I would. Cambridge supported Harvard, and was supported by the whole of Boston, so it was a large civilized community which had the possibility of supporting an original theatre of new verse plays, and this inflamed the imaginations of all of us, and we incorporated the poets' theatre. That's how it got started. Everyone got terribly excited about it. I had never seen such excitement in any other literary movement. It was unique to me, the amount of real, powerful enthusiasm. This resulted in quite a few works being done in three or four years. For the first five years of the theatre much was accomplished. But I regret to say that it lasted only ten years—ten or eleven—and is now moribund. It's too bad. We all thought we were going to have a theatre as good as the Abbey Theatre. We all wanted to be as good as William Butler Yeats, you know, and we really thought we could. But, there again, there's something very mysterious about literature and about poetry and about the production of literary works. It wasn't that there wasn't enough talent around; it just wasn't in the social situation. The social situation supported this kind of high but rather strange and particularized effort for a while, but then it faded, and nothing could keep it up. Technically, quite a few of the authors went away to other cities. The cohesion was lost, and then there were the inevitable political squabbles about the management of the theatre and that sort of thing—worldly problems. It was a great spurt of energy in this direction in this country for awhile. I'm very glad to say that out of this I have one book which came out a year ago, my collected verse plays. I talk about this problem in the introduction, and at least my effort is in that book.

Interviewer: Do you feel that there are any forces, individual or organized, in this country that are doing the utmost for the presentation and enjoyment of poetry today?

Eberhart: I try to look on the optimistic side of things. Maybe I'm too optimistic, but I think that poetry is at a high state of excellence, as I said earlier. I can see many reasons why this is so. Maybe you could take me to task for overemphasizing some of these things. Let's just take the matter of prizes. There are more good prizes in this country now than there were in 1930, when I began. It's possible for young poets to win prizes, and while the money is not enough to change their life, it does their ego a lot of good and helps them along the road of recognition. There is the whole institution of poets in residence, which is only about twenty years old. Now there must be ten or fifteen poets in residence at colleges where poets are allowed to make their livings and continue their careers. This was unheard of before. The administrations realized that the original career potential of the poet is quite as important as his ability to conduct a class, and they have poets at their institutions both for teaching and for writing. Well, this is a great thing. It wasn't true when Hart Crane was suffering in New York. There was no such thing. There are enormous fellowships. Who would have ever thought twenty-five years ago of $10,000 fellowships such as the Ford Foundation has given out to half a dozen poets at a time in various programs in the last few years? Now I don't say that a young man can aspire to these, because you may not be elected to one. But I say that they are there, they are in the air. There are fellowships that people can get. There are many more prizes. It seems to me that there are many more books of good poetry published in America than there used to be. As a matter of fact, it's appalling now, it's really rather frightening. Sometimes I read for some review at the end of the year all the poems of a year. I would say in the last five years—in every year—well, if you're really optimistic—twenty good books of poetry—and by everyone from the age of seventy down to twenty. It used to be that there were only two or three books of poetry in a year that were good. I mean that young poets have a better chance of getting published than they used to. Furthermore, another thing I would say of this vast change from when I was struggling in the Thirties, concerns the workshops such as at Iowa and other places around the country. There are workshops where people can live for relatively little and sometimes live year after year before they can find their voice and get up to where they aspire, and they can exist not quite from hand to mouth either. They can exist and talk ideas with their fellows, their peers and their teachers, and have a serious poetical career. All these I think are better situations than those which existed when I was young. It seemed to me you could count the poets on one hand when I began to write. There were fewer poets—that is, of any serious intent. Now that we are at a great, a vast plateau of excellence in the art, there are many excellent poets. I think that the peaks of poetic achievement are as hard to come by now as they ever were, and in any century there are only a few great poets. And I would have to hold, looking at myself and my contemporaries and the younger ones, that, since the great poets of the Teens and Twenties in this country, many of whom are now dying off—I mean since the careers of Eliot, Aiken, MacLeish, Marianne Moore, Jeffers, William Carlos Williams and Wallace Stevens and Cummings—it seems to me that we have leveled off—I would consider these as mountain peaks. Now we don't have the mountain peaks from my age down or at any age, I believe. We have a high plateau of achievement now. Maybe I'm being too modest, but I don't think I am. Who are the poets of my decade? Robert Penn Warren and Theodore Roethke, who died in August, Kunitz and Kenneth Rexroth—I always liked him. Well, how do you compare these with this older group? It's too early to say yet. And you have to jump down to Lowell and Wilbur, Nemerov, Shapiro. That's all sort of different plateaus, you see. It's harder to make any final assessment of them.

Interviewer: Which of your poems do you feel has the most meaning for you as an expression of both yourself and your attitude toward poetry?

Eberhart: Oh, you ask awfully hard questions, young man. I would like to end this interview by ending as a relativist, and to say that I have no dogma about my own poems and that I think they are all relative one to another and relative to the year, decade in which they were written and relative to my life in America, or as a man on the face of the earth. I am, after all, not so far removed from reality as not to be able to see a certain truth about my work, and let me just speak of that for a moment. When I wrote "The Groundhog"—the summer I wrote "The Groundhog"—I wrote three other poems at the same time and I thought all of these poems were equal in merit. Twenty-five years go by or thirty or whatever it is, and only one of these poems survives —which is "The Groundhog," with the exception of one which survives in a lesser way, which is called "In a Hard Intellectual Light," which Allen Tate liked enough to put in his anthology a few years ago, his *Mid-Century Anthology.* The other two are completely lost. I would have to look back in my chapbooks to find their titles. Now what do you make of this? I am forced to make of it that there must be some inherent objective poetic truth in poems that are considered best for the longest time by the most people. In other words, there must be something in "The Groundhog" that is deeper, more human, more nearly universal than in poem *x* or poem *y* which is dropped out. This has always troubled me, because when I wrote the four poems I couldn't see the difference. Isn't that an amazing thing from a creative point of view? The furor, the excitement, the interest, thinking you are putting down the truth, the love for what you are doing or trying to do was the same for all four poems, yet one of them gets to be a mountain peak, one of them gets to be a plateau, and the others undersea or underground. So, I don't know how to answer your question, except to say that, when you've lived as long as I have, you have to read a lot in yourself to find out who you are. In other words, I'm so aware of other poets and the general climate of America and literature in general that sometimes I have to sit down and read myself for hours to find out what I really am like. I have a chance of knowing myself less than you do—you students. And by the same token, I suppose I would have to admit that the best poems of mine must be in the best anthologies, and that if you look through all the anthologies of the last twenty years you could make up a core of about six, eight, or ten of my poems, which by that standard must be the best because they've been reprinted more, and more students have known them. I admire critical discernment enough to believe this, and I don't see why I should tell you that the poem that I like best of mine is so and so and then pick out one that nobody has enjoyed for twenty years. Wouldn't that be wrong? Maybe it wouldn't, but it wouldn't seem to be realistic. Well, I think there are all sorts of levels on which you can read poetry. If you want to read me or any other poet who has got to the point of collected poems—entire—and really get the man and make a study of him—that's one thing. But if you want to get the kernel of his work, which is what happens in all classrooms, you can get it from the best anthologies. Every poet can be reduced to a core of poems—that's what usually happens. I mean, when you think of Ransom or even Hopkins, half a dozen poems—you don't think of the whole work —unless you're a specialist or you particularly love to delve into that poet. Does that answer it? I don't know how you wanted it.

Interviewer: That's fine, yes. Well, I hope you enjoy your visit in Williamsburg, and I want to thank you for giving the *William and Mary Review* the opportunity of talking with you this afternoon. Thank you very much.

An Interview *(Pulse)*

Eberhart: I do not keep a notebook or a journal, and I have, I think, somewhat unusual ideas about the creative act. I have never understood it in my entire life and I don't understand it now. But I think of the creation of a poem as an inspirational thing at its best, that is, sometimes in your life. Now I can say that about a half a dozen times in my life a poem has been given to me, rather than had I tried to invent it, or make it with the rational mind. It is as if it were a gift of the gods, and as if the personality of the poet were a vein upon which a wind, a spiritual wind blows, so that in a sense the whole being is used by the poem. I don't mean by this automatic writing as Yeats thought his wife understood it. I don't mean quite that; but I insist that in at least half a dozen cases in my life some of my best poems have been given to me. They have come right out of the air. To give one case in point, "The Groundhog," which has survived now for a long time, was written in about twenty minutes of intense concentration and power, but without the necessity to change a line when it was done. Well, what a mysterious and remarkable thing. How could this be? And I remembered this time as one of great subdued joy, although it was talking about mortality. But it's so mysterious. For instance, in the summer or in the year that I wrote "The Groundhog," I wrote three other poems and my energy output was the same for all of them. And my belief in what I was doing was the same; and yet, of these four poems, two were never even published in a little magazine, one turned out to be "In a Hard Intellectual Light," which has been in quite a few anthologies but never achieved the prominence of "The Groundhog." "The Groundhog" was a mountain peak poem, the other one was a

First published in *Pulse*, Spring, 1973, pp. 10–15. The interviewers are Michael Cannito, Jo Ann Thrash, and Robert J. Barnes.

plateau, and the other ones were right down in the swamp. I thought a long time about this and I don't understand it. In other words, what I'm trying to say is that in one sense a poet doesn't know what he's doing. For instance, I had the same purity, the same passion, the same intense desire to say something about life in all four cases, and yet look at the great qualitative difference in all of the results. Now I'm talking about way back in the past, so you have to try to re-create when those four poems were written. I wasn't as far along then as I am now. So it was all very new, it was all fresh, it was all potential, and it was all creative acts. But, if you take the problem right up to 1972, if I had been writing a poem yesterday I would have no more knowledge of how it might fare than I did in those four cases. What I think I'm trying to say is that I don't believe in the rational intellect very much, and I believe that there is something irrational about poetry, or that it comes from somewhere beyond the mind; it comes from the heart, or the stomach, or the genitals, or the blood—Lawrence was always talking about the blood and the great blood consciousness. It has a lot more to do with the deepest parts of our nature and with the wholeness of these depths, to me, than it does with merely the intellect. And yet, the minute I say this I know that I'm in a sense limiting myself, but we are all terribly limited. I immediately think of somebody like Alexander Pope, whom everybody admires. I don't think that Pope would agree with what I've just been saying. Well, he would understand it, but I don't think Pope could give much credence to my theory. Because if you read his work as a representative of the rationality of the eighteenth century you could see that he believed in prose consciousness, and in sparkling diction, and in incredibly lively mental convolutions, but it isn't what I would call "inspired." I really still believe, and I think I'm one of the few poets of today who still likes this ancient word, I believe that poetry comes by inspiration. In other words, I ally myself more with Shelley, and with Hopkins, and with Blake and with Wordsworth, and maybe with Dylan Thomas a little bit, than I do with certain other kinds of poets who are more closely allied to prose. I think of poetry as a possibly joyful thing, and as ecstatic, and as high pitched, and therefore I have mostly written lyrics. So, that's sort of what I feel about poetry, that it's a very strange thing, and it's very mysterious, it's hard to understand. You don't know what you're up to, but the spirit speaks through you, and when you're in a mood to write your soul or your true being comes out; so that if you write through a whole lifetime, then you can study the work of this poet for decades and you can really get a long line on what his mind is like, and what his being is like. Let me say something against my principle for a moment just to show you how complex these things are. You would agree, all of us in this room would agree, that Chaucer is a great poet, the father of old poetry, let's say. He was nothing like this kind of poet that I've been talking about, I don't believe. If you read the *Canterbury Tales* you'll see that they were based on prose and story telling. And Shakespeare, except in certain passages in *Lear,* certain passages in *Hamlet,* and maybe some lines of the sonnets and maybe a few of the songs, was much vaster a character in his command of a totality of life than I am, obviously. It's absurd to mention it, but I mean it quite seriously—Poetry is such a huge word. If you think of Shakespeare as a poet, he took in all of this, you see. And also, if you think of Milton, he had very high passages, but there was an awful lot of hard intellect in most of what he wrote. In *Paradise Lost* and *Paradise Regained* and *Samson Agonistes* and all that, there is the wrestling of a mind with the Christian mythology and what it meant in his times. However, when you come up to Wordsworth and Blake, you come back into my orbit and you come into my court of the ball game, as it were. I could say that most of Wordsworth's best work fits into this inspirational orbit or gambit. And so too the lyrics, the early lyrics, and the great and marvelous "Songs of Innocence and Experience" of Blake. Well, I don't want to carry on too long with that but I think that will give you some idea of where I think I am. I don't think I could do anything about it. I don't think I could sit down tonight and write a poem that would last ten years or a hundred years. It would be absurd, it would be absurd to think of. On the other hand, I might write a poem anytime that might be as good as anything I've done, or maybe better. You don't know. Poetry has endless possibilities, and it's only limited to the hold your spirit has on the world in the few years that we live on this planet. It's all potential, and that's what I think.

Now let me go back a little on this "gift of the gods" business, or the inspirational thing. It makes quite a pretty picture to have said what I did, but there are some other complexities that have to come in here. Let us think of Mozart and Beethoven. Can you imagine both of them being little boys? Well they must have been. There must have been a time when young Mozart was taught the scales of the pianoforte. And Beethoven must have learned the white keys and black keys when he was three or five or whatever he was, and somebody must have taught them. So any artist has to learn his art. I mean, the picture I gave you was in a sense absurd, in that I'm trying to say that here's a flesh-and-blood man, full of humanity and muscle and force, writing a poem that, let's say, might live for hundreds of years *without knowing what he's doing*. Or that it is given to him by the spirit. I really believe this, and I've said it and I stand by it; but you have to understand that when a man is ready to bear this poem, his whole life comes into play, up to that point. And that includes learning the scales; or, in a poet, it includes imitating poetry from the age of fifteen, when I started. I learned to imitate and I wrote hundreds of imitative poems, and I imitated Tennyson. I go back as far as to have begun by imitating Tennyson; just think of that. Now they think it's very ancient to go back to Dylan Thomas, or somebody who's only been dead a few years, relatively. You have to learn your art. Every artist has to learn. For instance, there were years when I read the dictionary with the greatest attention. I just loved studying the dictionary. One of the great books of the world. If you just read the dictionary intensely you get a terrific education and you learn all kinds of words.

But let me put it another way, and I will use "The Groundhog" as one example. When the poem is ready to be born, it will be born, it will be born whole; and it will summarize the total life of the poet in some frame of reference, at that point. As we know, the two great forces of life cannot be stopped once they have begun, both birth and death. The physical act of death, once started, will not be stopped. A poem, by analogy, is born in the same way under my theory—that is, some poems. And it is born whole. It comes to birth. It comes into being. And there you are.

Let me just say something else. Because I want to be thorough about this. I tried to give you a theory of mine, which I think is true to me. But I would like to remind whoever hears this that I am talking about only a half-dozen of the best poems of my life. And yet think of all the poems I've written. I wouldn't know how many, but I suppose over a thousand, probably. And many of these if they are good poems, and they are published in books and they are enjoyed by people, are composed in an entirely different way. You see, I want to make sure, that you couldn't—I can't imagine anybody, even Shelley, being always this ethereal spirit, who's a godlike person, who has some hold or direct line from the ultimate creative principle. It's too high an idea. So, then, in my own case, there's an awful lot of hard work on the majority of my poems, and there are many poems which have endless scratchings out and re-makings and many, many copies or many times before the poem is presented to the public.

Interviewer: I'll use an analogy here, but would you say that this more difficult work of yours is some sort of "honing of your edge" for the moments when the best of your poetry comes?

Eberhart: I don't think I'd say that, but it's a very good idea. I don't know that I could say that. I will say that I think some of my best poems are what I call "inspissated" poems, and I like that word. Do you happen to know it? From *inspissare* in Latin, it means "to thicken." Inspissation is the thickening of the context. Well, I like thickened poems and I've written, I think, quite a few crabbed or thick poems, from a grammatical point of view. But I've noticed, invariably, that these are never the ones best loved by the poetry-reading public, or that ever get into my books. I'll give you an example. If you read every poem I've written, you'd find that some of them are pretty dense; and yet, when James Laughlin asked if he could put out a paperback of me, he thought it was high time, and we agreed and the publishers agreed and I said O.K. Mr. James Laughlin, the editor of New Directions, an old friend, took all of my books on a boat one summer and went across the ocean to see Ezra Pound—he's the chief publisher of Ezra Pound and he loves the *Cantos* and everything—and Laughlin had the horse sense, or the clarity of judgment, or the editorial acumen, since he was going to put out a paperback book of my poems, to throw out categorically all the heavy poems, or the inspissated ones, or the dense ones. And he put out a little paperback of what he would call the "purest" ones, which were invariably short and invariably lyrical. And his book won the Pulitzer Prize, much to the consternation of the Oxford University Press, who wouldn't even bring me out in paperback. So that's one of the jokes of my literary career, I mean the joke was on them. But this is very serious and this book has sold very well ever since. He just knew that people don't have the concentration—except a few highly learned people in universities—don't have the brains to want to read heavy poetry all the time. They want something that's more easily assimilable and that gives instant pleasure, or existential joy, or whatever you want to say. And, just to follow up, I have a new book coming out next month, it's supposed to be out on November 9. It's the wrestling with the publishers, which I've always had to do with every book that I've brought out; there were about ten poems which I wanted in which didn't get in this book—and I'm going to get them in my next book, or I'm going to get them in my complete works, or my ultimate collected—because they just thought they were too dense. Now they wouldn't say they weren't good; and after all they have to sell the book. When you think of the perilous life of a poet and the perils of publishing, it is really crucial what goes into a book. It either makes your reputation or kills you, or it makes you worse or better, and the publishers have to take the responsibility for presenting you to the world, so they should have a lot of say about what goes on. So I couldn't even get some of the poems that I've written in the last three years in this new book that I

wanted in. But we never have drag-out fights. We always have intellectual discussions about them and there's always a give and take, and
I say, "Well, then I'll put in this one. You give me that one. I'll give you
this one." So the books that are published under my name really
represent a unanimity of judgment for the moment, but with a little
argument on the side.

Interviewer: I wanted to ask about "New Hampshire, February."
How did you come about writing it; what inspired it?

Eberhart: Many of my poems such as that, that have been used by
students for a long time now, come from real events. So that this poem
came from a real event just as "The Groundhog" came from a real
event and "The Fury of Aerial Bombardment" and a lot of these
poems, "The Horse Chestnut Tree," for example, "The Cancer Cells,"
many of these poems of mine have come from actual physical things
that have happened, but then, the making of them into a poem is this
undefinable or unexplainable thing.

Now let me tell you about "New Hampshire, February." I was at
that time as yet unmarried. I was a bachelor and was teaching at St.
Mark's School, and I was given a house by one of the masters up there
in Kensington, New Hampshire, near Exeter, in the winter. I think it
was January. He gave me an old farmhouse to go up and live in, say
for ten days, during a vacation. So I went and I went alone and I was a
studious and meditative man. I lived alone. I took all my things. I
didn't see many people. I took a lot of books along and I was wanting
to write poetry all the time. Well actually, wasps did fall out of the
ceiling onto the stove. But then, from there the poem is my origina-
tion. And that is a pretty good idea, I mean, I don't think I would have
dreamed up the idea of wasps dropping down on a hot spot. Now I
could. You could. But with almost all of these anthologized poems
that people know, there is a basis of reality which is then embroidered
on, or made more of. You see, so that poetry is then putting it all
together in some new context. So this idea of pushing them over and
then pushing them out and all that sort of thing, and then the ending
of it and the ideas, are out of my ratiocination. Now, I'm afraid, I
wouldn't say that that poem was a poem of inspiration, the way I was
talking about "The Groundhog" and some of the others. That poem
was a *made* poem. The poetry itself—*poesis* means "to make" in Greek,
the poet is the maker—this was the making. This was making something out of something else, or out of the wasp idea. And the same
with the horse chestnut tree poem. The tree still stands. I saw it only
yesterday. It's right outside my mother-in-law's house on Lake View
Avenue in Cambridge. The very tree that these boys came—they

really came and threw sticks and stones at the tree. That one even had more basis in fact than the wasp one, because it was really a recounting of what actually happened. So maybe that would give you some idea. I think a lot of my poems are grounded in anecdotal reality, or in a story of some kind, or some consecutive acts of some sort that seemed significant somehow to me, and then you build a poem from them. But, I don't know, they're not all that way.

Interviewer: You've already anticipated many of our questions. Well, here's an obvious one: who would you say is your favorite poet?

Eberhart: I don't have a favorite poet. Let me speak to that, though. I think I'm peculiar in that you have to remember I started quite a long time ago, and I'm still raging on the world, but I started way out in Minnesota where there was no poetry. I started in high school, where the only book in our family library on the desk was Tennyson, as I said before. If they had T. S. Eliot I would have probably started imitating Eliot, but Eliot would be later. It was before that. Well, no, it really wasn't before *him,* but he hadn't got out to there in my family's estimation, you see. And then I went to Dartmouth, and then I went to Cambridge, and Harvard, and all that. You know the whole story, I suppose, the biography; there was one out last year, as you know. I think I was fortunate in being moved, I would say, first by Wordsworth, second by Blake, and then a little later by Hopkins. Those were, and I guess they still are, my three gods. That is, I read all the other poets, but I wasn't moved so much by Spenser; I wasn't a Miltonian. I was really taken by Wordsworth, and if you read my first book, *A Bravery of Earth,* you can see that it was an imitation, one long poem, a hundred and thirty five pages, of the growth of my mind, or a young person's mind, and it was modeled on "The Prelude" and "The Excursion." So Wordsworth was the deepest influence on me. And then Blake hit me like wildfire. For at least the first half of my career everybody thought I was like Blake, they kept saying, he has Blakean feelings or inputs. They don't say that so much any more. And then Hopkins later, but Hopkins to a lesser extent. So that's sort of strange; but I'm so lucky, I think I was terribly lucky not to have been influenced by Eliot, or by Pound, or by Stevens, or by Hart Crane, or any of those people just before me. You know, a lot of people have been ruined by that sort of thing. I mean, I think I was lucky to go way back to some prototype long ago.

Interviewer: Do you think there's been any kind of cross-fertilization between you and any of your contemporaries, like Frost, say?

Eberhart: I don't think very much. I think that a few of my poems were influenced a little bit by Stevens. There were a few years there when I was terribly enamoured of him. As a matter of fact, I had a marvelous friendship with the old man. He was twenty-five years my senior, but in the last eight years of his life we had a friendship, and he wrote thirty-five letters to me and I answered them and these are all known now. I also had a friendship with William Carlos Williams and I liked him a lot, but Stevens was closer to my aesthetic feelings than Williams. But Frost was always around like an old shoe. He was always there. He was in the back of your head; one read him early. And there he was, we knew him of course. He came to our house several times. And he came to Dartmouth all the time. You'd see him every year, a couple of times. Then I succeeded him at the Library of Congress, in that job of consultantship in '59–61, and he was there a great deal. So I know Frost as a person, but he was so much older than I am that it wasn't very close. As far as the words go, I think I have an early sonnet that's sort of like him, called "The Village Daily." No, I wouldn't say there's much cross-breeding there.

Interviewer: In your recent poem, "The Other Gerard" (written to Gerard Malanga about Gerard Manley Hopkins), you seem to come out openly against the undisciplined chaos and superficiality of what one might call *now* poetry of the "now generation."

Eberhart: Well yeah. All I'd say is, it's just one poem. Maybe it preaches a little, but I shouldn't preach too much. I think you just have to read that along with a lot of other poems, and you've got to read that with all the new poems in my new book to see how I fit it into my canon. I think I'm still growing. I feel very much alive to the world and I've really been given to write a lot in the last year. I mean, I'm very delighted that I still have a lot to say. For instance, I have a long poem which was written too late to get into this book; it came out in the *Harvard Advocate* this summer. It is a long poem and it's called "Love Sequence with Variations." Let me just read, since we're talking about Hopkins. I put Hopkins into this poem. You mentioned "The Other Gerard" and what a modern Gerard would write compared with Hopkins; I put Hopkins into this one and I'll read you this little passage:

> But of Hopkins the sufferer I write further
> And think of his manuscripts, precise, intent,
> Who died unknown at the age of forty-four,
> As the scandal of genius, the secret heart of man,
> For this man, lost before reality's hardship,
> Buckled before his ability, and gave us his poems
>
> Shining in reality like the life of his Master,
> Peculiar, odd, differing, lovely and enlivening,

> And there is no madness, despite Plato,
> So rewarding as a true originality of nature
> Perceiving subtleties, central truths of nature,
> And there is no poet today so exacting as Hopkins.

So I'm glad to pay my tribute to him once more. And I notice, since life is so dynamic, and poetry also, only two days ago I received the new *Oxford Book of English Verse,* just brought out by the Oxford University Press, by Helen Gardner, and I note that in this book it is thought that Hopkins was one of the four greatest poets of the nineteenth century. What do you think of that!

Interviewer: There seems to be a tendency toward primitivism among some modern poets today. In the winter, 1971, issue of the *New York Quarterly,* in which your own "The Other Gerard" appeared, poet Jerome Rothenburg, in a craft interview, said this:

Poetry, it seems clear to me, grew out of a tribal and communal situation —even while going into the ages of literacy and the political stages—where we lost track of its beginnings, there was always a memory of poetry from the first civilization on. Poetry in a certain sense is a non-civilized thing. It is primitive in the sense that it is one of the first high developments in cultures that have not developed a political state. I don't think it ever really, in any significant sense, goes beyond that development. It always remembers its roots back in that primitive culture. It is a way of being in the world. . . .

California poet Gary Snyder also speaks of poetry's primitive, even "paleolithic" values in what he calls the "ecstasy of the tribe." What is your opinion of this new primitivism?

Eberhart: Well, I like what he has to say, and I subscribe to it heartily, and I feel these primitive urges in myself. I think that probably this inspiration that I was talking to you about, in going beyond the head to other lower and deeper regions of our being, comes along with this. Also, I've always loved and admired D. H. Lawrence a lot, and I think he is a gut, or sex, or primitive poet who understands the dark flow of things and the creative urges of man. On the other hand, I would like to respond to your question by announcing what maybe you've discovered already—maybe not quite yet, you haven't found me out entirely yet—I am really an ambivalent person. I used to say "schizophrenic" but that's an old-fashioned word now. I mean, I can see two sides of every question. And while you were reading those really pertinent things said by Rothenburg, which I love to hear and I thought have a lot of truth, you know what was running through my head all the time you were talking? The word *Mallarmé.* O.K., there's Mallarmé too. And Mallarmé is a great poet, one of the greatest. He's an enormous mountain, against which you have to come sometime in

257

your thinking. A man as sophisticated, as dense, as inspissated and as curious, and as complicated as Mallarmé would be at the opposite end of the poetic spectrum that he (Rothenburg) is talking about. But that's real too. I mean, Mallarmé is a great poet too, and he is of the coldest intelligence. I mean, the most crystal clarity—of course, behind his worth is a lot of confusion, and there may be a lot of this dark interplay, too, like in the one about the faun, *L'Après-Midi,* there is a great deal of the subconscious, erotic, dream-power in Mallarmé too, but I think of Mallarmé in the world, mostly as the intellectual poet par excellence . . . hard brained . . . so what can you answer? There is no dogma about poetry that covers the whole house. Poetry is a house of many mansions; it's so great a thing. And there's not a one—you take Eliot's principles of the impersonality of the poet that ruled the roost for thirty years, we were all raised on this; golly, how false that is if you believe in Shelley, say, or if you believe in yourself maybe. So I don't think it's impersonal at all. I think it's terribly personal. It's hard to talk about poetry at all, it's so complicated.

Interviewer: How do you personally define the role of the poet, what he is and does?

Eberhart: I don't define the role of the poet. I guess the role of the poet is thrust upon him. If Dylan Thomas, just for one part of his personality, if he hadn't had such a great voice box given him by God, probably he wouldn't have had thrust upon him the enormity of his success all over the Western world as the finest vocalizer of poetry of these times. And I don't know, some people become public poets; some like to stay private. Auden wrestled all his life with the idea of the public stance and the public man and he became the public man. Dear old John Ransom, whose picture you have up here, who is still alive, is a shrinking violet by comparison. He stayed all his life in Gambier, never liked the big fanfare or the big time; he's an excellent poet, but he kept it off—he's an esoteric or he's an ingrown or a small college orator-poet. And I'm not enough of a psychoanalyst to know why we become what we are. I wish I did know how any of us become what we are. Look at Robert Lowell. He's a powerful man, my student. What a strange role he has in the world, getting more complex all the time. He's now given up America. His life is disorderly.

And look at our Russian friends, how they get on or don't get on. Like Voznesenski, who was over last year—just last fall he came to Dartmouth. We had a fine time with him then. I introduced him—I guess he's the best poet there. He has so far not offended the Russian state enough to be thrown out; but he's always sort of on the verge. He has to be very careful. But they dislike the fact that he knows French poetry. He's been in Paris; he's been in London. He loves the London poets, he loves the American poets. You know they find this hard to take; so they like better Yevtushenko, who is, from the American intellectual point of view, not considered so good a poet, but who has a much wider audience. He speaks the language that the Russian state wants to hear and he loves his mother country, there's no doubt about it. But he's also sentimental. He's really a sentimentalist in some ways, compared with Voznesenski and now with Brodsky, who's been invited to leave Russia and has come over to the University of Michigan. So just think about that for a while. What is the role of the poet? It depends in a way on what country you're speaking of. In America, I rejoice to say, we still have freedom and may it long be with us, and one of the greatest things we still have to worry about in this country, politically, I believe, is the danger of a certain part of our national psyche coming into undue prominence. And I mean the vigilante part, which is very deep in America from early times. Or if you want to use a harsher word, the possibility of fascism or a repressive state, you know. I just would hate to think we'd go that way. But there are signs of it already. You know that. And that's what we have to worry about. This very campaign (Autumn 1972) has to do with these things, in my view. But I don't want to talk about politics here. But I think it's fine that American poets can do anything they like. If I didn't want to come down here I didn't have to accept the invitation. If I don't want to go around giving readings I could be a more private poet; or maybe I could be a much more public poet if I tried. I still feel that their freedom is the marvelous thing about American poets. You can do—you want to grow up like a flower, you want to flower out—you want to do your thing, you want to be the best you can. But you can do it in your own way. And that's what I love. I mean, every poet is different. All of us, all the people who are now speaking from my age down to thirty, or even way down to twenty, are individualists. I love the idea of individualism. I don't like the idea of schools, I never belonged to any school of poetry. I don't like to think that they're like schools of fishes. But we pride ourselves on what's called the New York School, all those fellows like to be in that. They go under one sort of heading. You know, there's one thing against individualism, that poets from a career point of view are much better off if they are allied with somebody else. I go back when I was at Cambridge to the beginning of the Oxford School. And those names are on everybody's lips forever more: Auden, Spender, Day-Lewis and MacNeice. Think how much good they all got from their names being associated. They really did. Although I think Spender wrote an

259

article about three or four years ago that amused me very much. When somebody asked about the "Oxford School," he said, and astounded everybody, that those four human beings had never been in a room until about 1950 together. The schoolroom wasn't very densely inhabited way back in the Thirties when their names got used together so much, you see. And you think of poets like this: Eliot and Pound, Stevens and Williams, Lowell and Wilbur. Oftentimes you get a lift if you're paired with somebody else. I was never paired with anybody else and I'm glad I wasn't. Neither was Dylan Thomas.

Interviewer: In much of your poetry there seems to have been a continual dialectic between humanism and mysticism, a *thisness* and an *otherness*. Could you elaborate on this? Do you feel that you have reached a resolution?

Eberhart: No. I think I know what you're talking about. No, it's totally unresolved. It probably never will be. Yeah, I think I'm alive, mentally and as a poet, because I have not been able to solve the questions that I want to solve, or that's one way of saying it. That the challenge is always there and you never can get the answers; or one is totally dissatisfied. I don't think I've written a good poem yet in my life—well that's going too far; I don't mean false modesty, but in some profound sense you feel that you have to keep on trying, you want to do it, you want to find the answers, see? I think the metaphysical is strong in me and I think the humanist is strong too. I don't know how they ever—they just get together in various ways in various poems. I think to read poetry you have to read a great deal of any man, that's if he has a lot of poems to show. You have to read. It's not fair really to only know anthologies. Anthologies are good because for one thing students can't afford to buy all these poets in whole books, you can't shell out six or seven dollars for every book, and you can get a very good education by reading a half-dozen of the best poems by all of the poets who are considered good. But I think the more you can read of one poet, the deeper your knowledge will be. At the end of reading some whole poet, like Auden, you may come down to only four or five poems, but at least you know the brunt of the man. You know his whole problem.

Interviewer: In two particular poems, "The Humanist" and "Mysticism Has Not the Patience to Wait for God's Revelation," you portray the mundane aspect of humanity as "an ape at the fair" and "the eternal ape on the leash." Could you clarify this image for us?

Eberhart: I think man is pulling along his past and he can never get rid of it, maybe something like that. On the other one—I can't even remember much from that poem—what was the line from that?

Interviewer: "The eternal ape on the leash/drawing us down to faith," I believe it was.

Eberhart: I think that's a rugged sentence and I think it means drawing us down to accept the whole of mankind including the ape. We can't be too far beyond . . . you can't be . . . I gave you all this airy stuff before but how many people ever get up into these airy reaches? And then, the good thing about mankind, I suppose, is that we are limited and that we have—well, I don't know, I shouldn't get into this theology. I hate to say it because I'm so much worse off than every one of you in this room, timewise, but probably it's fine that life doesn't last forever. Just think of that. You know, you live for two years or you live for seventy; or you live for forty-four like Hopkins, thirty-nine like Dylan, twenty-six for Keats, wasn't it, thirty-one for Shelley, or eighty-nine for Frost, or seventy-five for Stevens, it's still an awfully small bit of the reality of the world, isn't it? When you think of Mr. Leaky, who unfortunately died the other day at the age of only seventy, whom I heard gave a lecture in Seattle last spring on his discoveries of our true ancestors, as he thinks, just millions of years ago in East Africa—how small a span of time any of us has to figure out what it means to be alive, don't you see? So I think the poet should rejoice in our humanity, including the worst part of it, the lowest as well as the highest.

Interviewer: In one of your poems, "The Soul Longs to Return When It Came," you portray a modern individual participating in the primal ecstasy of nature's worship of the Earth Mother, saying:

> I flung myself down on the earth
> Full length on the great earth, full length,
> I wept out the dark load of human love,
> In pagan adoration I adored her.

Early in this century Swiss depth psychologist C. G. Jung expressed the notion of an archetypal woman with his concept of the *anima*; poet Robert Graves, in *The White Goddess*, examines the importance of such phenomena in poetry; more recently, Erich Neumann, in *The Great Mother*, almost comprehensively catalogs the myriad cultural expressions of this timeless archetypal woman-mother. You also deal with the idea of the Earth Mother in your brief, pretty poem, "Cover Me Over," and again more explicitly and powerfully in "The Soul Longs to Return When It Came," where you conclude:

> I went away,
> Slowly, tingling, elated, saying, saying,
> Mother, Great Being, O Source of Life

> To whom in wisdom we return,
> Accept this humble servant evermore.

Now, what in your opinion is the significance of this eternal return to the Great Mother for man in general and in your own art in particular?

Eberhart: When you were reading the first part of the lines about throwing himself down on the earth, I thought you were going to ask me some critical question about them, and I was going to say: The words say it all; you can't say any more; they are all there; it says itself; it's absolutely true; you can't improve on it. I mean, it's absolutely true to this profound experience. So what is the use of talking? I had not read Jung, I had not read Graves, when I wrote that poem. And the last thing you mentioned I don't think I even know. I think there is this. I believe that my poem fits in, as you said, to their principles; but the poem was from an immediate experience and had nothing to do with them. That's all I can say.

Interviewer: One last thing. What would be your advice, if anything, to beginning poets, people that are trying to learn to write now?

Eberhart. I guess that would depend upon my mood. If I were in a gloomy enough mood, and I must say I've been pretty gloomy the last few months, for all kinds of reasons, especially the way I look at the world. And every time you open a paper you can feel worse. Look what we did, bombing the French Embassy yesterday. I don't know. In my gloomiest and most pessimistic, I would not want anybody to write poetry. I wouldn't suggest it. I'd say, forget it. Any young person, don't do it. It's nothing but suffering and sorrow. It comes from suffering and speaks of suffering; and, paradoxically, it's supposed to give pleasure or joy. But it can't give pleasure or joy unless it understands the whole scope of man. And he is a suffering creature; and he early recognizes death and pain and sin, and he spends most of his time in his life trying to make some accommodation to these. Now, that's when I'm feeling my lousiest. If I'm feeling good, or if I'm sort of more rational—the world is a fine place and all that—what would I tell them? I would say that it's legitimate to imitate people slavishly, when you're in high school, say. And that the people should study the language. They should read poetry handbooks. They should learn all the forms, the beautiful very complicated forms there are. They should experiment with sonnets and villanelles and triolets and rondos and God knows what, ballads and everything, sestinas—that would be a little later maybe, but they should start by imitating old forms. I don't think they should start by writing right out of their heart, because they haven't had enough experience yet. So they should try to learn the language of poetry. And then gradually and painfully they should try to get their own style. And of course, the greatest thing is if somebody can finally master a style of his own, so that he doesn't sound like Ginsberg or Ferlinghetti or whomever it may be, if it were a few years ago. Or if he doesn't sound like whoever are the ones they would most imitate now who are, say, twenty-five to thirty. But I wanted to say, before we end, that I teach, and have taught for many years, creative writing or the writing of poetry at Dartmouth and at other institutions, and I assume when a man or a woman comes to a college, which would include yours here, that they are beyond what I've just been talking about; that they should do all that, theoretically, in high school, say from the age of about fifteen to eighteen. From about eighteen to twenty-two, I refuse to have any classes—well, I do it sometimes as a sportive gesture—but I, by and large, refuse to make them write sonnets, to make them write all these forms, because I think that's just too much playing of the scales. By the time they're eighteen to twenty-two, a human being's had quite a lot of experience by that time and what they ought to do is start telling their soul. They should put their hearts on paper, they should put their passions, their feelings, their whole reactions to life. And that's been the theory of my teaching, and I think they like that. Now sometimes we play games and everybody writes a sestina or something, but that really doesn't do them that much good. What they've got to do is to learn how to turn their feelings into some kind of a variable grammatical entity that will be pleasing as an English poem, or a poem in English—I mean an American poem. O.K. Well, thank you very much. You ask very good questions, I must say, very good questions.

An Interview (*American Poetry Review*)

Interviewer: You talked about pushing up daisies—going back to the earth and pushing up daisies—you think good people push up daisies further than—

Eberhart: Oh, heavens no! Good heavens, no! No, no—absolute materialism. It's just a matter of material. I think bigger people push up more daisies than smaller people.

Interviewer: How do you define a major poet?

Eberhart: These major words about poetry have always intrigued me—another one that I suppose you should ask me is, "What do you think about great; what is a great poem?" I think it's easier to define a minor poet than it is to define a major poet. And yet it seems simple if you look at the *Oxford Book of English Verse*—if you look at the history of poetry in any of the languages that I know anything about, the Western ones, you know who is a major poet and you know who is a minor poet. You know, for instance, that Shakespeare was a major poet and you know that there are all kinds of minor poets, compared with Shakespeare. You know that Dante was major. If you want to get it on the highest level, even in high school we learned that there are three major poets, Dante, Shakespeare, and Goethe, in the whole Western world, but you and I wouldn't draw it so fine as that.

Interviewer: Well, you were compared with Shakespeare recently—

Eberhart: Ah, yes, in one poem. I don't know, I don't think there's anything scientific about it—who gets called a major poet and who doesn't—but it's the critics who put people into categories. Now, for instance, I think very highly of A. E. Housman, and yet I have heard it said that he's not a major poet. Well, if he's not a major poet, who,

First published in *American Poetry Review* 6, no. 3 (1977): 30–36. The interviewer is Irving Broughton.

amongst the people of his time, was? You hear it said that Hopkins was certainly greater than Housman; Hardy is considered a major poet, and by many people Housman is considered major, but there are other people who don't—they think he is too thin because he didn't write enough. Auden and others have held that to be a major poet you have to have a great deal of quantity—of course, the quality goes without saying—but that you really can't be major if you write one or two or three or four or five poems. To be a major poet presumes a large nature and the large expression of that nature. So it's very hard to say. There's an anthology right now called *The Major Poets of England and America*—uh, well (chuckles) some people spread a wider net, some spread a less wide net, you know.

Interviewer: George Cannon spoke in his memoirs, saying no one ever taught him to view a painting, a building, a tree—

Eberhart: Well, that's like saying that you cannot teach poetry. I don't believe that at all. I think you can.

Interviewer: Why do so many great writers consider themselves failures?

Eberhart: I think that's a very hard kind of question to answer. I thought at once of Melville. People say now, this late, that Herman Melville was a failure, or thought he was a failure, and we know that his fame came after his lifetime and now he's considered absolutely great, one of our greatest writers, and yet he had difficulty in having his books published and all that sort of thing; he didn't have any *éclat* or any big doings when he was alive. But then I don't know—to answer a question like that just on one man would presume a great deal of knowledge which I don't have. You know, you have to know all about him, all about his attitude to his writing, all about his psyche, and I just don't know. Poe thought he was a failure, although he succeeded quite a bit, and he was always a desperate man, and drank himself to death.

Interviewer: What about suicide?

Eberhart: I think you have to die for poetry, but I don't think it should be literal. If you have to die for poetry, that's too bad. If you have to put your head in the oven and turn on the gas, as Sylvia Plath did, to become famous, or to be read at all, because—well, she was just starting in the usual slow, hard way of going up the artistic hill when she had six months—toward the end of her life—of tremendous illumination and outpouring of her kind of uniqueness, and during those few months she wrote her best poems.

She has a very harsh voice. I remember the last time I heard her, on the gramophone, I could hardly stand it just because of the harshness

265

of her voice, the lack of humanity, the lack of warmth, the brittleness, the terrific passion of this woman. Well, I'm not here to say, about her poetry, its ultimate value now, but I take her seriously, and all the professional poets do, and she now has quite a high place in the pantheon of American poetry. As a matter of fact, some people say she's great, or she's—you know—she's going to be permanent.

I want to go on record as being against suicide. I think, from a rational point of view, we have a right to do it. We didn't ask to be born, we know we have to die, and if you want to take your life by reason, it seems to me you have a right to. I wouldn't object to that. What I object to, in a poet, is the idea of thinking that suicide is the way to the meaning of poetry. It seems to me it should be just the opposite. Sylvia Plath should not only be alive, and less famous today than she is, but she should be struggling for the next twenty years to write more and better poetry, and maybe by the time she was fifty or sixty she would get to be known to be as good as Elizabeth Bishop or Marianne Moore, or whoever you wish to name. But that wasn't to be, in her case, and I never can read her poems without dissatisfaction over her end. And you know, suicide is getting to be quite a thing these days . . . I don't know, you have to have a pretty good sense of humor to get through literature. A. Alvarez gives a list of the famous recent suicides, and he knew Sylvia Plath well, and he was with her almost at the time; he knows a great deal about her, and he mentions Berryman, the most recent one, but he doesn't mention Winfield Townley Scott—so there are hierarchies, even within the suicide list.

So, as opposed to suicide, I'd like to propose the unpopular side that I'm on, always have been on: I've always believed in an Elizabethan kind of fullness of life, and I think that artists should be whole people rather than hurt, broken, mad, or demented ones—as they often are—and that they should have every experience that they want or can get in life; that they are not odd, not strangely divorced from the rest of humanity, but that in fact they are richer in sensory equipment, and as intelligent as any, and can and should live a full life. Out of fullness of life, a lust for life, if you like—a joy in life—the great art can come. So again, you come and find that there is just as difficult a thing to try to decide, as learners, about what kind of poet, or what kind of composer or painter, you think would represent life best: the outgoers, the full-bodied ones, the richly sensory people, or the crabbed and indrawn, subjective, the quaint, the odd.

Interviewer: You wrote a poem about a suicide.

Eberhart: That's about a woman we knew, who had survived Hitler. If one survives Hitler, and comes to this country and has a new life and lasts for ten or twelve or fifteen years more, wouldn't you think pretty well of that person? You know, you'd think that this would be a conquering of her terrible predicament. And yet there are delayed time bombs, there are delayed realities. She was as much a victim of Hitler as if she had been thrown into a furnace in Germany, at Auschwitz. Fifteen years later she couldn't take life anymore. We knew her, she was a poet, she came to the poetry readings at Dartmouth.

Interviewer: Who was this?

Eberhart: I can't remember her name. She was a beautiful Jewish woman, a very short woman, who had a child, one child about twelve years old, and had a husband in Lebanon, but then he vanished; nobody could have foreseen this, but she finally took a hand gun and blew her brains out.

Interviewer: That doesn't seem natural to me.

Eberhart: Oh, but I think Hitler won. This was the history of Hitler twenty years later. Well, I don't blame her if she felt that way. I just felt sad about it. I didn't have any intention that I was going to write the poem, and I hardly knew her, but I wrote the poem out of sympathy and empathy.

Interviewer: How important is encouragement in writing? Do you need it as a writer?

Eberhart: I think you do, I think most poets do. If you fail as a poet, it is a bitter pill, a very long and bitter thing. You have to succeed, you have to win credence for your ideas, you have to have your say among people who will listen to what you say and who will grant that you are saying something valuable to them, or it's a disaster.

Interviewer: Do you believe, with Blake, that if the sun and moon should doubt, they would immediately go out?

Eberhart: Oh, yes, absolutely. That's a most nonscientific sentence. This is subjective, he's talking about the imagination. What is it again? If the sun and moon should doubt, they would immediately go out? That's just absurd, isn't it, absurd; it posits a human mind to inanimate planets, you know, so you have to make a move there to—you have to reach through the credibility gap, right there. But then obviously, if the sun and the moon didn't believe in themselves subjectively as you or I wouldn't, why, naturally they would be nothing, so in that way it's true. It's a poetical proposition and assertion.

Interviewer: Borges is troubled by Blake because he feels he lacks modesty.

Eberhart: Well, I don't know Borges enough to know why he should be so modest himself; maybe there's a lot in virtue that we don't have in the North so much. That moves right over me without touching me at all. I think modesty covers over the truth, and Blake is a man who gets directly to the truth, so he wouldn't have to have modesty. In other words, Blake would say modesty, I suppose, was a false value.

Interviewer: And you would also?

Eberhart: I would tend to, yes. It depends on what you think about society. For instance, let me say that when I lived in the intellectual society of Cambridge University when I was a young man, and when there were no wars at the moment, and when there hadn't been the crash of 1929, but it was imminent, and when there was a highly stylized cultural situation in England, and to some extent in America, too, when we hadn't entertained, say, the black questions in the West, we hadn't—it was such a structured and bland and old-fashioned society that, for instance, if you were a man in Cambridge University at that time, and you felt you had a sort of elegance about you and you were quite aware of your personality and of yourself and of your position in a more or less stable society, then you can afford to be modest. Not only can you afford to, but to be modest is just one of the forms of being polite. You are polite with others because the structures of society haven't been undermined. So you live these elaborate rituals of the gentleman. I remember those very well, the sort of gentlemanly conduct of the young intellectuals. So it depends on what you think of society, and what it actually is like at the time.

Interviewer: Would you explain the "desert island trick" of evaluating poetry?

Eberhart: Oh, yes. That's just a way of getting an absolute. Everything is so relative in connection with poetry and the values of poetry that one way to try to force people to make up their minds is to pull this trick of saying, If you had to go to a desert island and, let's say, if he was a professor and had twelve poets to choose from, you'd say, which one or which two would you take to live with for a year? So it is a trick, but it's a viable one, and it makes people think what they would slough off and tries to make them instantaneously decide what are the best values of literature. Like somebody might instantly say, I would take Homer, the Bible, and Shakespeare. That would be a conservative view, but he would be wise to take all three of those. It's just a little tricky way of trying to make people be precise.

Interviewer: Did you invent the twelve times test?

Eberhart: Oh, I don't have any idea that I did—I don't have the faintest notion that I did. Why, do you think I did?

Interviewer: I think you did. Or the twenty times test.

Eberhart: I don't know. I must say, I've used that idea quite a bit, but I don't believe I invented it. Somebody else must have thought of it.

Interviewer: You say everything's fair in love, war, and poetry.

Eberhart: In love and war, and I guess when I added poetry I meant poetry is a ruthless business too. I don't think that's too profound, though, when connected. I do think there's some truth, though, in love and war. But I don't think it's quite right to add poetry, because it's a much more complex thing—anything does not go, in poetry; there are many things that do not go; many things that go better than not. So I don't think I should have added that one. Or, if I did—after all, I have a certain facetiousness in my nature, too, or a certain comic sense. Maybe I mean that in a lighthearted way. To stimulate people to think a little bit. They can knock it off themselves.

Interviewer: What about the two theories of how poetry is derived: the pain theory and the energy theory? Aren't some people sort of born with pain—without a specific trauma? In other words, isn't it conceivable that some people be born of pain, have pain sort of ingrained by other than experience?

Eberhart: I think Housman must have suffered a general pain like you're talking about; he was a misanthrope, misanthropic because he disliked mankind in general, but he probably had specific troubles in his adolescence that made him take badly to mankind.

Interviewer: Of these two theories, the pain theory and the energy theory, to which do you subscribe?

Eberhart: Oh, well—I subscribe to both and I find them both in my own nature, and I think it's a perfectly arbitrary dichotomy. But it troubles me that I never go around with trichotomies or quatrochotomies or whatever, that I never get over a dualism which is basic in my mind, and—I'm afraid—is somewhat basic in the whole Western mind. I think both are very true, but I have always had health and vitality, and when I was starting to write in high school I threw off poems by the dozens, if not by the hundreds, with the greatest of ease—and with a tremendous verve and pleasure and joy. It was as easy as falling off a log, as they used to say, although I never fell off a log, but—you know, it was easy, and so in that sense poetry was play, it was a kind of play with words and it was easy to do and it was fun and pleasant. Beth Bentley recently expressed the idea that poetry, for her, was play—that's interesting. I think it's much more than play, but she stressed the idea of play, playing with words as if they were easy counters and as if it were a kind of light operation which you could truly manipulate. It seems to me you must write poems beyond the age of twenty, or twenty-five, or thirty, or whatever arbitrary date you want to put on it, because of some profound malaise within your being or something split in the soul, as I like to call it, some psychic split or Freudian split or whatever, maybe going back to the year one or the year two or three, or maybe a trauma that you never knew you had, during your adolescence, or maybe some actual trouble that changed your life in the real world. Well, I suffered some of these things myself and it took years to figure out the significance of them, or what were the operant powers of them, but I know that both these things are true within my own self, and there's always a tug between them. There are the death poems, if you like to say, or the death wish or the fact that you only write when you're in fatigue or when you feel defeat or when you are destroyed to some extent and yet you have enough force to try to push up a flower out of the dungheap —something like that. It's something to right your mind when your mind feels incapable of order but is not in total disorder, and yet you want to withhold yourself from being too orderly so that you may not yet come up to order—that kind of subtlety operates.

Interviewer: Well, you're healthy. What effect does your good health have on your writing, on your life?

Eberhart: You never can say. It might have been that I would have written much better and much more and I might be much further along in poetry if I had been ill half the time. Quite possible, because I know the whole creation comes from states allied to that. On the other hand, if I were too ill, I wouldn't have done a thing—I wouldn't have the energy either to do it or to care. Furthermore, you say I'm healthy—well, how healthy am I? I don't know . . .

Interviewer: You've never been to the hospital.

Eberhart: I've been to the hospital for checkups. I've never been in the hospital, no. Except when I was about twelve and had my tonsils taken out.

Interviewer: Don L. Lee, who's a black poet, says that white po- ets are obsessed with death . . . do you think this is a weakness of white poetry?

Eberhart: That sort of puts me on the spot as to how much I know about black poetry.

Interviewer: Well, do you think it can be a weakness of poetry?

Eberhart: I don't think it's a weakness. I think death is one of the great topics of poetry, because it's one of the great things of life. In a way you can say it's the greatest thing about life, because it's the only thing that we absolutely know that we absolutely know nothing about. We don't know whether we're going to be sitting here—you don't know how long we're going to live—you have nothing to say about it. It is one of the great final things, and I can't imagine that whites have the only lien on this topic. But I don't think I know enough about black poetry per se to know whether they use it less. I was thinking of Dennis Brutus, and I think in his poetry there's as much recognition of death as there is in mine, as far as I can see. He may not write typical objective death poems, but there's the sub-stratum of feeling that the black people in South Africa live close to death—they are right on the line of life and death all the time—if you take imprisonment and the taking away of liberties and everything like that as being a deadly act.

Interviewer: Are you a hero worshiper?

Eberhart: I think I was a hero worshiper when I was growing up. But I don't think I am anymore. For instance, in college, I was a hero worshiper of Nietzsche for years. I read everything he wrote, I adored everything he said. I understood it only in a small way, as I look back at my life from, say, twenty or thirty years later. I thought his ideas were absolute, but if you read Kazantzakis right now on Nietzsche, or if you read historians of Hitler and Mussolini, who hold that they got their ideas from Nietzsche, you feel differently. I wouldn't say that he was the precursor of Nazism, although he did talk about a mas-ter race. But he talked about it in a different way. Yes, I certainly hero worshiped him a lot. Oh, I had fleeting worships of many poets—I remember worshiping Keats, you know, lots of people go through this. I remember first going to England and going to Keats's house and looking at where he sat and seeing his manuscripts with absolute adoration. But that was rather ephemeral. I don't know if worship is tl.ᵒ right word—I don't think I'd say worship—but the three poets, as you know, who influenced me really were Wordsworth, and then Blake and Hopkins. I think I had Buddha as a hero for a long time. When I went around the world on tramp freighters, I faced up to seeing tens of thousands of Chinese people who had never heard of Jesus Christ, under whose system I'd grown up. That led me to think a great deal how well these Chinese pagans went from birth to death, and it made me denigrate Christianity for a long time. Then I read Buddha—I was, in fact, enamoured of Buddha for a long time. I guess I worshiped him. More than, say, Mohammed or Taoism, or more than Confucianism. Confucianism is a practical polity, but Buddha is one of the great ideas. I mean Buddha was daring enough to say that you can only seek peace or be at peace if you escape from the senses entirely—well, that's a pretty big thing to think about. What do we have but senses? We have a sensory organism—which is your body—and he in effect says all desires are bad, all bodily desires are bad, and that you have to get away from them, and you can only get away from them by silence and by prayer. And in a way he goes beyond Christ's religion, which is an activist one, that you should go out and love your neighbor, and you should do something for others, you should help others and all that—he goes into the shrinking, that you should be self-enclosed within your own personality, own psyche, and have nothing to do with anybody else. If you have something to do with somebody else, you'll probably get into trouble, desire will come, warfare will come, killing will come—and I always loved the story about the Buddha who was a prince, a handsome young prince and had a princess and a small baby, and one night he was walking in the gardens of the palace and he saw three sights: he saw an old man, and he saw a sick man, and he saw a dead man. And being of a sentient nature, he realized that all of these things would happen to him, and he shuddered at the possibility of being old, sick, or dead. So he then got his big idea, and he left his wife and his child, he left the sensuous world, the world of procreation, all that, and he walked out of the palace grounds forever and never returned, and spent seventeen years meditating under the tree to get away, to try to divorce himself from the possibilities of old age, sickness, and death by trying to become as much like nothingness as possible . . . I mean, to become the way we will be when we're dead. As far as we know, the world will still be here, there will be time and space, there will be a universe of some kind, and—but he thought the way to be happy was to seek Nirvana, which has been equated with our heaven, but not an active thing with actual angels around. Nirvana was a state of ultimate grace and negation and of peace and harmony and oneness, and nothingness. Those ideas powerfully influenced me for a long time. But in the West, you can't be a Buddhist; there are now hundreds of Buddhists around, thousands of them, but I don't want to be a Buddhist. I enjoy his ideas, I know what they are, but you have to partake of the nature of the times.

Interviewer: If you were elsewhere, if you were overseas, do you think you could be a Buddhist?

Eberhart: Oh, I think if I'd stayed in the Orient I might have become one—something like that, yes.

Interviewer: Do you think you've been judged harshly by critics?

Eberhart: No, I don't think I have been judged harshly. I don't think I've been—I think that's too harsh a word to say. I don't think anybody has been harsh enough on me to ruin my words. Maybe time will do that. I think I had to struggle so hard within myself and against society when I was young, also through the Thirties and Forties up to

World War II, that I'm tolerant about what anybody says. Like most men, if they praise, I love them; if they hate me or dislike me, I tend to ignore them. You know, I probably hate them back, but I don't, so I try not to say it—and you have me sitting here in a very good situation because in a way it's much better to be where I am, right now, than it was to be a poet ten years younger, even, than I am now. Or certainly twenty years younger—when all these things were matters of life or death. If you're older and have more perspective, you think, "Oh, well, let him say what he likes, that's only one review . . . there are going to be other reviews." No, I think the worst thing for a poet is to suffer indifference. If somebody criticizes you harshly, at least they are laying on with their forks and knives and their bludgeons, and that's a sign of life. What hurts is indifference. If you were not noticed, that is the most galling thing. And that's what happened to Emily Dickinson. There was a woman who knew Emily well, and used to stop and see her at Amherst, had several books out and was sort of the reigning successful female poet of the times. Well, it must have been galling to Emily to know that she was not only as good, but better than this woman, and couldn't get a hearing. So it's all very relative, but I don't think I have been dealt with harshly. I believe in the central compulsions of poetry. I'm glad that I write a lot, that I've published a lot. I think it's a sign of a fullblooded life. But I know other poets who write very little and are splendid. I don't say that one course is necessarily better than another.

Interviewer: Stanley Kunitz?

Eberhart: Stanley is a splendid poet, one of our best, and he's written relatively little. He's a perfectionist and he's getting high praise for his work and he had the kind of temperament to be able to withstand silence for decades and go about his business in a quiet way, exacting his own demands from himself. But I would say this, that you'll note that although Stanley Kunitz is my own age, he is flowering now, and he's flowering out mightily and I'm glad he is.

Interviewer: Leila Rogers told the House Un-American Activities Committee that she considered *None but the Lonely Heart* un-American because it was gloomy. [Laughter] Is it un-American to be gloomy?

Eberhart: I think that's a silly question. [Gales of laughter] Oh, gloom is all right in its place. Nice to be gloomy sometimes. Why not?

Interviewer: Seems like most of your Maine poems are very definitely rooted poems, I mean they're rooted in a locale—they're a little bit easier to get handles on in certain respects—do you feel this?

Eberhart: I feel that there is a group of maybe twenty or twenty-five poems about places in Maine, but I think that's just part of my work. I don't make anything about that. I don't think that—if I had to think of a place where poetry is, it's in the mind and the heart, it's in the psyche. I mean, I used to say that Frost was the New England poet, he had to be a New England poet; well, maybe that was true, but I wouldn't like to limit him that much.

Interviewer: According to Borges, William Henry Hudson was trying to read Hume or Spinoza and couldn't because happiness kept breaking in.

Eberhart: I like that. But I think I would immediately see just the opposite. I like to be happy, I think that's great—to have happiness break in and you hope it will last a long time, but let's take it the other way around. What if you were a happy mortal, wouldn't you be delighted, maybe, if a little thought broke in sometime, and you were hit by the profoundest thing ever said by Sophocles, that "Best it would be never to have been born; next best, to go back fastest whence ye came"? I can see an analogy there, and I don't see that it's necessarily better to see it on one side than on the other. I suppose Sgt. Calley was a happy man, wasn't he? Dumbbell, who just killed when they told him to, didn't seem to have any moral conscience.

Interviewer: Is poetry anti-democratic?

Eberhart: What a marvelous question! That is a powerful question; I congratulate you on thinking of it. I suppose then you have to decide what you mean by democratic, but let's take the common meaning that everybody understands, more or less. I think it is from this point of view, that if you look at the best poets of any thirty years, these high names—they get there, they get where they are in the anthologies and in the history of literature of this country by superior powers; they have more intelligence, by birth probably, in the first place; they have more highly trained intellects by study in the second place, or by going to universities. So, in a way, this seems undemocratic.

I have kicked against this a lot. I mean, think of a man as lofty and noble and great as Wallace Stevens. He was a businessman and lived in ordinary American society, had a nice house, had a wife and child, and he wasn't a snob when you met him—but there was an absolute superiority to his mind and to the quality of his imagination which in my view rode over hundreds of other people—thousands of other poets, if you can imagine that many—so that, yes, it is absolutely undemocratic, he simply can't—you can't call him a commoner in this art; he was a great particularist. He was a mountain peak—and you could say this of several others, obviously; I just mention him—so that in a way it does seem very undemocratic. It seems not aristocratic, which would be the opposing word, because we don't have any aristocracy in society, but you could use that word a hundred years ago, or two hundred years ago. It did come from *aristoi,* or the more highly educated, rather than from the *plebes* or *plebeians, hoi polloi* to use the other Greek word.

Now let's take a question on the other side—should it be democratic, or is it democratic? Again, I've named a man at the top of his profession, in our time, one of the half-dozen I can mention; and yet isn't it a grand thing from a cultural point of view, that there are so many hundreds and even thousands of young poets writing poetry all over America? Isn't it splendid that the University of Washington, to name only one, has such a lively input and outgo, outflow of poems and poets, and that is on the democratic side, I would say. Isn't it fine that they have me here? That's a democratic thing. Don't you think that it's splendid that there are twenty or thirty poets-in-residence all over America today? That's sort of spreading it out, it's saying how far each poet may or may not get, and that maybe one of them will win a Pulitzer Prize or something, some day. I'm not being that particular. But I think there's a great hope for the democracy or the democratic idea of poetry in its widespread use, and I really am for that. The longer I live the less I like elitism or snobbery. I have known that too much, earlier in my life. I saw that implacable power of the elitism, you know, and so I like the generality of poetry.

Interviewer: Why do you say that?

Eberhart: Well, I think the great poets will be the great intellects, the great poets will be the people who can assemble the ideas of a whole century. There are few people who understand Wallace Stevens, but many more people could read, twenty-five years ago, Carl Sandburg. He could be the closest example of what we have as a poet of the commonality, a poet of the people; and yet his poems are so simple that you can't read them many times. You read them once and you have them. Wallace Stevens gives us endless delight because his subtlety and fineness, refinements of his poetry, allow you to get more pleasure out of the twentieth reading—so you see how I'm always in the dichotomous business; I can't answer these questions black or white. I want to say this, since you've got it on record: I would like to hope that this country could sometime, maybe in this century, produce a universal poet. And like you might think of Shakespeare in the sixteenth and seventeenth centuries, when he came along this universal poet would appeal to people on all levels, the high and the low, the highly educated and the lesser educated. And maybe he would come out of the cornfields of Kansas, but it's more likely he'd come out of Harvard. I hope we do, but I don't think it's very likely. Stevens was great but he wasn't universal; Sandburg is also great—though not so many people say so—but he was—a hundred years from now he'll be just as great; he'll have said his thing about America in 1920—but then he only spoke to the workman; he didn't speak to the learned intelligence. There's a dichotomy that you can't get around.

Interviewer: Your poems talk often of love.

Eberhart: That is a big topic. I think it's a kind of generalized love, I mean, I don't think I write poems about specific love objects or specific acts of love. I think I use the word in a philosophical sense, or maybe in a religious sense, in that man must love his neighbors; you must love mankind and you must love your brother, and so forth. I think it's love in a kind of basic, universal sense that I mean it, rather than in specifics—although I do know the love of a man for his job, for instance, or—you know—love of animals and all that, love of man for a woman.

Interviewer: Where would man be without the faculty of imagination?

Eberhart: He'd be back in the cave state somewhere; maybe he wouldn't have invented fire yet, or if he had fire, maybe he wouldn't have gone any farther than that, but—oh yes, just as I hold two hundred million Americans can live well without ever reading a poem. Which in a sense they do; only a small percentage of the vast millions of Americans understand what we're talking about today, or know about serious poetry.

It's not a direct analogy, but I can see an analogy here, that man, if he didn't have imagination, might be a very successful animal on the face of the earth. He wouldn't have written the Bible, he wouldn't have produced Notre Dame, he wouldn't have produced Shakespeare, he wouldn't have produced Beethoven. You almost intrigue me into saying he might be better than with it. Because it is through his imagination that we have got almost to our apocalyptic end, and it's through the imagination that we invented the atom bomb, and if we don't have reason enough to control that and not let it control us, we'll blow the whole thing to smithereens. And then where's man with all his imagination? He will have annihilated himself.

I'm not a great lover of the primitive, in one sense—I haven't denied society and gone back, like Gauguin, to the Polynesian canoe life or something like that. But it is sort of intriguing to think of man, from what you know about him anthropologically, in a much simpler stage than we are, where he might have actually been much happier; his mind wasn't so developed, therefore he didn't have such a keen sense of good and evil, therefore he didn't know anything about sin, for instance. And no imagination to worry about these things. So you intrigue me into an answer I didn't know I'd give you, on that.

Interviewer: Your childhood seemed to be one of camaraderie—can one in later years ever replicate this?

Eberhart: I think maybe you try to all the time. I'm not enough of a Freudian psychologist, but I did have a glorious childhood, it was Edenic, it was like total happiness—it was like heaven on earth. And then one suffered the fall of man, and the falling away, and the death of parents, the loss of material goods, and then you had to struggle, try to find out what life means. No, I don't think you could ever get it back, but I think you can dream it back, and that's what I do in some of the poems I read in public, which hark back to childhood, you know, some of those early poems. And maybe the fact that I had such a good childhood and youth is why I still love mankind, in the sense that I love social events, I like to be with people. I'm not a loner, I like to live in society—maybe I'm secretly hoping to bring that kind of happiness back. I don't know.

Interviewer: Could you be a hermit poet?

Eberhart: No. I don't think I ever could . . . no.

Interviewer: Not at all?

Eberhart: Oh, yes, maybe for a month, a year—even a year. No, no, a year is too long. I'd like to be a hermit for, say, three months— live absolutely alone and think and write.

Interviewer: What do you think about these secrets people have for living to an old age?

Eberhart: Who can say why a man lives to be a hundred and two? He probably doesn't know himself, you know—maybe it's just a genetic thing. I believe in heredity. Maybe his father and his grandfather, you know, gave him certain stamina, a certain cast or make of body that lasts longer than some other make. My mother was a beautiful woman, but how—why—she got cancer at the age of forty-eight nobody could ever tell. It killed her. Why should she get it at that age? These are mysteries. Everything in the world is mysterious.

I think the more we know, the better off we are. And yet I almost despair of the mind. The older I get, the less I believe in the mind per se. It seems to me you have to work your mind so hard to know anything, and to know everything about any topic is—it's almost impossible. So I don't believe in the mind so much. I believe in what I call the whole being, the whole man—I believe in the senses, the total senses, your whole walking on the face of the earth. All of your organs. I'm much closer to D. H. Lawrence and to the sexual drive or the stomachic—I consider myself a stomachic type—I mean the love of sensory experiences. It seems to me that's closer to the nature of what man is than the intellect, which gets so trained in universities that it becomes apart from mankind, too often. This may be just a rationalization, because I know that I haven't got a brain as big as Einstein's; maybe when we make any of these pronouncements we are trying to defend ourselves against our lack. Or, to put it another way, if I had a critical mind as advanced as that of my friend and mentor, I. A. Richards, I would probably think much better of criticism, you see? So in a sense a poet defends his own energies, he defends his own feelings, and his own particularity on the face of the earth, and he can only write out of himself, he can only write what he is.

Interviewer: Did you ever meet Lawrence?

Eberhart: I remember seeing D. H. Lawrence as far away as you are from me at the back of this room, no farther than that, and he was just as his pictures depict him, he was lean and nervously alive, sort of a very energetic, quick-moving man, not too tall and not too short, with a red, red short beard, sort of blazing eyes, a terribly animated man, and, well, I could have gone up to say hello to him—lots of other people did—but it might amuse you to know that I felt so sophisticated, with my friend then, that we did not deign to walk twenty feet to say hello to D. H. Lawrence. And that was an example of our princely sophistication. We thought we were too elegant or too— I don't know what words—too Cantabrigian to bother to go and say hello. We could see him, that was good enough. We saw his paintings, we saw what was going on—but I now wish, of course, that I hadn't been such a snob. In Lawrence's book there was a passage toward the end where the reading was pretty racy, and the bookstore in Florence had received, say, a hundred copies of this book right away, and when I got there, to this bookstore, just innocently going into it, there was a queue of at least forty people lined up and there was a post from the ceiling to the floor around which was a wooden table, round table like this, where you could lean and read, and the unexpurgated copy of this book was chained to a post, and here were people queued up to get their read of this book. And of course they were all reading this purple passage, or blood passage, in the back —and really it was the strangest thing in the world how eager people were. They had heard about this, it was wildfire, you know, all very new and all very daring and very exciting. Well, I waited in line and queued up and finally got my two minutes' worth of reading a chained book by D. H. Lawrence . . . I never forgot that. Does this mean anything or not? It always struck me as probably deeply meaningful that a man like Lawrence, who spent all his life talking about sex, probably wasn't very good at it. I mean, this often happens, I think . . . I mean, if he'd been more normal he would probably have been a good father, a good husband, and a more regular kind of man. But then he wouldn't be D. H. Lawrence. You can psychoanalyze him a great deal, he was a very passionate man and had tremendous abilities, but I've often heard—I've met people who knew him, out in Taos and they said it was electrifying to be with him. I mean, he thought so fast and talked so hard and was so alive, and he was so vigorous in his whole being; but he was sort of like a different kind of man, he really wasn't like the rest of mankind in some way. And that always struck me as one of the prime paradoxes, that his whole thing was talking about sex and yet he had no family, raised no family, and didn't know what it was to be a father. Well, I think he admitted that women were the stronger of the two. I think he thought that women were the more powerful. That man was a kind of man who never gets over being a little boy.

Interviewer: You write a lot and publish a lot, and you've been criticized for that.

Eberhart: I guess maybe it's part of the insecurity; if you write widely, and you publish widely, maybe you could say it's because you haven't the patience or the security to perfect some jewel-like final object. On the other hand, maybe this audacity, as you call it, is a pugnacious refusal to accept any of the prevailing modes. Maybe what keeps me alive as a poet is that, to this day, I do not know where I stand—and maybe if I knew where I stood I would be dead, that would be the end of me as a creator; whereas, if the world is always open, always possible, and always potential, you go on creating, trying to make the perfect poem which you know you'll never achieve. And I like to think of it in this second way, because—who are these masters of the poetry of the time? Do all of us, when you're coming along, say, when you're coming up, do you have to bow down to somebody else's idea of what poetry is like? Now, that's what I dislike. I don't say it in a vainglorious way, but I'm glad that I'm an individualist, as an American and as a middlewesterner to start on, and I think I would never be taken in by Eliot or Pound. I never belonged to any school—it's a lucky thing that I never did—hundreds of poets were ruined, about thirty years ago, by writing like somebody else, like belonging to the Eliot school or the Pound school. And there's the whole business of the New Criticism, and the New Critics set a rigid notion of what a poem should be and should not be. Well, I never fitted in any of those schools, but maybe that's just good luck. Maybe it has something to do with idiosyncratic ego, or God knows . . . something much worse than that.

Interviewer: What about those who don't stick at it?

Eberhart: T. S. Eliot wrote nothing after *Four Quartets*—why? The next twenty years of his life, from his fifties up to his death, he was not an active poet. He finally married his secretary, a beautiful woman; he wrote a little poem to her that was feeble, although his love for her was great. And how can you account for a man as powerful in mind and poetic consciousness, as strong as Eliot, coming to an end, as it were, long before the man; whereas, to name some other oldsters—it's fair game in these things, I guess, not to mention younger people who are still at it so much—but Robert Frost wrote at the age of eighty-eight one of his best poems, "Away," two years before his death. A saucy poem—that whole last book had excellent things in it. And Wallace Stevens was writing right up to his death at seventy-five. Bill Williams, as we affectionately called him, was writing—he wrote "Asphodel, That Greening Flower" and the love poems, some of the best love poems written by an American, when he was over eighty. I'm for the people who go on, I'm for that, but I simply do not know why—I don't know.

Interviewer: You said T. S. Eliot was insecure—you once told me a story about how he was always holding his wife's hand.

Eberhart: You know, the truth is very hard to come by. Now you've already given a false impression. I only knew T. S. Eliot very little, and at one dinner party at Robert—Elisabeth Lowell's at Marlborough Street before the Lowells went to New York, Betty and I had the pleasure of dining with Mr. and Mrs. Eliot, and Ivor and Dorothea Richards—and that was a magnificent evening, and I don't think that I have the time here to explain all the things that went on, but I was surprised that Eliot, after dinner, held the hand of his wife for hours—he simply couldn't let go of it. It seemed so abnormal a thing—he was married to her, after all, but he had this great need—it was the most pathetic thing I ever saw. And I think it made the audience, the others, a little restive, but what could you do? That was his thing at the moment, and he needed it very much—but I don't know, I wouldn't deign to say whether he was insecure or not; I haven't the faintest idea. I just mentioned that as a phenomenon, but it should be seen in a larger context, and it wasn't all that important.

I think your single question builds it up to mean more than it did.

Let me say one thing on this: This whole thing of autobiography or of biography is fraught with difficulties. For instance, is it in good taste for me to say what I have said? Was it in good taste for me to tell you this little anecdote? Who am I to talk to the public or to the future or to whoever's going to listen to this, about some little thing like that in the personal life of T. S. Eliot? You know, maybe this is in the worst taste; maybe I shouldn't have done it at all. How do you know what is true, what is the truth? And what should you say about other people, what should you say about yourself?

Interviewer: I think there's some other word besides "taste," though—I get a little confused and troubled by "taste"—what is your definition of taste? It seems a very casual word, you know—what is good taste.

Eberhart: Well, I think it has to do with not offending others. Good taste certainly would be some kind of elegance or restraint, where you wouldn't offend other people, but you would be saying what you thought was the truth within limits.

Interviewer: What are our obligations to history? Do you save your papers?

Eberhart: I think it comes down to a matter of personality or type. I happen to be a saver, so I save every scrap of paper, so there are huge archives now in the Dartmouth library. If you want to come, you can spend weeks wandering around in these papers of thirty years. Other people are the opposite. I remember that Ted Roethke was also a saver—I don't know whether he ever told me—I knew him at Yaddo for six weeks in the Fifties, but anyway, I guess if I were telling this on the record in print—that he saved every scrap of paper; and yet there are poets who throw away all the first drafts of poems, just throw them away. I think Auden did that, because I watched Auden for five or six weeks just a year after he'd been in this country, and he would throw things in the scrap basket all the time. He'd throw away whole versions of poems and keep the latest one. And I'm going to name, lastly, a long-time friend of mine, I. A. Richards, whom I have long admired, began to admire at Cambridge and still love him—he's called the father of modern criticism, so he's much greater as a critic than as a poet, but he is a poet too—and I was talking with Richards about a year ago about this. He's absolutely adamant—he throws everything away—he won't save anybody's letters, he doesn't keep carbon copies of his own letters, he doesn't want any of what he'd call trivia around, at all. All he wants is the books, what gets into the books. All he wants people to know about are his writings. A very severe and austere idea.

Interviewer: What obligation has the writer to history?

Eberhart: I don't think he has any obligation to history. I think he has an obligation to his own times. I think he has to speak for his own times, and I think this gets limited to about two decades. It seems to me in thinking about the poets of my time, for instance, it takes some probably two decades to get up to a plateau of their career, then they flourish for about two decades, and then they wane and die. There are a few at the top of every age who flourish for, say, four decades at the peak of fame, like Eliot and Pound and a few people like that. I can't imagine a poet trying to think exactly what his position would be three hundred years hence, because there's no knowing. He may have an inkling. Eliot must have known he was a major poet, he knew that all the time; he was the master of the age, he was the Dr. Johnson of the twentieth century, he must have known that he would be read as long as literature is read and he'd be studied. But already, only a few years after his death, he's fallen down in reputation so much farther than anyone would have predicted.

Interviewer: Emerson used to say, Always do that which you're most afraid of doing, and I think he gave Goethe as an example; but Goethe was afraid of heights and falling, and so he forced himself always to go up to great heights and towers. This idea, this Emersonian idea of doing that which you most fear in life—what do you think of that?

Eberhart: I don't believe that. I wouldn't do that. I think you should do what you can do best, and you should strive for that. I don't go for this . . .

Interviewer: What about prizes?

Eberhart: Having sat on the boards, practically all the judging boards for the major prizes in this country, I have a sort of divided opinion about these boards, and also about prizes in general. And now you see I'm being a speculator, or I'm being a professor. T. S. Eliot said, at one point in his career, that there's no competition in poetry, that is, there's no competition between poets. Well, all of a sudden, out of the blue, like being struck by a poem from the sky—and I've expressed sometimes that this has happened to me in the writing of poetry— I had a flash of an idea, an idea came to me right on the spur of the moment, and I said, "Well, why don't we give it to Robert Frost?" And all my colleagues, almost within one minute, conceded this, that this would be a good thing to do. We didn't really seriously judge the others. We knew, we knew their excellences, we would have had a long hour's talk about the other books, but Robert Frost was in the hospital, in Boston, and everyone on the board knew that he was one of the great American poets, that he had never won our highest prize, strangely enough; he'd never won the Bollingen Prize, although he'd won the Pulitzer Prize four times, the only man who ever won it four times, to my knowledge—and we also were aware (certainly, I was aware) that old Frost probably felt badly in his later years that he never won the Nobel Prize, the highest prize in the world. So, apparently I had a flash, an intuitive flash, that the next-best thing to giving him the Nobel Prize would be to give him our highest American prize, the Bollingen. And it was a *fait accompli* in a very few minutes. I was elected to call up and speak to Robert first, because they seemed to think I knew him best. So I called him in the hospital, and he was in his hospital bed in Boston, and his voice was strong, and he had at least some of the old Frostian wit—that is, not only did he thank the board, but he said, "What will I do with the money?" At eighty-nine or so, whatever he was, he was still pretty spry—and so then everyone in turn spoke with him. John Hall Wheelock, an elderly man now, too, and one of our excellent poets, who had won the Bollingen prize with me in 1962, John said he had never met Frost, which was sort of incredible, but apparently he had got through life never seeing him. With characteristic Wheelockian modesty he wanted to talk to him last, and he said—all the rest of us talked to him in the personal way, because we knew him—and then Mr. Wheelock talked to him and met him over the phone. The reason why I'm making quite a bit of this story is that two weeks later Robert was dead. So I thought that was one of the best, if I may say so, I thought that was one of the luckiest strokes of intuition I've had.

Also, in my case, when my first paperback book came out—I believe it came out in the fall of 1966, and it sold, not only well, as you would expect—I wasn't interested in the sales, I learned this later—but it sold quite well. And then, just as James Wright must have got a telephone call yesterday announcing his victory, I got one at my house, and the telephone rang continuously for twelve hours, and calls came from all over the country and from very distant places. Well, inside of a month, I think it was just a month, the sales of my book jumped up to ten thousand—they'd sold a few thousand before that, and it sold like hotcakes for months, and still is selling. Now, what does this mean? Does it mean that the poetry is any more valuable than it was before a prize was stuck on it? It can't, because the words were the same. The most charitable way of looking at it, and I've heard people use this argument, is that prizes like the Bollingen and Pulitzer are good because they point out to the public that there is an excellent book here, or that this man is an excellent poet. That's a very charitable way of looking at it. That, say, hundreds of people, say thousands of people, wouldn't have read my book at all, or maybe they wouldn't have read it until much later, if it hadn't won a spectacular prize. Well, how do you assess that? The worst way to look at it is that it is an elitist victory given to you by peers, and that it's a political prize with which you'll be dubbed and known the rest of your life, and maybe in some profoundly serious way you would have been better off without it. They do mean a great deal if you are a worldly person, and yet a lot of poets are not very worldly, so I suppose it depends upon what grasp you think you have on your life and the life of your times—what value you place on these things.

Also, a few years ago, on the board of the same Bollingen Prize, I tried to get the judges to give our highest literary prize to Carl Sandburg . . . Carl Sandburg was not admired in the academies, he was not read very much in them, there weren't hundreds of papers written about his poetry because it was so simple that if you read it once you had exhausted it and there was nothing more to be said about it. On the other hand, Wallace Stevens became the darling of the academy, and he is so complex and so ambiguous sometimes, and so powerfully evocative that intellectual people and learned people adored him, and still do. I'm troubled as a teacher because the academy, or the people who are supposed to know the most about poetry, don't admit Sandburg yet to the sacred grove. Now maybe he will be admitted in years to come, but if you went around to the English department and asked colleagues of mine, you might find many people less tolerant than I am. I don't know . . . but you see, when a man goes beyond the academy and is accepted by the world, the academy has to preserve itself by keeping him out. Isn't that pretty interesting?

Interviewer: Federico Fellini said that an artist can no more judge another artist than one child can judge other children . . . .

Eberhart: Oh, I'd be definitely against that. I think one child judges another child very quickly and accurately and totally, and so do artists judge each other, absolutely and intuitively . . . .

Interviewer: Poe said that poets are irritable. He said that the man who is not irritable is not a poet. How would you answer that?

Eberhart: I agree with that. I think some of them are too damned irritable. I think John Berryman was about the most irritating man I ever saw. But he had this divine discontent, if you want to call it, *terribilitá* is another word the Italians used to describe it—this terrible something. But you see what it did for him—he jumped off a bridge and ended it all.

Interviewer: Did you have any intimation of Robert Lowell's greatness when he was your student?

Eberhart: No, certainly not. I had an intimation that he and Frank Parker, his friend, were two of the brightest young men I'd ever seen, or been with, and I admired them no end. But frankly you couldn't tell when a boy was only sixteen or eighteen, you couldn't even imagine what he'd be like when he was thirty. I knew he would be a brilliant student when he was in college, that he'd go to Harvard or somewhere else. But beyond that you couldn't guess. No, I really don't think so. It was his flowering that seen in retrospect was inevitable, but seen when you knew him as a rather heavy boy of sixteen or seventeen you couldn't imagine that he'd be so brilliant.

Interviewer: What do you mean, heavy?

Eberhart: He had a heavy being. He looked serious, he looked heavy, he walked heavy, he was a heavy creature. He had no lightness, no gaiety, hardly any spontaneity. He was a sort of brooding, heavy-walking young man thinking all the time. He was terribly adolescent when I knew him.

Interviewer: Did he really look up to you as a mentor?

Eberhart: There's no doubt about it. He said so in print.

Interviewer: Are you a restless kind?

Eberhart: Oh, very much so. I've always been very restless.

Interviewer: How does it manifest itself?

Eberhart: I think in sporadic action, all kinds of sporadic actions. Also, I think one of my greatest traits, I'd call it a weakness really, is impatience. I've always been very impatient somehow with the world. Straining at the leash, trying to get on and fidgeting with things as they are and yet not knowing where to go or how it would be any better any other way.

Interviewer: Voznesenski says, "If I'm late for a date, it could be because I'm writing a poem." Has that ever happened to you?

Eberhart: No, no, I don't think so. I usually get to dates on time. I like to be on time and I've never torn myself away from writing a poem to get in a car and go somewhere or go have a date or something that I'm supposed to have. I don't think so. I think when I write there's a time freedom before and after—there's a stasis in which one feels free and has no compunction of time.

Interviewer: Could you explain that a little more?

Eberhart: Well, I was just saying that it seems to me that mostly when I write it's in some time of the day or night when I know there are hours ahead and there is plenty of time. I don't have to feel any coercion about time. I can be completely absorbed in the poem.

Interviewer: You told of making a shape and then writing a poem to fit it. Isn't that a kind of gamesmanship?

Eberhart: Yes, it is and I think it's a valuable kind of gamesmanship but I don't think it is ultimately valuable. I think it's part of poetry as play or as intellectual grace. I used to do that quite a bit, to make up an arbitrary form, a fairly complex form, and then see if I could write a poem to fit it. I really like that idea. It's as if you had a preconceived architecture in mind. Suppose you were an architect and you wanted to make that building over there that you're seeing right out of this window in Seattle, which has just been completed. More than the poet, the architect would have to be controlled by absolute necessity, because I think you would have less initial freedom than the poet. To get that building started at all, the architect has to envisage it. He has to have the prearranged *a priori* form in mind. And then it's just a matter of putting it up. Well, I think there's an analogy with the sometime writing of poems, but I think the poet has more freedom, even if he preconceives a kind of form—he has more freedom in building into it or changing it as he goes along. But to come back to your original question, I don't think any of my best poems or what I consider my best poems or, in fact, what the world considers my best poems have been written in this way. I think there are some of them I could probably find in the collected poems that were composed this way, but it's more as an initial stimulus or kind of an intellectual play, a pleasure, a look of elegance in an unworded shape and then you flesh it in with the words.

Interviewer: How do great poets respond to criticism?

Eberhart: I don't know. I think of Auden. He was an absolute chameleon. He would change his colors instantly and I thought that was a very fine thing. A lot of people wouldn't do that at all, but he was—you'd be sitting with him in a room, as I was at St. Marks for a whole month, day after day, more or less, with his books all around him, and his writing table full of papers hand-written on, and he'd show you a new poem and if you didn't like a line he'd strike it right out. "Why, yes, I see that exactly," and he'd take it right out and he'd actually mark through it. And he would invite you to criticize his poems and he would act instantly either for or against, he'd either accept what you said or not. He was completely limber, absolutely fluid, and wonderfully sensitive. I thought that was interesting, but he is the only other poet I ever saw write a poem—I mean any poet of stature, actually in the act of writing them, and so I can only say this about him. I wouldn't know how other people do it. I just know a few things like Eliot told me when we had a dinner party that Betty and I went to on Marlborough St. at the Lowell's, when Cal was still in Boston before they went to New York, the other couple being the I. A. Richardses. Eliot told me, I can't remember whether it was before or after dinner, but he said he wrote very slowly and that he envisaged words as a bricklayer might envisage bricks, or as you could see a bricklayer making something very deliberately, setting one precisely on another. I had the feeling that a word for Eliot was a plastic thing, and that it was solid, and that he had a heavy, massive mind which could put these counters down slowly and adjudicate all the subtle ramifications of their meanings in his mind while he was doing this. And that enchanted me! It's so opposite from my kind of being that I was simply fascinated. It is more as if he were writing as a prose writer. I don't think Eliot had anything of the creative frenzy or the divine madness, as the Greeks called it, or the terrible immediacy, or the all-in-a-rush-with-richness of Hopkins, that sort of thing. I don't think he could be overwhelmed by a poem, or have so much going around him that he could hardly get it out. He wrote very deliberately, and that interested me very much. The only other thing I can think of to say along this line, which is also fascinating, and again it's a case in which my own mind—and we are all interested in ourselves—is different from that of Robert Frost. Old Frost told me one time, I can't remember where this was, but he said he could be walking along in the woods, and a poem would form in his mind, and he would, let's say, actually still be walking and compose it in his head as he was walking, and I remember, he said, sometimes it would be as long as thirty lines and these lines as they came into his being, or as they came into his consciousness, would be so graphically formed that he knew them absolutely by heart, as he made them, and that he wouldn't have to write them down, and that he could carry a poem of, say, twenty-five or thirty lines for maybe a year in his head, and that then sometimes, if he was quiet or in some mood, this poem would come to him again, and he could draw it right off and write it down. What an amazing thing; it absolutely startled me. It's just incredible, this heavy deliberate graphic sense of language as a malleable thing.

Interviewer: What was Robert Frost really like?

Eberhart: Oh, I couldn't tell you, I'd have to talk an hour about what Robert Frost was like. His biographer, Lawrance Thompson, whom we knew, has brought out a recent book as you know in which he lambastes him pretty severely and makes him into a Satan, an absolute devil, and it's after his death, so I guess he's fair game after death. It doesn't matter; you can say anything. No, I only saw the side of Frost that most people that I know saw in him—simply the marvelous man, the wonderful man, the friendly and nice, fine man. And I must say it's worth saying in 1972 that when I saw Frost in the last five years of his life—he was always coming back to Dartmouth, twice a year, or I'd see him in the Library of Congress or somewhere—he was really sparkling in his conversation.

Interviewer: How did you feel, as a young poet, when Robert Frost mentioned your poem "The Village Daily"?

Eberhart: Oh, I felt just great, I felt wonderful, fine. I mean, I didn't know enough about Frost to know whether he should have mentioned another poem or what the significance of this was. I was a very youthful, energetic, and life-loving chap, and to be taken up or mentioned by Robert Frost, whom then we thought was a true poet, was wonderful. I never did anything about it; I don't think I met him until years later. I guess I must have seen him once when I was an undergraduate but I never had any friendship with him until long after that. Oh, incidentally, let me tell you this story. Once in about 1948 when we were living on 10 Hilliard Place in Cambridge, it was a few years after the war—it was just about the time of the writing of the "Horse Chestnut Tree"—I was invited to meet Robert Frost and then have dinner and attend his reading. He lived on Brewster Street in Cambridge nearby. I remember going into this anteroom where they were passing around sherry, as the Harvard boys did, with great decorum, and nothing as wicked as scotch and soda, but a little something mild like sherry. I brought this little book, this very little book in which he wrote the Introduction, and it was even then a rare volume and now it's rarer still. And I asked Robert if he remembered this book. Well, he perked up rather markedly. Oh, he said, yes, he did, very well, and he looked at it and turned it over and he knew who I was and it was a very pleasant thing. And then he signed it. He was delighted to remember it.

Interviewer: You seem to like the finite creatures, the small animals, in your poetry.

Eberhart: Yes, and maybe it's because of Edmund Burke's definition of the beautiful in his "Essay on Esthetics." He has the idea that beauty is small, round, and smooth. Small animals are more beautiful than big animals. Roundness is more beautiful than angularity or jagged things; I think he mentions the moon, the sun, the earth, a breast, and the womb. All these prime symbols of the universe are more or less round. Of course, you have a gibbous moon when it's not quite round, and so on. And the ideas of smoothness, smooth skin, a woman with a smooth face is more beautiful, or thought to be, than rough skin. Maybe it has something to do with that. Well, I don't know. I'd like to write a poem about the greatest whale in the world, but I haven't yet.

Interviewer: Do you agree with Goethe that the strong man is at his mightiest, alone?

Eberhart: You bring in the damnedest things. I don't know whether

Goethe said that, did he? It's so dramatic and Teutonic, it sounds like the old Germans! You see, I don't believe enough in the mind to think you could give an absolute answer to that. I rather think the strong man is at his mightiest when he's least alone. I would think a strong man would be at his best when he was most social, operating socially. "Alone" sounds as if it were Hitler, always being there alone, ready to kill six million Jews, which then he would go out and do. So I don't think I believe that.

Interviewer: Your poem "Love Sequence with Variations" includes a lot of forms in one poem. One senses that you're still experimenting.

Eberhart: Well, I don't think it has all that many, but I am glad that there are several in that poem. The thing that interests me the most about it was that when I got writing on it, just the charge of what I had to say seemed to come off in bulks of about fourteen lines, so then I had enough wit to make them fourteen lines all the time, while this seething thing was going and to draw it off this way. And then when I got the poem written I was astounded to see that I'd written double sonnets in a couple of cases and a treble sonnet in one; instead of having fourteen lines, you'd have fourteen and then do it right over and have twenty-eight, and one time there were three of these sonnets all strung together, talking about one sort of thing in one section of the poem. Then it is lightened up or varied with more limber passages. But I'm glad you noticed that, I think it is experimental to some extent. I'm very anxious to see it. I wish it would hurry up and get here. I want to see what it looks like in the *Harvard Advocate*.

Interviewer: Don't adjectives help the celebrating process?

Eberhart: I don't quite see it—with description? Not necessarily. I don't see why it couldn't be just as good without them, actually better.

Interviewer: "Chocorua" perhaps reminded you of the limits of the imagination. You said in doing that you couldn't know what the Indians did and how they lived.

Eberhart: I simply didn't know and don't today know enough about the decor of Indian life in the New England of two hundred years ago to make a viable play, and I didn't have the energy or the will to study it enough. I wanted to say something about the chief's life and death because it was like a Greek tragedy. And I tried to write this thing in the tiniest possible way. In other words, a minuscule play. It's a little, minuscule play with several little two-minute acts. But I don't think it works. It may work as a reading play. I mean, you can read it. At least it preserves his story, the true story, which is in history, and I guess I wrote it at all because I've seen the area, the mountains, we have

289

driven by it many times. My wife, as a girl, climbed up it all the time. And it always intrigued me that you could see the very place where he jumped off, and killed himself and made great anathemas of the whole white race for mistreating the Indians.

Interviewer: Do you consider yourself a preserver of history?

Eberhart: No, not in general. I think the point of this one play was to preserve the history and to show the people, if they read it today, what was going on in the life of an Indian chief back there. But let me come back to your statement. In one sense, any poet, if his works live or are going to live, preserves history. Yes, I certainly believe that. Just take the one poem, "The Groundhog," today; it was written in the mid-Thirties. It's almost forty years old, and people read it all the time and say this is just as real as it was then. But it's preserved the attitudes of a poet writing way back then. So in that sense all poetry preserves history. And when you read poetry of the past, say Whitman or someone, you get the feeling of those times. I have no doubt if they read any of us of the middle part of the century, fifty years from now or a hundred years from now, they won't be able to escape the feeling and temper of these words and that would be one reason for reading them. When you read Poe you get a sense of the mid-nineteenth century, and so on.

Interviewer: What about taking risks in writing?

Eberhart: Well, that's a mighty interesting question. I never know what it means. I think it's great to take risks. For instance, if I'd never taken any risks beyond the age of high school, I would have still been writing imitations of Tennyson four years later as a senior in college, in which case I would never have won the prizes of college and I would never have dared to go on. Pardon me for harking back to my own life, but I can see that in some ways you have to take risks all the time. The risk I took with my young life was to go to Cambridge at all. And that paid off enormously, because it was the most exciting intellectual milieu I had ever been in and it was from growing up and flowering in that environment that my whole career began and was made possible. But I think you're thinking of the technical point when you actually write a poem—how much risk are you taking in the way you write it? That's what the critics usually say. And I don't know how to answer that. I don't think you sit down and deliberately say, "Now, I want to take a big risk—I'm going to take a big risk," and then you write a poem in some new way. I never think it's that way. I think it's much more inner and much more compulsive. You're compelled to write it, then afterwards you'll see that the risk has been taken. Twenty years later they'll look back and say, well, he did write differently from the rest of them of the time. Or he had something else to say or some different kind of drive. And that peculiarity is what makes him have a name now. I'd like to warn in a way: in one sense there's a paradox that maybe the greatest risk of a young poet today would be to take too great a risk. I mean, you shouldn't take too great a risk, you should preserve, you shouldn't make it too risky because you might lose too much. If some student today studies Pope enough—one of these young people writing in my class, say—he might change the history of poetry for the next twenty-five years by changing the way they write now, this flat, open, non-structured writing. That would be to take the greatest risk of all, although he would appear to be doing the opposite, he would appear to be going back to do the most regular thing, to study the resources of the English of another century when there were set forms.

Interviewer: What about people who write their epitaphs?

Eberhart: Oh, I think that's fine. It's great. Do you know what mine is? Ruth Hershberger got up a little printed thing a few years ago, she got all the poets, twenty poets that we all know, and they wrote their epitaphs and she printed them in different color ink each in a different way. "Here lies Richard Eberhart./When he ended he thought he was about to start." That's my epitaph. Never been published yet, but I think it's pretty good. What it says to me is that life is too short, whether you live to be ninety or twenty or thirty, and it also has a slight, I would say real, but a slight Christian implication. There's a slight hint that maybe there's something else over there.

Interviewer: Do you think that?

Eberhart: No, I don't think it with my rational mind. I think you're dead as a doornail once the breath goes out of you. But, I think, this is the biggest question you can ask: there probably is another world, maybe there is an afterlife, maybe there are all kinds of future lives. The Orientals, the Buddhists have this great chain of being; you go around and you suffer in one life and you're put in a certain position and through millennia you get further on and so on. Nobody knows at all and nobody likes to think that your death is the end of the whole show. It's sort of inconceivable, why should we be here if it doesn't mean any more than that? And if you're a Christian they tell you that you're going to live forever if you believe in Christ. Well, I'm very sympathetic to all spiritual ideas, I must say; I take it very seriously. But the best I've been able to come up with *vis-à-vis* Christianity and the afterlife is that I don't believe it when I enter a church door because I've got a very hard head, and I can see when I go in the door of, let's say, an Episcopal church which we half belong to—it's the one that's closest to us—that two times two makes four. But you take the Catholic church, the Mass, well, I do that and I don't know why I do except that I just let my mind go, I don't have any mind anymore. I park my mind at the door, I park it on the curb step and when I come in I'm a child, I'm willing to take it all in, I'm willing to suppress my ego and not to be the me that you're talking to now, or the me who's on the covers of these books. I'm willing to be totally and simply human and accept what they have to say about it. And then I can take the wafer and drink the blood of Christ. But I don't want to think about it. I do it as an act of spiritual grace. And then I suppose I do it because my grandparents were very religious people. But here I am; every year I get a year older. I'll bet if I live another ten or twenty years I'll never get any closer to answering that question. And then the end will come and nobody will know the answer anyway.

Interviewer: Some have considered you a religious poet. How do you answer that?

Eberhart: Well, we're talking about that sort of thing now. I think I am. I don't know what you mean by religious, but I certainly am not an anti-religious poet and I'm not a grossly materialistic one. I think my poetry is spiritual in the sense that it's hazy or it's ethereal or skyey or it's evanescent—I've used that word—it's fragile, it's probing, it's, I think, imaginative and I think it's religious without belonging to any set church. I don't think it's dogmatic. I don't think I have any dogmatic poems. I have one poem in the new book, called "The Meditation of God"; it's about what God is saying to man, and I speak as if I were God and I talk down to mankind, and wish that I had the failure of mankind because, if I had the failure of mankind, I would never know the ultimate answer and I could always grope, but I would always be held between good and evil, and I would know sin and I would try for redemption, but my humanity would be in this eternal struggle—it's always about these things and it's never resolved. So here I write a little poem, about so long, about God wishing that he were human. If you're God, you know it all—if there is a God—and it must be terribly dull, it must be awfully dull in heaven. Hell is much more interesting.

Interviewer: You're being a devil's advocate.

Eberhart: Yeah, well, God wants to be man so he can suffer as man. And also the idea that the theologians say—I often try to get their answer to this—that there's no way even though God is absolute that he can take away from man his sin once he fell. And that's pretty deep. I often used to think in my simple way, Adam and Eve ate the apple and it all changed, and forever after we suffer and we're sick and we die and we have sin and we have all this other. Well, why didn't God just make them all pure again, why didn't He take it all back? But there seems to be the idea that even God couldn't do this. So then all He can do forever is to look at mankind as his children, whom He theoretically loves, but He can't help if they make war. People used to say why doesn't God stop the war right now? Well, He can't stop it entirely; he can look down and see man doing all these things, but He can't really tell them what to do.

Interviewer: Robert Graves said that his writing was a painful process of corrections and persistent dissatisfaction.

Eberhart: Well, I'm on the other side of the fence on that for the most part because I believe, for instance, that when you revise you have a 50-50 chance or a toss of the coin of making it worse. Why is the assumption that in revising you will always make it better? So there is a chance of making a line or a stanza or a whole poem better by hard work on revision, but maybe you'll lose some of the original flavor of it, the original musical value of it, in tampering with the words. I don't know about Graves, but we all know Yeats was the best at revising his work and he made one of his greatest poems, "Leda and the Swan," many years later out of an inferior poem. At its start it was inferior and then fifteen or twenty years later he took up the idea when he was writing *A Vision,* and made it into one of his most famous poems. At least a half-dozen times in my life poems have been given to me, as if the whole being was a weathervane played on by the wind of the spirit. It's hard to say this just right because I don't believe in automatic writing but I do believe in some kind of possession, that you are possessed by the poem, and then I also believe that when some of these poems are given in this way you couldn't stop it—I like to use the analogy of either birth or death—when birth starts it's irreversible and it's absolute, when a child is ready to be born, it's born; and death we see as irreversible when we see it coming, when it's there, that's it. And by the same token I think sometimes, when a poem is ready to be born, it will be born whole, without the need to change lines or words. "The Groundhog" was one of the poems given to me in this way: it was written in about fifteen or twenty minutes of intense absorption, an intense, marvelous sense of control and power or pleasure or joy in the writing. One knew that he was speaking with absolute ability, clarity, and meaning, so maybe I'd say sometimes your mind is at its best then. Now I would say that of all the poems I've written a very small percentage were done in this way. So that most of them come from a welling up of memory in some mysterious way. I don't understand how.

Interviewer: Has your reading of your poetry influenced it?

Eberhart: All I can say in answer to that is that I've found some are better for reading publicly than others, and it would be folly to read some of my poems in public because they would be the ones that are too hard or difficult; I found out that certain ones go better than others, and I learned how to read them. I don't think the fact that certain poems read well in public today influenced me in what kind of a poem I think I wanted to write the next time I felt like writing a poem. That would be the farthest thing away from what I was thinking.

Interviewer: Which of your work do you prefer—the old or the new?

Eberhart: I always like my newest work best. I'm rather put out and amazed by some critics who every now and then come along—I don't think they've said this much in print—but I remember I read a letter several years ago, a serious letter, saying they liked my earlier work better than my later. Well, that shook me. I'd much rather have my later work be better than my earlier work just because when you're quite young you wouldn't think you'd have as much to say as when you're older. But this one fellow liked to read my early poems, when I was in my twenties and early thirties. I don't go for that at all.

Interviewer: Robert Frost talked about the joke that God played . . .

Eberhart: I always thought that was a blasphemous poem. Those two lines were blasphemous.

Interviewer: Why?

Eberhart: They're so cruel. It's all right to say them if you're Robert Frost, but I wouldn't say it.

Interviewer: Is metaphor, by its nature, a kind of euphemism?

Eberhart: Not at all. Metaphor by nature is essential. It's essential to thinking. It's very profound in our consciousness, saying one thing is another, or it's seeing likeness between two things. It's very deep. I don't think it's a euphemism at all.

Interviewer: Belloc said that the more enormous one's output, the more the publishers get to regard you as a regular milk cow. Do you think this happens?

Eberhart: Once in 1961—I guess it was—during my second year in the Library, I came to New York to a publisher's party that the head of Holt Rinehart gave for Robert Frost. They were putting out a new edition of his work, or a new volume, I can't remember which. But that was very interesting, and I remember Marianne Moore was there, and Frost and Marianne sat together for a long time on a divan. I watched them from about twenty or thirty feet away with great admiration and didn't want to go bother them, but I talked with the head of the company and he gave me all the materialistic wonderful news about how his company had done with Robert Frost since 1912, it was now fifty years later or so and they had done just fine, they were very proud and very jealous. They loved every sale.

Interviewer: William Empson was a classmate of yours back when. Did you ever pass any poetic notes?

Eberhart: That I can't remember. I don't think we passed any poetic notes, but we talked a lot about poetry. I never had any lively correspondence with him, but I always had a casual friendship with him after Cambridge days because, I remember, when I was teaching at St. Marks he was returning from Japan, where he taught for a while, and he stopped here on the west coast and went east and I got in touch with him and got him to come to St. Marks, which is an odd thing, a secondary school like that, to read to the boys, and that was an exhilarating experience. I remember he had an affection of his eyes that was disturbing but fascinating; he blinked his eyes all the time, as if it were a disease or a tic, and yet he didn't do anything about it. But it was sort of painful to watch him, he was a very high-powered, intellectual, then youngish man, but his eyelids were just going all the time. I often wondered how he made out with that, whether he got over it or whether it was a nervous tic, or whether that was just part of his peculiarity—he batted those eyes all the time.

Interviewer: Have you ever wanted to be a musician?

Eberhart: No, except I used to play the piano when I was six to fourteen and I can still play one little piece on the piano, and I played the saxophone in high school a great deal, an E flat first, then my father or mother or both got me a C melody. I was very proud to have a big C melody. I played in the high school band and I played a little at college at the Alpha Delta Phi house.

Interviewer: Did it ever influence your music in poetry? Is there any connection?

Eberhart: No, but I really enjoy music very much; one fair question about poets is, what stimulates them? We know, for instance, that Hart Crane wrote with the gramophone on full blast and a lot of whiskey inside him. He used alcohol a lot. I guess some poets used drugs. I never had to do either of those, but I must say I love to listen for long periods of time to certain composers; in recent years, principally Ives. I can sit in my house and, if alone, listen to Ives by the hour and sometimes that releases the being—it really does aid you—and you start writing. You want to write. I don't know what you'd call that; a drug? It doesn't really stimulate you so much as release inhibitions.

Interviewer: Does the spirit die with the flesh?

Eberhart: Does the spirit die with the flesh? The mysteries of the origin of the universe, of God, are still maintained, you can always speculate on them. But you can never find out for sure. The carbon atom is said to be eternal because it never changes. It's the only changeless thing in the universe. We have carbon atoms in our kneecaps that are eternal, and they will be there when our bones are in the earth. If our bones are completely resolved, these atoms will be somewhere else in something else and they'll be there forever. They are inexhaustible. They're never changeable—but that sort of gets far afield. But that kind of question does intrigue me because the relations between the flesh and the spirit are primary to my speculation and I never solved anything about it.

Interviewer: You're an old 10-flat-hundred man—a physical person as well as a spiritual one. Does this dichotomy bother you sometimes?

Eberhart: Oh, yes, I think there's an absolute, a total tug that goes on all your life, but it's much easier for me to believe in the flesh than in the spirit. One is always conscious of one's body. What else have you got? We're in these shapes, we're in our physical being, we live with it every day, we see it change, we keep it up or it breaks down, we never can get beyond the body in a way, so the spirit is something different. It's obviously attached to your body, I suppose, but I don't know what it is. Maybe there's no such thing as a spirit, maybe it's a fiction. That's what Stevens said—Stevens thought of the imagination as the supreme fiction.

Interviewer: Tell me, did you organize this Poets' Theatre?

Eberhart: There are several written accounts on the founding of the Poets' Theatre and I wish I could tell you where they are, but there are records of how this all happened and I'll try to give you an idea. We were living at 10 Hilliard Place, which we bought a couple of years before 1950. I think we bought it in 1948; we lived for two or three years up in grandfather and grandmother's house, and then we bought this little place on 10 Hilliard Place. I was working at the Butcher Polish Company and it was right in the middle of Harvard Square, so I was enmeshed in all the goings-on of the University and Boston, in art ways, and in June of 1950 a man named Lyon Phelps came to see me. He was very excited about writing verse drama and he was a nephew of William Lyon Phelps, the old professor at Yale who was still alive. Young Lyon Phelps was an interesting, somewhat decadent young man, but he had quite a lot of force in his interests, and ideas, and there was a fascinating woman named Molly Howe, who was the wife of a law professor at Harvard, whose name had been Molly Manning in Ireland, who had been an actress in William Butler

Yeats's theatre, and she was around, and keenly interested in the theatre, and suddenly there was a whole group. There was a sort of mushroom maybe, there were twenty young men and women and after, older ones who were all of a sudden talking about verse plays. It was amazing how it caught on like wildfire and everybody got terribly excited and there were a lot of people around there at the time. Ciardi was around, MacLeish was there, Dick Wilbur was around there, and Cal Lowell and who else . . . John Holmes, so there were a lot of poets around. Actually Lyon Phelps came to our house a number of times. By the end of school, about the third week in June, a nucleus of us had decided to see what we could do over the summer, whether we could write a verse play. Not a one of us up to this point had written a verse play, but we were all poets, we had all written lyrical poetry, but we'd never gotten behind the idea of manipulating characters on stage, which is very exciting and very difficult. Bill Matchett, who is a professor here right now, was in Cambridge then. He was one of our members, and Donald Hall was around, because I remember he played in one of my plays. There were all kinds of lively spirits and they were all quite young then. So we found we had so much going for us in the fall that we decided to incorporate, to have a real theatre. We spent a couple of months trying to figure out where to have it, which plays to use and whose plays would be given first, etc. Frank O'Hara was there; he had one on the first night, and I had one. Thornton Wilder was giving lectures there, he was a great stimulus to us, he was very excited about it and we got the theatre going by January '51. In other words, about nine months after it was first broached, there was a meeting in Christ Church, I think, and I remember Thornton Wilder got up and gave an impassioned speech about the theatre and said this was the grass roots of a new drama in America, and then he passed the hat and everybody put in a dollar or a quarter or something. It was simply fantastic and the excitement was terrific. Then they put on these little ten- or fifteen-minute plays. Well, to make a long story short, we finally incorporated, and I remember going to some law office in Boston—I was the first president—and the president and treasurer had to sign their names on a paper of incorporation. And Bunny Lang, who, alas, died shortly thereafter, whom I much liked and to whom I dedicated one of the poems in one of my books— Bunny Lang was one of our best patrons and actresses and she was the secretary. My play, *Visionary Farms*, was put on in the basement of the Fogg Museum, and I think some other plays were there too. We finally got a theatre of our own behind the Harvard Commons, in a little alleyway. Then that burned down, and we moved to some other one.

One of the most interesting things was when Dylan Thomas came and stayed at our house once and I remember we were walking down Brattle Street with him and we had all been drinking quite a lot and were feeling rather jolly. Then I introduced him in Brattle Hall, where he gave the first and only reading he ever did from dramatic works and he thinks he was stimulated to do that by the Poets' Theatre. He did it to raise money. For instance, only five minutes before we left the house to go to Brattle Hall, Dylan said, "Do you have a Webster?" Well I, of course, had a Webster and rushed upstairs and found it, and within one minute he picked out exactly what passages he wanted to read from Webster's *The White Devil*. He had such a quick mind. Then he said, "Do you have a Beddoes?" and I said, "Sure, I can probably find a Beddoes." I got my Beddoes and he turned to "Death's Jest Book," and I introduced him that time. He went on and spoke, he had a marvelous audience, it was terribly exciting and he read English drama for forty minutes or so. Then he read some of his own poems at the end, and that was another memorable occasion connected with the Poets' Theatre. Thomas was writing *Under Milk Wood* and we put on really the first production of *Under Milk Wood*, though in the history books you will read that the first production of it was a week or ten days later in New York at the YMHA. But people who are in the know know that the first one when it was still less perfected was in our little theatre. A week later he was all the rage and they got the YMHA to put it on in New York, and he was there and he took a part and he was still making up the final lines when he went on stage in New York. I can't tell you how heady an experience it was and how wonderful it was to be breaking out of the lyric into a massive form that had endless possibilities in trying to relate human beings to each other on a larger stage. But, alas, it didn't last but seven or eight years. Finally, it petered out. When we were going strong we thought we had a movement that would be as significant as the Irish renaissance in the theatre in Ireland. But it didn't prove so.

Interviewer: Do you think that verse drama affected the persona in your poems afterward?

Eberhart: No, I don't think so. I do think I became a more realistic writer, I might concede that. I don't know how, but I think in dealing with verse drama you had to be more realistic. You had to think of people walking around on stage and saying things to each other out of their mouths and you had to make up the words to work and it had to be viable. So maybe that helped me get my own poetry out of the cloister or out of the perfumed areas a bit, and into the common thoroughfares.

Interviewer: What of the oral tradition of American poetry—it seems that more people are reading than ever before.

Eberhart: Oh, I see, reading and speaking, yes. There has been much more of that over the past twenty-five years. The fact that there are circuits for the reading of poems and almost every poet reads his poems and gets better at it the more he does it, and the fact that you see poets on stages all the time is, I think, all to the good. There are some poets who still refuse to do this, though, and I'd like to name one, my friend Phillip Booth. He is an excellent poet, but he has something in his being that inhibits him from it, or maybe that's not the word, but he just refuses to read his poems. Well, to what extent that is harming him in his career is hard to say. But most poets like to read their work, and many of them are very good and others not so good. For instance, in my time, Marianne Moore was incredibly famous and much beloved by everybody, but she was about the worst reader you ever heard, and yet people came anyway because they loved to look at her and the mystique of the personality was so great. And the tricorn hat, and just the way she looked and moved, but her voice was flat and nasal and nobody ever said she was a good reader of her poetry, so there you are.

Interviewer: Susanne Langer says that the need of symbolization is a primary need of man and really differentiates him from other creatures.

Eberhart: I would agree to that all out. I certainly do. That's a beautiful statement. I don't know what she was thinking of by "symbols," because I don't know her work well. But it must be that the caveman saw the actual sun and the actual moon, and when he saw the sun rise in the morning perhaps he let out joyful cries and perhaps that was the first lyrical utterance; when his baby was killed or his mate was killed he felt sad and he lowered his voice and perhaps that was the first eulogy or first death poem. That seems a natural progression, and it seems splendid, and I think the symbols are very beautiful things.

Interviewer: Are you a new man after writing a poem?

Eberhart: Sure, I go out and celebrate, I kick up my heels; of course I'm a new man. No, to be serious, I suppose I feel good after writing a poem, if it's a good poem, because it's a continuation, it's not new or old, it's a continuation of the problems that I've faced all my life and the effort I've put forth to conquer them or make something out of them. I believe that Blackmur was more nearly true. Dear old Richard Blackmur, a friend of ours who is just my age, born the same year, died a long time ago, and who said you can't expect a professor to have a new idea after the age of fifty. So if I write a poem I rather tend to agree with that. If I write a poem at sixty it won't be exactly new, will it? It's going to be a continuation of the whole meaning of your life.

Interviewer: Somebody compared you to Shakespeare and Arnold recently.

Eberhart: Yes, Shakespeare, Arnold, and I—isn't that terrific! That was nice to receive from a grass roots critic who's a banker in Birmingham, Alabama. It was very nice to receive, but I must say, it makes me laugh. Isn't life strange? Supposing you could imagine yourself being sixteen years old, full of energy, bursting with desire and to have somebody say, before you die, somebody is going to compare your poems, or at least one of them, to Shakespeare. Well, do you know what I would have done? I would have gone out and run the hundred-yard dash in four and four-fifths seconds, instead of ten flat. But now, I actually got such a letter. While I took it seriously—well, at first I thought it was a joke, and then I could see he was serious—I must say, I'm enough of a radical—I'm glad to put this on tape—I'm enough of an anti-establishment radical to admire the fact that that criticism came, not from a professor, not a poet, not a member of the establishment, not the winner of a Pulitzer Prize, none of those things. It came from a supposedly good, straightforward, honest, intelligent man in the South, who really believes this, because his mind is not cluttered up with a bunch of books that all the rest of us had read in the last thirty years. He hasn't read all those books I'll bet, but he has read some of these poems. Nobody will pay the slightest attention to it, it won't be known by anybody. The critics won't have a chance to knock it down or pick it up, it doesn't have any clout, as they say now, but it was mighty sweet to receive. Of course, it may have been a joke after all. If I ever meet him, maybe he was pulling my leg, you know.

Interviewer: Do you like warm colors?

Eberhart: I like blues and yellows. Blue would be a cool color. No, I think I like cool colors. I'm partially colorblind or I have minor red-green genetic colorblindness, so I can't really see what I think you call warm colors. So I'm very conscious of yellows. In the evening light, yellows and blues and black and white, but I don't get reds, embedded in browns, very well. You know, some of my colleagues died in the Pacific theatre, in World War II, of bombs on carriers, and I might have been one of those. If I had been sent out on a carrier, I might have been dead inside of a month. The fact that I had minor colorblindness meant that I had to be kept on shore, shore duty, and I had to be kept as a teacher, so probably it saved my life.

Interviewer: But you could see those cancer cells bursting out?

Eberhart: Oh, yes, sure.

An Interview (*New York Quarterly*)

Interviewer: Would you describe the physical conditions of writing your poetry? Are you always at a desk? Do you do first drafts on typewriter or with pencil or with pen? On what kind of paper? As poems progress, what do you do with worksheets that you no longer need?

Eberhart: I almost always write with a pen on typewriter-sized paper, or in a large notebook of that size, am often at a desk, or sitting in an armchair. I save first drafts—as a matter of fact, I am a saver and keep all changes in any poem, whether few or many, and have always been fascinated by the look of the text as it develops. I believe in the mystery of creation and have gone on record that some of my poems which are considered my best ones have been given to me, as it were, as if the poem used the man, not the other way around, or as if the personality were a vane on which the wind of the spirit moved to make the poem. Not automatic writing, but I use an old and now little-used word to convey the meaning, the word "inspiration." These moods are strange and not to be accounted for by strict rationality, yet the idea of inspiration where poems come whole from the spirit, the hand being the agent of communication, has governed I should say a small percentage of my poems. Therefore there is a kind of sacredness to the markings on the page when inspiration has been the compulsive force, and I look at these pages sometimes with amazement. I would not change a word or stroke of the original manuscript due to my belief in the value of the mysterious origins and strange making of a poem. "The Groundhog," for instance, now over forty years old, was given to me in the way suggested and composed in perhaps less than half an hour, without the need to

First published in *New York Quarterly* no. 20 (1978): 17–25.

change a word, or perhaps one word was changed, I cannot remember. I used to study the manuscript closely, but alas somewhere in time it disappeared and is lost. In most poems there are few or many changes and all changes are kept to study with a cool mind. Many poems have undergone revision, light or heavy, but because of the ideas I have just expressed, I have often been doubtful about the value of revising one's initial force or thrust in writing the poem. It has occurred to me that there is no guarantee, in matters so subtle and delicate, that one can necessarily improve his work by taking thought, by using a cold, rational, intellectual gaze at the display of words, for any single change ramifies through words, sense, and lines and may decrease rather than increase the effect desired. Yet it is obvious that in many instances one can improve poems by careful analysis of every option available to thought. I am not dogmatic about anything, but, being a subjective rather than an objective poet, I value what comes from deep compulsions, from the subconscious essence of being or soul, I respect what is compelled, and I have been, as I said, in some instances afraid to change a word in some poems where the poem was the gift and I its vehicle.

Interviewer: When you are away from your desk or writing area, do you carry a notebook with you? What do you do with thoughts or impulses that come to you when you are unable to record them easily?

Eberhart: When away from my writing area I do not carry a notebook with me. Once Eliot told me that he wrote slowly, word to word, like (but he did not use this comparison) a bricklayer cementing one brick to another with great care. Once Frost told me that he would be walking in the woods and a whole poem of, say, thirty lines would form in his head, and that he had so much control of the lines that each was etched definitively on his mind and he felt no compulsion to write them down. He said that sometimes he could draw this poem off maybe ten years later precisely as it came to him in this way. In both these instances I was amazed and realized that my mind was of a different kind. I felt that my mind was wild and tempestuous in the comparison, volatile and Shelleyan. When words were flowing and churning, sometimes, I would lose a poem or part of one if pen and paper were not to hand. I would have to catch the poem out of the air immediately or it would be lost. "Hardening into Print" deals with this problem.

About catching words out of the air, I recall waking at dawn once with a line, "The river of sweetness that runs through the meadow of lies," unaccountably repeating itself. I was half awake and in a kind of panic because I knew I would lose this line unless I found pen and paper at once, which I did. It caused the poem entitled "Hill Dream of Youth,/ Thirty Years Later," which would not have been written except for the strange eruption of this line out of the subconscious when I was half-awake. To answer your question directly, if I could not easily record my sometime thoughts or impulses, I would lose them forever. It would be impossible to get them back. The creative word-cauldron is something seething, sometimes, I do not say all the time, which has always been a mystery to me.

Interviewer: What would you say about revision? Is it a creative act with you? Have you written anything that did not need extensive revision? Do you have any special procedure for revising a poem?

Eberhart: I have talked about revision; I do not have any special procedure for it. I can see that revision can be creative too, its aim is to create something better. I conceive of revision as coming from your best, cool and rational mind, but I do not believe entirely in rationality. Indeed, I think irrationality works in the seething cauldron theory, although I wish I could invent another term for what I mean.

Interviewer: What do you feel is the value of poetry workshops for a young poet? Did you take any when you were beginning to write poetry? What do you feel about student criticism of each other's work?

Eberhart: When I began writing there were no poetry workshops; it would have been an unthinkable idea. We were fewer in number as poets and seem to have been radically individualistic. I feel now that workshops can be valuable for a young poet. Immediate student criticism of each other's work is now taken for granted and must be of great help to the beginner. Criticism is essential to poetry. Poetry is inconceivable without criticism. It cannot live in a vacuum of itself. Culture intends that the poet and the critic should go together. Just as men and women in the real world create the future of mankind by producing children, criticism brings to birth the future of poetry by preserving the best works written at a given time, insuring the pleasure of readers in a long extension of time.

I think of criticism in two main categories. First is professional criticism, which explains and evaluates the poetry of a time or age, and may be written by competent learned persons or by great perceivers such as Aristotle, Sidney, Dr. Johnson, Shelley, Arnold, and others. The second category is the criticism of the poet himself. He cannot create a poem without the critical awareness of what to leave out, as well as what to put in, or without using his rational mind, however irrational his creative impulse may have been, in perfecting every line and phrase and word of a poem. The Lockwood Library at Buffalo has Thomas manuscripts showing over a hundred changes in a poem to perfect and produce the final poem Dylan Thomas wanted to express. Likewise, most of us have examined elaborate changes made by Yeats in some of his poems, changes dictated by the critical intelligence.

Poetry is complex, very ancient, going back to primitive responses; it is deep in us and essential to us, and it is married to criticism as I suggested in the analogy of men essentially connected to women.

One of the many great things said about poetry by great critics was the statement Coleridge made in the *Biographia Literaria* that poetry gives most pleasure when only generally and not perfectly understood, thus giving on to endless delights of speculation and contemplation, making criticism a continuous, living thing.

Interviewer: Do you ever experience a dry period in writing, and if so, what do you do about it?

Eberhart: I have written more or less continuously since I was fifteen or sixteen and have never had what I would call a significant dry period. In late years I have recognized what I would call long swells of ups and shorter periods of downs. This is somewhat perceived after the event, as it were. There might be a year of intense upsurge of creativity, then a corresponding downthrust of creativity, maybe of a few months; but I would not characterize the latter as dry, rather a difference of intensity due to unanalyzable reasons, just as I never could understand the long uprush periods, either. These fluctuations have to do with one's entire life, over which often we have little control, although we live as if we seem to have control of our lives and know what we are doing and why we behave as we do.

Interviewer: Do you ever play games with the craft of poetry, prosody, for the fun of it, or for what it might lead to? Anagrams, palindromes, etc.?

Eberhart: I used to invent arbitrary forms for poems, an abstract *a priori* structure, then invent lines to fit this architecture. This would come under the rubric of poetry as play, about which much has been said. In my entire life, however, this means would be rather slight.

Interviewer: What do you feel about the need for isolation in the life of a writer? How does it affect personal relationships? Professional activities such as teaching?

Eberhart: I cannot speak for other writers. In a sense Hopkins was isolated all his life, except for communications with Bridges, Dixon, and Patmore. If he had become poet laureate, as did his friend Bridges, would he have written better poetry for being a public figure? Probably isolation made and saved him. Take the other side of the coin; if Auden, coming to New York in 1939, had written little and been known to a few poet friends, would his work have been deeper? It is impossible to say. Isolation is relative, in any case. Whitman partook of his times and the war but was isolated from the fame he now enjoys until long after his death. And it is difficult to think of Emily Dickinson as anything but an isolated poet. We do not think of her in the context of the worldly success of a Millay.

Some poets thrive in isolation; some do not. In a sense Jeffers isolated himself from mankind in favor of the vast impersonal realities of the California mountains and ocean. He had none of the social charm and social beliefs of William Carlos Williams. Frost, early thought to be isolated on New England farms, came to woo large audiences, college presidents, and a President of the United States.

For me there has always been the tug of the spirit and the world. To live only for the spirit would be to be isolated in some sense. My nature turned me to the world, but realism without spiritual meaning is devoid of something sensed as deep and primitive in all of us. I have never got out of dualism, the dualism of spirit-flesh, time-timelessness, tragedy-comedy, hope and despair, sorrow and joy, hatred and love. In "A Way Out" I went to nature as a unifying principle.

Some say one cannot teach poetry. You cannot teach genius, maybe you cannot teach talent. These will emerge and reveal themselves beyond the teacher, no matter what the means and the enthusiasms. Teachers can instruct in techniques, in systems of thought, in evaluations of meaning, in subtleties of being and feeling. I was delighted to be taught poetry when I was young and to teach it in the last twenty-five years of my life.

Interviewer: Have you ever received lines of poetry which you were unable to incorporate into a poem? What would you do with them, as a rule?

Eberhart: I said something earlier about catching lines out of the air. There are many lines you write which you reject, for one reason or another. These are discarded and do not get into poems, but the pages are kept for study. Recently I sent a poem written in Florida to Spender, suggesting that I should excise the third line from the bottom. He objected, said I needed this for the rhythm. The poem is entitled "Night Thoughts," recently published in *TLS*.

Interviewer: If a poet is about to fall asleep and suddenly thinks of an interesting poem or some interesting lines for a poem, what should he do?

Eberhart: This is rather whimsical. If he is sleepy enough he will fall asleep and lose the lines. If not, he may wake up and use the lines to whatever problematical effect.

Interviewer: What reference books do you feel are useful for a young poet to have on his desk for consultation?

Eberhart: What a question! The *OED* and perhaps Hutchins's hundred books, but he couldn't afford them. He could look out the window and read the book of nature. He could look in his heart, as has been said, and write. Returning to the isolation problem, if he were to live on an uninhabited island for a year, should he not take the Bible, Shakespeare, Dante, Milton, the Greek dramatists, Wordsworth, and I would take along Blake? But think how many great exemplars this list leaves out! What about Buddha and, if he were a practical young man, Confucius?

Interviewer: Do you feel we live in a particularly permissive age as far as education and discipline in craft are concerned, and if so, what effect is this having on the present stage of poetry being written today?

Eberhart: I believe that poets cannot escape their time, indeed, are enmeshed in it. Poets of the Thirties wrote differently from poets now writing in the Seventies. In the Forties and Fifties they would have been influenced by the New Criticism and the so-called well-made poem. Poetry reacts to the acts of every man and woman in the society. These acts vary, and one decade is not like another. Since World War II poets have written without rhyme, in long lines, about anything in the world, in what I have termed spewed lines. The poems in this fashion may be as excellent as those of the well-made poems of the middle of the century. There is no reason to limit the styles and force of poetry. Everything changes, including poetry. I am reminded of Dame Fortune, the Lady of Permutations:

> All earth's gear
> she changes from nation to nation, from
> house to house,
> in changeless change through every turning year.
>
> No mortal power may stay her spinning wheel.
> The nations rise and fall by her decree.
> None may foresee where she will set her wheel:
>
> she passes, and things pass. Man's mortal reason
> cannot encompass her. She rules her sphere
> as the other gods rule theirs. Season by season
>
> her changes change her changes endlessly,

> and those whose turn has come press on her so,
> she must be swift by hard necessity.
>
> (Ciardi's translation)

Interviewer: What poet do you feel would be a good model for a young writer to begin learning about poetry?

Eberhart: Each young poet will choose his or her model or models by preference or by chance. Since there are so many poets it would be futile to name any one model.

EPILOGUE

National Book Award
Acceptance Speech

Mr. Chairman, ladies and gentlemen:

There ought to be a suffering meter for poetry. But what a joke. How can you judge the amount of suffering in a poem?

Poetry is like fighting. "Sir, there was in my heart a kind of fighting." Hamlet was not averse to killing. But it is more like shadowboxing. The poet is a self-knower trying to get out of himself.

I wrote a paper for this occasion but would like to summarize it instead.

Thanks to the judges for the National Book Award. Best wishes to my colleagues who were also nominated, especially to Muriel Rukeyser. I reviewed her first book, *U.S. 1*, in the late Thirties. I have always loved the warmth and depth of her poetry. Everybody knows that to be nominated is tantamount to election.

Now for the summary:

Poetry is a natural energy resource of our country. It has no energy crisis, possessing a potential that will last as long as the country. Its power is equal to that of any country in the world. Poetry is written in America by thousands of young people today as a natural expression of their perceptions of life. They invite the future.

I call for a more democratic attitude toward poetry than is found in the academy. It is hard to square elitism in poetry with democracy. Our greatest poet, Whitman, was no elitist but a poet of the people. Yet the academy, the universities, have mothered and best nurtured our art in my time.

Let us rejoice that we are free and that nobody will dictate to us what we shall say or write. While millions do not listen, American poetry attests to the great idea of democracy and freedom.

Speech delivered in New York, April 13, 1977.

Some of our best poets have died for poetry by suicide. Poets should not die for poetry but should live for it. I deplore the suicides of these poets.

Speaking of the struggles of life, and against suicide, I would like to close with a five-line poem entitled "How It Is":

> Then the eighty-year-old lady with a sparkle,
> A Cambridge lady, hearing of the latest
> Suicide, said to her friend, turning off
> TV for tea, "Well, my dear, doesn't it seem
> A little like going where you haven't been invited?"